OASIS JOURNAL
2008

Stories
Poems
Essays

by New & Emerging Writers Over Fifty

Edited by Leila Joiner

IMAGO PRESS
TUCSON ARIZONA

Copyright © 2008 by Leila Joiner

All rights reserved. No part of this book may be reproduced or transmitted in any form or by any means, electronic or mechanical, including photocopying, recording, or by any information storage and retrieval system, without permission in writing from the publisher.

Published in the United States of America by:

Imago Press
3710 East Edison
Tucson AZ 85716

www.imagobooks.com

Names, characters, places, and incidents, unless otherwise specifically noted, are either the product of the author's imagination or are used fictitiously.

Cover Design and Book Design by Leila Joiner
Cover Photograph copyright © Roswitha Laminger-Purgstaller

ISBN 978-0-9799341-8-6

Printed in the United States of America on Acid-Free Paper

In loving memory,
for the good times & all the good stories…

Richard Dershimer
1926 – 2007

ACKNOWLEDGMENTS

I want to thank the OASIS Institute, all the judges who have generously volunteered their time to select our contest winners and comment on the work of our authors, and all the writers over fifty who continue to contribute their work to *OASIS Journal* every year.

May we all have many successful years ahead of us.

LIST OF ILLUSTRATIONS

"Fresh Plums," photograph by Heike Kampe, p. 22

"Snow Goose in Flight," photograph by Elemental Imaging, p. 36

"Molotov Cocktail," photograph by Jazavac, p. 44

"Ice Cream Van," drawing by Sean Gladwell, p. 50

"Retro Leaving Room," photograph by Özgür Donmaz, p. 56

"Paternal Pride," photograph by Pum Rote, p. 84

"Solace?," photograph by Pum Rote, p. 97

"On the High Seas," photograph by Carole Ann Moleti, p. 106

"Machu Picchu? Where?," photograph by Marshall Bruce, p. 132

"Passport," scanned image courtesy Irene Etlinger, p. 150

"Immigrant Life," photograph courtesy Joan E. Zekas, p. 158

"Poulain," photograph by Alain Vigneron, p. 164

"Welcome Home," drawing by Annette Stovall, p. 253

"Gopher Tortoise," photograph courtesy Mary R. Durfee, p. 284

"George and Trudy," photograph courtesy Trudy Barton, p. 296

CONTENTS

EDITOR'S PREFACE	15
WINNER: BEST FICTION CONTEST THE PRICE OF PLUMS *Janet E. Irvin*	23
ALL THAT GLITTERS IS NOT *Ellaraine Lockie*	29
WINNER: BEST POETRY CONTEST AS A CHILD, ENTERING THE CELLAR *Kathleen Elliott Gilroy*	30
FRAGMENTS OF CHILDHOOD *Marlene Newman*	31
JOURNEY TO CONTENTMENT *Evelyn Buretta*	35
GOOSE CHASE *Jan Rider Newman*	37
ORIGAMI *Judy Ray*	43
1ST RUNNER-UP: BEST NON-FICTION CONTEST A CHILD OF THE FIFTIES *Jo Wilkinson*	45

2ND RUNNER-UP: BEST NON-FICTION CONTEST 51
   THE ICE CREAM MAN
Dolores Geuder

COLOR COORDINATED? 52
Helen Jones-Shepherd

THE DIFFERENCE 53
Marilyn Hochheiser

1ST RUNNER-UP: BEST POETRY CONTEST 54
   JUST SO STORY
Esther Brudo

2ND RUNNER-UP: BEST FICTION CONTEST 57
   IN HER MIRROR
Ronna Magy

AT FIRST LIGHT 60
Joanne Ellis

BENDEMEER'S STREAM 61
J. R. Nakken

LIFE HANDED ME A MEMOIR 64
Diana Raab

TIME OUT 65
Louise Larsen

WHEN IN DOUBT 68
Carole Kaliher

MY LITTLE RED WAGON 69
William Speight

IT WILL NOT LAST LONG 72
Kathleen A. O'Brien

THE CHASE FOR SOMEBODY 73
Ruth Hohberg

AUTHENTIC SELF 77
Lolene McFall

AT THE GAZEBO IN LARCHMONT *Sandra Sturtz Hauss*	78
MY DAD *Janet Kreitz*	79
HARVEY LEVI *Jolly Ann Maddox*	82
A CONGENITAL LIAR *Elisa Drachenberg*	85
CAPSIZED *Mimi Moriarty*	98
SERENDIPITY *Helena Frey*	99
ON THE HIGH SEAS *Carole Ann Moleti*	107
NEAR POINT LOBOS *Claire Livesey*	112
CLOAK OF FIRE *Marilyn J. Morgan*	113
CELILO *J. R. Nakken*	116
DAWN IN THE WEST *Andrew J. Hogan*	117
OCTOBER WOLDFIRE 2003 *Bobbie Jean Bishop*	128
RING OF FIRE *Toni Timmons*	129
REMOTE *Tillie Webb*	133
FROM RHODES TO THE BELGIAN CONGO *Albert Russo*	135

2ND RUNNER-UP: BEST POETRY CONTEST THE SCORPION *Ruth Moon Kempher*	146
VANITY *Jane Boruszewski*	147
ENEMY ALIEN *Irene Etlinger*	150
AN IMMIGRANT LIFE: SNAPSHOTS *Joan E. Zekas*	155
QUESTIONS *Dorothy Boggs*	159
AT AN AGE WHEN *Annette Stovall*	162
MAY DAY *Eleanor Whitney Nelson*	165
AGING HORSE *Sheryl Holland*	174
LIFE'S HARVEST *Sally Carper*	175
MOTHER EARTH *Helen Benson*	177
FRUITY FREEBIES *Marian Wilson*	178
"LEMON JUICE, THAT'S YELLOW ALERT" *Janet Thompson*	179
AUDIENCE *Judy Ray*	184
THOSE LETTERS FROM SALLY *Jean Ritter Smith*	185
MY UNCLE JACK *Esther Brudo*	190

DAY *Janet Kreitz*	192
JUST ANOTHER DAY AT GOLDEN ACRES *JoAnn Sunderland*	193
AH, THOSE LOVELY GOLDEN YEARS *Gloria G. Ammerman*	199
AT THE Y *Shirley Oppenheimer*	200
KIDS AND CARS *Frank Frost*	201
DUCT TAPE SAVES A LIFE *Diana Griggs*	206
FRAGILE WINGS *Diane L. Rau*	207
THE ULTIMATE SONG *Megan Webster*	218
THE PERFECT GIFT *Leila Peters*	219
ANOTHER SPRING *Kathleen A. O'Brien*	222
WINNER: BEST NON-FICTION CONTEST ONE MINUTE YOU'RE A WIFE, THE NEXT, A WIDOW *Vera Martignetti*	223
ACROSS *Constance Richardson*	234
RETURN TO PROVENCE *David Ray*	236
A SESTINA FOR MY SON *Adrienne Hernandez*	242
WORDLESS *Lena V. Roach*	244

ANGELA *Christy Wise*	245
IN MEMORIAM *Anne Whitlock*	248
AFTERMATH OF A HERO *Annette Stovall*	250
THE BALLAD OF A SOLDIER *Emily Keeler*	254
VOICES *A. G. Deutscher*	258
I DON'T REMEMBER *Diana Griggs*	262
DANDELIONS FOR BREAKFAST *Joanna Wanderman*	263
WILL YOUR DESTRUCTION MERGE WITH ANOTHER VOICE AND ANOTHER LIGHT? *Lucille Gang Shulklapper*	266
CHANGELING *Joan T. Doran*	267
NAILS *Rita Ries*	268
SHADOWSMITH *Neal Wilgus*	270
NIGHT TERRORS *Kathleen Elliott Gilroy*	271
MESSAGES IN THE WIND *Peggy Joyce Starr*	275
JUNK MAIL, THE GREAT BEYOND *Marilyn Hochheiser*	276
MESSAGES EVERYWHERE *Carolyn Kaliher*	277

WHEN A GOPHER WALKS ACROSS THE ROAD *Sheryl Holland*	280
A MIRACLE OF FAITH AT THE BIRD SANCTUARY *Mary R. Durfee*	281
THE SNOW GLOBE *Margaret E. Pennetti*	285
THE CHRISTMAS TREE *Mitzie Skrbin*	289
IN A SORT OF CHRISTMAS CARD *Manuel Torrez, Jr.*	295
I MET MY MILLION DOLLAR BABY IN A FIVE AND TEN CENT STORE *Trudy Barton*	297
THE RING *Lois Chorle*	299
THE PRINCE OF AMOUR *Lolene McFall*	300
PORTRAIT OF A LADY IN RED *Adrienne Rogers*	301
END OF SUMMER *Jean Doing*	310
THE LAST LETTER *Michael B. Mossman*	311
ON THE SOFA TOGETHER *Irma Sheppard*	316
LOVE REMAINS *Nancy Sandweiss*	317
PRIZED POSSESSION *Natalie Gottlieb*	318
THE ROOM I GREW UP IN *Ron L. Porter*	319

WHAT A BLESSING *Barbara Watson*	321
TWO ROADS DIVERGED *Susan Cummins Miller*	324
SHARDS *Teresa Flanagan Sheehan*	326
TOO LATE FOR HELLO *Eleanor D. Little*	327
LOVE, TAI CHI, AND REGRET *Steve Snyder*	328
1ST RUNNER-UP: BEST FICTION CONTEST SECOND CHANCES *Richard O'Donnell*	329
CONTRIBUTORS' NOTES	337
ORDER INFORMATION	359

EDITOR'S PREFACE

This seventh annual edition of the *OASIS Journal* sees some subjects falling away and new themes taking their place. This year, participants are writing less about their war experiences and more about personal connections. Loss of a loved one at any age, young or old, is high on the list. And, for the first time, I'm seeing an interest in after death communication. Love is another prominent theme this year—all kinds of love. Romantic, parental, filial. First love, everlasting love, requited and unrequited love. As long as the human race is capable of love, there may be hope for us yet.

Below are the judge's comments on the winning entries. I'm leaving the Fiction Contest for last this year, because Nancy Turner was kind enough to send in comments on all the published stories, winners and non-winners alike (there are no losers!). She and I both feel that everyone can benefit from delving into what makes a good story even better. However, you may want to read the book before you read the judge's comments, as there may be some spoilers here, especially in the fiction comments.

NON-FICTION: Judge, Sheila Bender, an award-winning poet, essayist, and book author and past contributing editor to *Writer's Digest Magazine*, who has written eight popular instructional books on writing from personal experience.

It wasn't easy to settle on first, second, and third place winners in nonfiction. Since I like reading personal experience, every essay you sent me was a pleasure to absorb. And that's the highest order of reading for me—to absorb another's history, viewpoint, and way of evoking experience. When forced to choose winners, I look at the shape of an essay, the way it makes me return to the writing because it holds an insight or universal human experience I want to retrieve and am grateful for having had someone articulate. I am quite sure that these three are not the only winners in the group, but here is why each is especially meaningful to me:

WINNER: "One Minute You're a Wife, the Next, a Widow"
The author's account of the days just before and after she lost her husband to cancer tackles difficult territory with grace and honesty. The essay successfully uses details and particulars to formulate a tribute to the author's husband and the way he prepared for his impending death and separation from his family. It is also a tribute to the way family, friends, and communities help those who are grieving. The essay contains the kind of information needed by any who might live through the pain of losing a long-time mate.

FIRST RUNNER-UP: "A Child of the Fifties"
This essay delivers the historical events and emotional side of life in 1959; it also reminds us about who we are beneath our political viewpoints and how we separate ourselves from others. The essay joins narrative about the author's twelfth year with details about the McCarthy era. It joins a young teen's awareness of being different from her peers with awareness of people's breaking points. It spotlights what adults say to comfort children against the darkness of violence.

SECOND RUNNER-UP: "The Ice Cream Man"
Today, many nonfiction publications look for what they call "flash nonfiction," short pieces of writing or small vignettes that carry a big punch. This account of a child's first encounter with prejudice makes readers wince. It reminds us in one page how ugly prejudice is, how wise children are, and how much they understand of how they will have to cope.

POETRY: Judge, Dan Gilmore, founder of the *OASIS Journal*, author of *Season Tickets* and *A Howl for Mayflower*.

I'd rather defend poems than judge them. All poems deserve defending. They exist to counter our human tendency to kill the world's soul. One poem is not better or worse than another. Like those who use dating services, poems are looking for a match with the right reader. In this edition of the *OASIS Journal* all poems, when properly matched, can change a life. But my job was to select three that spoke to me. To do this I read all the poems aloud three and four times. To my ear some potentially brilliant ideas reverted to poetic bedazzlement instead of accuracy of statement. To those poets who labored so hard, I apologize for not being bedazzled by bedazzlement.

WINNER: "As a Child, Entering the Cellar"
I chose this as my favorite because I liked its efficiency and deceptive simplicity. Its clear images evoke the magical grace of a childhood that sees through dark fears into "sparking light on packed jars / of summer-sweet peaches."

FIRST RUNNER-UP: "Just So Story"
I liked the imaginative leaps of this poem. The poet uses the umbilical cord in a surrealistic but clear way to move time forward to the exact moment a mother's love for her child is awakened. I choose it for second place.

SECOND RUNNER-UP: "The Scorpion"
The poet juxtaposes the cosmic Scorpius with the lowly scorpion that "retreats / under stacks of coffee cups," and suggests that, sometimes, to "see how the stars have tilted" we must first experience the "disconcerting grace" of sacrificing small lives. A big thought. A strong third place.

FICTION: Judge, Nancy Turner, author of *These Is My Words, The Water and the Blood, Sarah's Quilt,* and *The Star Garden.*

First of all, I want to thank all the participants for submitting stories. These obviously represent a great deal of work, thought, and, no doubt, hopes, too. I also want to state that my opinion is not the end-all of opinions and, as with any editor, teacher, or writer, there are things I may have a subjective review on that may strike someone else differently.

The hardest thing for me was deciding what criteria to use. I finally decided on these things (not in any particular order): Active voice, clean description, readability, characterization, plot/subplots, accurate use of point of view. Then I asked myself: What is the author trying to do and has it been accomplished here? It was a tough call all around, because some stories held together one way but not another. The choices eventually came because, with each reading, some moved toward the top of the list as having achieved these goals.

Here are my choices for this year's Fiction Contest:

WINNER: "The Price of Plums"
An easy winner, *highly publishable as it is* with tight writing and rich in details. This tragic coming-of-age tale is beautifully wrought, full of symbolic nuance and real characters. It has room, I think, for a little more fleshing out, particularly where the transition from moving out to taking up their new lives and the news of Kate's having a boyfriend all happens in a single paragraph. You don't want to disturb the great rhythm here, but I believe another sentence or two wouldn't hurt—at the very least, break up the paragraph, "I knew better than to talk back…" into two or more, with an extra sentence about Ross. I love the language—things like "flimsy fourteen-year-old dignity" and "that cheeseburger grinning up at me." One suggestion: this story could hold some grit—indeed, it already has some in its very premise—instead of having Uncle Johnny shout something inaudible (which seems to

the reader a bit of a fade-out of the author's prior strengths), use his words and make them harsh ones. Standing ovation!

First Runner-up: "Second Chances"

The strengths of this story are numerous; the style and tone are true throughout. Descriptions are good. The pretext of the story works well. The potential exists for it to become a very strong work. Here are some things I would ask the writer to consider: 1) Nothing happens in the "present" tense until nearly four pages in. Consider moving all the backstory to sometime later, or have it be recalled as a flashback. I understand the purpose of the laddering of events, but it's all a sort of writerly "wait here until I get done with this…," which makes the reader want to ask why. Could you show these events happening in their own present time, rather than the recitation technique? Or have mother tell them the same way as Aunt Ellen recounts her own life? 2) Consider doing the whole thing in 3rd person, which will ease the reader through a difficult transition into the last section. Doing this might also make suggestions in (1) work well. 3) It's a tricky thing to maneuver the shift from point of view and character/narrator. Kudos to the writer for trying. Perhaps give us a glimpse of "he" before the abrupt change—another section back and forth might work. Also, in the last section, "he" throws around a great many names except his own. Please give him one. High applause!

Second Runner-up: "In Her Mirror"

I chose this story for placement because the imagery was beautiful, and the writing clean and clear. The voice was so right for the telling. Here are some things the author should consider: 1) This needs a stronger plot line and a sense that something is going to happen, then, indeed, does happen. It is not a clear cut story, but more of a series of scenes. It is essential that the main character or events evolve, change somehow, more than just growing older. Push the character to have some abiding need, some inner *something* at stake, so that we watch the transformation as she becomes *more* than she was at the beginning. 2) Remember, a narrator who is a character cannot know what is in other characters' minds. Rather than have "…whisper of Claudette Colbert flits across the…spaces of her mind…," perhaps Mother could speak aloud: "Daddy says I look like Claudette Colbert in this dress." More high applause!

Just a word about the other stories. These are collectively the best technically worked out stories I've ever had to judge—you all know your bits and pieces very well. It is obvious, too, that each writer spent great effort and showed control of the work. Here are suggestions for the remainder as I would give if we were workshopping these in my classroom:

The closest in caliber to third place is "Just Another Day at Golden Acres," which boasts good strong writing but, again, is a slice of life without a definitive change in the characters. The people are believable, but they would benefit from having more at stake than a good night's rest. The author brought in that the narrator was having cancer treatment—a built in "something at stake"—but the issue never impacted the story at all. Consider pushing these characters for all they're worth.

"Goose Chase" – This story is intriguing, highly imaginative, readable, and carries a nice plot. While you do have a change at the end, somehow it needed to "hang together" more. Suggest you drop the first paragraph and begin with the second, which is a powerful opener, and rewrite the end—it wraps up with the whole world in it just a little too neatly. This needs to be longer—give us more, more, more of these characters, so we have to sympathize even more. You are really onto something here, so do rework this one.

"Dawn in the West" – Use more active tense rather than passive. Frank's story is dynamic, but the first section sets up a story that doesn't affect the rest. Please don't give up on this—it has potential—but do rewrite the ending, which comes a little too close to a deus ex machina.

"Portrait of a Lady in Red" – The characters are interesting, the settings are great. Title's been done, but that's a small thing. The opening scene sets up one story as if we are going to get into Milton's life, but the real story is something else, not really about Milton, but about Nadia. It would make more sense for Hilde to commit suicide if we knew before the fact that she had cancer—be sure not to make the reader wait for information. There is not enough real basis for Hilde to trust Nadia with her "mission" so quickly. Milton is the strongest character at the beginning, but he all but fades from view—take him through to the end—make him the active role—and we'll all go gladly with him.

"Those Letters from Sally" – Perhaps it is the letters themselves, but the whole story is rather more explained than shown. Almost everything is past tense, and some things way past. "…That was about ten days ago…" is an example. Yes, that is the way letters are, but this is a story. Second, it is a personal hangup of mine for a writer to ask the reader direct questions, such as "Can you make sense of this one?" Doing that takes me out of reader's position. The author is supposed to be the leader here. I get what the writer is doing, and maybe some other reader would adore the chummy style.

"Aftermath of a Hero" – Good honest style here, and fantastic potential if you will rewrite with an eye to what happens beyond the job hunt scene. But the story lost momentum as, more and more, Arthur took in what his parents said and finally considered himself "the handicapped." We don't really know for sure that he got the job; it was just "I'll keep you in mind...," which doesn't mean "Show up at seven tomorrow, son." Readers want to like and empathize with a main character, but Arthur is lost in his anger and becomes more pathetic than likeable. Use a light touch with the colloquialisms, and remember not to have people 'start to' do something or 'begin to' think—just do it, think it. This story has the chance to have Arthur find real purpose and growth in his life and, in doing so, become heroic in a new way, and I think this may happen if you write what happens next: on the job, meeting a girl, etc. Movies are full of hard-luck-turns-to-make-good stories.

"A Congenital Liar" – This story could benefit from being written in active voice rather than passive. Show us rather than explain as in "...truth would not have served..." Give us scenes rather than past-tense accounts. The last line feels as if the author were stepping in under the curtain and saying "Ha-ha-ha! This is really me!" whether it is or not. Even so, it is also past tense. Consider having the character enter a writing contest instead of winning one 'last year'. Have all the characters do things rather than tell them.

"Cloak of Fire" – a brave try at a fantasy-style story. Applause for taking a risk and stepping out with this work. This one would benefit from clearing out *all or almost all* of the adverbs and adjectives. This type of story is difficult to carry off at best, and usually a clear-cut writing voice is a great asset to a story in which the reader is asked not just to suspend disbelief but to accept an alternate reality.

Thank you, again, for allowing me to judge this year's contest submissions. I hope you will all continue to pursue your obvious gifts in writing. A good short story is a thing of great joy!

And a heartfelt thank you to all our judges for volunteering their time and expertise. I hope the stories and poems herein bring you great joy as you read them.

L.J.

# OASIS JOURNAL

2008

Stories

Poems

Essays

Winner: Best Fiction Contest

The Price of Plums

Janet E. Irvin

> Dedicated to Cathy Smith Bowers for her generous permission to use her poem "Groceries" as inspiration.

The day we ran away from my father, I climbed to the top of the sycamore and let the wind blow me over the city like a banner. It was still dark, just past five in the morning, and no one saw me shimmy my way up the trunk, not even nosy old Ellie Richley, and she saw everything that happened in our neighborhood. I imagined her thin, nasal voice coming at me like a pair of hedge clippers, her words slicing up my flimsy, fourteen-year-old dignity. *Big girl like you oughtn't to be scaling trees like a boy. 'Tisn't proper.* Maybe she was right, but it didn't matter. After today, we none of us would ever be proper again.

I climbed until the branches thinned out, and the trunk swayed under my weight. Gripping the sturdiest branch with my legs, I spread my arms and embraced the damp and foggy air. Tears peppered my cheeks and flung themselves across the last of the green leaves. When Mama called, I hugged my way down, snapping off one of the thin lower limbs as I dropped onto the scrub grass. The broken branch bounced off my head and settled into the dirt beside me. In the driveway, Mama put her finger to her lips, covered my sleeping brothers with her tattered wedding quilt, and shoved the last of the boxes into our red Duster.

"Hurry, Kate," she hissed, handing me the door key. I ran up the sidewalk, looking over my shoulder just in case. But Daddy was gone to the mill. Only the scent of his pipe and the stale alcohol smell lingered in the hall. I turned the key three times, straining to make the lock work. The bolt refused to slide into place. The house didn't want to let us go. Mama hissed at me again, so I just shoved the key under the fraying welcome mat and sprinted back to the car. She looked past me, her eyes narrowed into slits, her mouth a knot of hardness and determination. I nodded like I'd taken care of things. When she eased the car onto the street, I glanced back. The door hung open, swaying in the light wind that scattered leaves and rattled the loose mailbox lid.

Our new house, a Cracker Jack box nestled between a carpet warehouse and a corner store that sold candles and incense burners, reminded me of a Stephen King novel. The roof bowed in the middle, two garbage cans minus tops squatted at the curb, and what I could see of the back yard looked crowded with scrap lumber and old tires. Two sharp blasts of a train whistle made me jump. The railroad tracks were only a hundred yards away.

Mama pulled onto the gravel driveway and turned off the engine. She and I sat there with Sammy and Robert still asleep in the back, staring at crooked curtains and paint peeling off the siding that stared right back at us from under the light cast by a front porch bulb.

"At least it's something," Mama said, straightening her shoulders and shifting her hips under the weight of her decision. She reached over the seat and shook Sammy's leg. "You all get ready for school now."

I knew better than to talk back, but I was tired and my stomach growled. Mama hadn't packed any food, and I was certain there wasn't any waiting in that ugly knob of a house. I wondered when we were going to eat. And I wondered what Ross would say when he saw where I lived now. His family, three generations of jewelers, owned a big brick two-story on the west side of Steeltown, where the streets were tree-lined, the homes freshly-painted, and the families still intact. Maybe he wouldn't want to be my boyfriend anymore.

Four days passed before Uncle Johnny found us. I woke to the sound of him and Mama arguing outside on the square of concrete that pretended to be a porch.

"Come on, Zoe, you know Cal don't mean anything by it." Uncle Johnny's words sifted through the uncaulked window. "He's just hot-tempered, is all. You know he loves you."

"Love ain't enough, John," Mama said. "You figure I should stay until your brother kills me?" She sounded strong and brave, but I couldn't stop shaking. It wasn't a minute before Sammy and Robert sneaked into my room from their bed on the couch. I welcomed them under the covers, and we strained to hear the words.

"Cal won't chase after you," Uncle Johnny said, his voice low and ugly. "You cut yourself off from a proper life, Zoe, and you get no help from anyone. Come back or stay here and starve, it's your choice."

"Will Mama make us go back?" Sammy asked, his voice heavy with longing and fear. I remembered the bruises, still purple below her right eye and along the curve of her shoulder blade, and I held him tighter.

"Back where?" I asked, but it was one of those rhetorical questions my teacher, Mrs. English, always talked about. I knew the answer.

"We're not going back," Robert blurted into the darkness. I felt him scratching at his forehead, fingering the lumpy scar hidden beneath a patch of dirty blonde curls.

"No," I whispered. Sammy grabbed my hand and cradled it next to his cheek. Robert nestled his head against my ribs and repeated "twinkle, twinkle little star," pausing after every line to listen for footsteps. The front door slammed open, and Uncle Johnny shouted something I couldn't hear, but it sounded pretty final. Then Mama groped her way to us. The bed sagged as she climbed in and curled her arms around our shoulders, and I knew, we all knew, we weren't going back. What I didn't know was how we were going to go forward.

Ross had told everybody at school he liked me, but we didn't actually go out or anything until after the move. The first time he came to see me at the house on Byer's Lane, I swept the front steps and raked up the trash that had blown into the yard. Then I found two old white plastic lawn chairs in the junk pile in the back yard and set them out on the porch with a pot of wilting pansies between them. And I waited.

I heard his truck before I saw it. The twin mufflers roared on the second-hand, sweet, dark purple Dodge pickup, their growl competing with the railroad whistle that announced the four o'clock was right on time. He didn't get out right away, just leaned his arm out the opened window and squinted at me.

"Want to go for a ride?" He lifted a bag from the seat next to him and dangled it out the open window. "I got brownies."

I shuffled my way to the curb. "Can't," I said, my mouth watering at his look and his smell and the thought of eating a brownie. "I have to watch the boys." I glanced back at the house. Sammy and Robert stared at us through the grimy picture window, their faces scrunched up into frowns. I looked back at Ross's earnest brown eyes and his wide, casual mouth, and a deeper hunger gnawed its way into my mouth.

"That's all right," Ross said, turning off the engine. "I've got enough for everybody."

I touched his hand with my own. "C'mon inside."

He didn't say anything, just stroked my fingers with his thumb and looked at the house, but I knew. Later, when he bent to kiss me, his mouth warm and chocolate and still hungry, I didn't think about saying no. That's how Mama caught us, leaning against the side of the house, my hips raised to meet his, and the odor of brownies swirling around us like a mist.

"Go," Mama said, pointing toward his truck.

Ross stepped away from me. "Pleased to meet you, ma'am," he said, cutting his eyes away from Mama's sour face.

She tried to stay angry, but work and worry had claimed all her fire. I stared after him until he pulled away from the curb. Mama smoothed my hair away from my face and grabbed my hand. "Remember what I told you." She pressed down on my fingers, her hand hard and heavy as a club. "Save yourself for a better time."

"So, I'll see you tonight?" Ross leaned close to me, his brown eyes pleading, his slender lips pressed tight so he wouldn't beg. The gym rocked with the strains of the school fight song, and I wanted to go with him to the Burger Bar, to watch the other girls watching me, to feel his arm slip round my waist as he walked me into the restaurant. To eat. I had to swallow hard to keep from thinking about the taste of a cheeseburger and the way the grease dripped onto my fingers every time I took a bite. I had split my peanut butter sandwich between Sammy and Robert every day this week and taken the smallest portion of soup at night. Mama said things would get better, and I just had to tough it out, but I didn't know if I could.

"Mama works late," I told him, turning away so he wouldn't see my eagerness or my apprehension.

"I get off at ten," he said, sliding his hand into mine.

Robert and Sammy wrestled on the scuffed pine board floor, the static on the small black-and-white TV underscoring their slaps and yells. I felt light-headed, weak, restless. Mama called to say she was working a double shift and wouldn't be home until eleven, to say *don't you go out with that boy, Kate,* but I kept picturing the Burger Bar and that cheeseburger grinning up at me from the white plastic plate they served it on. I must have fallen asleep. So did the boys, their slim, nine-year-old bodies reminiscent of my father's slender frame. How could a man so slight create such a big hole in our lives? Mama said she loved him once, when he was younger, kinder, less beaten down by the bills and the booze, but I couldn't see it.

The sound of the screen door flapping against the back of the house startled me awake. I looked up to see Ross's face pressed against the storm door glass, his nose and lips like suction cups.

"Jesus! You scared me." I held the door open as he slipped past me, his arms full of grocery bags. I peeked into the living room, saw the boys asleep on the sofa cushions they'd dragged onto the floor. I turned off the TV and covered their sleeping forms with an old Army blanket. In the kitchen Ross was rustling the bags.

"What's that?" I asked, pointing at the bulging sacks labeled Gorilla Market.

"Fridays we go through the stock, fish out all the damaged goods and set them aside for the trash pickup." Ross shrugged his shoulders and looked at the refrigerator. "I thought you could use them, is all." He stepped away from the table and waited.

I stared at the bags, thinking about my father and our old house and climbing trees and the hunger that clawed at me. It was like I had x-ray vision and could see the cans of soup, and the taped-up boxes of macaroni and cheese, and the squashed bottle of dish soap, and the half full bag of rice. I looked at Ross, at the question hanging on his lips like one of Mama's cigarettes when she had her hands full doing something else.

"You don't have to if you don't want to," Ross said.

I looked at the clock on the stove and the fire in his face that matched the one burning its way down my belly and nodded.

"I'll be in the truck," Ross said, easing his way through the door. I walked back to Mama's room, picked up the wedding quilt and turned off all the lights.

Our tennis shoes crunched over the gravel path that led up the siding to the empty boxcar. It was a clear night, and the stars hung above my head like a checkerboard. I tossed the quilt in first, then Ross lifted me up, and

I scrambled ahead of him into the darkness. I heard a scratching, and a dove, disturbed by our arrival, took flight right over my head. Ross hoisted himself into the car, took my hand and hugged me. Together, we spread the quilt above the straw and feathers and bird shit, and I spread myself out to the night and the boy and the black veil of the moment. When he rocked me in his arms, I felt the sway of the sycamore and opened my arms to the wind once more.

It wasn't quite daylight when Ross lifted me down from the train car and we made our way back to his truck. When he dropped me off, I shook Mama's wedding quilt to free it of the straw and folded it into a small square of regret.

Mama was waiting, standing in the kitchen, the glow from her cigarette and the shine of the night-light glancing off the grocery bags still sitting on the table. She didn't say anything, just fingered the cans and boxes and soap powder she had lifted from the sacks, her face a road map of shame and hope and hunger. She took the quilt out of my arms, kissed my forehead and disappeared.

My pants were wet from the damp air and sex, and I shivered in the stillness. Rummaging through the grocery sacks, I found a can of plums, dented in two places. You shouldn't eat food from damaged cans, I'd heard, but I was too hungry to care. I fished around in one of the drawers for the can opener, twisted the handle until the lid popped off, and stuffed a plum, juicy and full of sweetness, into my eager mouth.

All That Glitters Is Not

Ellaraine Lockie

Sun like oil slick on water
polishes icicles that hang
from the eave above the cabin window
Where there were none this morning
An act by the divine creator of art
And perhaps compensation

for last night's view of November rage
As though the devil ripped
my grandmother's handiwork from the table
And flung it in miniscule motifs
over and over against the glass
His hellhole howl as chilling
as a cat in an all-night heat

Stillness now except for prism light
dancing carnival colors across
the oak plank floor in front of the window
I'd believe that Good won this round
in the ongoing battle between forces
If I didn't remember a mittened hand
holding an icicle

The danger sign parents flashed
when 20 below turns icicles adhesive
The dagger point that might have served
as omen if I hadn't been seven
With eyes that saw diamonds
and with a mouth parched
by summer's want of a popsicle
If I hadn't paid with skin and blood
As we all have traded pain for forbidden pleasure
ever since sweet juice ran down Eve's chin

Winner: Best Poetry Contest

As a Child, Entering the Cellar

Kathleen Elliott Gilroy

Ice crusts the outside cellar door.
Minute icicles hang from the latch.
I snap them off with a nearby stone—
pry up the hasp,
lift the door up,
brace it against the snow-crusted house.

As I slip inside, scents of must
rise up like steam from a boiling kettle
of mason jars.
There are undoubtedly spider webs,
nests for families of wintering mice,

but I, moving low on the steps,
see only the glint of winter sun
sparking light on packed jars
of summer-sweet peaches.

Fragments of Childhood

Marlene Newman

Places
It should begin where I began in

Riverhead

Where the north and the south forks of Long Island meet on the Peconic Bay
But remembrances of things past fade as I cling to fragments.
December night…peanuts at a movie house…a bellyache…a long ride to the hospital…my arrival.
The happy days of their marriage…the dinner parties…the good friends.

I crawled inside the laundry bag only to be lifted and carried over his shoulder as he played the game of how heavy it was, and how I'd laugh at his mock surprise to find me hiding in the wash.

Long, long train trips to the house filled with aunts and uncles and cousins and Nana and Pop or visits to the other grandma who kept tins of candied orange peel tucked on a shelf within my reach, and the uncle who played the piano as he called through the swampland for Chloe.

China rabbits played instruments so tiny that only stuffed dogs and dolls could hear. I played with the rabbits until I had chipped or broken or lost her little orchestra. But then our lives were already chipping and breaking by the time we left for

Buena Vista Avenue in Yonkers

The 'good view' was of the Hudson. I watched the day liners sailing north from the city. At night, I watched the strings of lights that outlined the boats as they floated back down the river past my window.

Still, through the eye of my child's mind, the room had three walls, the dormer ceiling creating an illusion.

A birthday party for a three-year-old. How vivid the memories of lollypop and marshmallow dolls that Cousin Ruthie fashioned with toothpicks and gumdrops. What fun was had by all. A happy time. A time of love. And still the rabbits played on the shelf.

It was early, early in the morning. They were asleep. I took her rings from the dresser and played with them and then...and then...I remember like it was yesterday...and then...I put them on top of the green blanket that was folded over the radiator that sat beneath the opened window. And that was the last of them. I didn't throw them out the window. I didn't. I know I didn't. I put them on top of the green blanket that was folded over the radiator that sat beneath the opened window. I remember...I remember the cherry tree on...

SOUTH 6ᵀᴴ BETWEEN 4ᵀᴴ AND 5ᵀᴴ IN MT. VERNON

I played store with the cousins. We'd pull the weeds in Nana's yard and sort them into little piles to sell for pebbles. I remember the taste of vegetables—carrots and peas, potatoes and beans—cooked straight out of Nana's garden, strained through her Foley mill.

Oh, best of times in Nana's kitchen. The pan under the icebox was filled to the top as she carried it to the same sink I was bathed in, sometimes, with the cousins while I looked up at the stamped tin ceiling and wondered.

Pop was a plumber, busier than the shoemaker whose children went shoeless, so hot water ran in the toilet when I pulled the chain.

Snoony was a stray wolfdog puppy Pop brought home. He grew savage in appearance and manner. Still, I could reach deep into his mouth to retrieve and share his scraps as disapproving grownups looked on in anticipatory horror.

Most happy times in the house on South 6ᵗʰ. Most happy times of aunts and uncles and cousins and Nana and Pop.

I don't remember the trip from South 6ᵗʰ to

SHAKESPEARE AVENUE IN THE BRONX

I don't remember how we got there. It was almost at the top of the hill. A long hill that reached up from the park where I'd roll over and over the newly mowed expanse and breathe in the sweet smell of the grass.

The hill led my father from the elevated train station to our door. Up the hill, he would carry me home as I'd pretend to be asleep and he'd pretend not to know.

There were jacks and jump ropes and potsies. We would save the foil wrappers of chewing gum—juicy fruit and mint—and fold them into a square heavy enough to toss onto the chalk-numbered box on the sidewalk. When the war came, we had to collect the foil to save the world for democracy.

There was a chaise lounge near the window of their bedroom and I would climb onto the sill and step down between the spikes of the railing that enclosed the privet hedge, in and out, because I could. But he was too little…I told him he couldn't…he was too little…I told him…I did. But he followed me out…and he slipped and the spike pierced his thigh.

They rushed him to the doctor and I hid under the big mahogany bed. I told him not to…I told him he was too little…it wasn't my fault…but it was. So I hid under the bed.

And they came back with a small bag of candy for me and a small bag of candy for him. They understood, but I didn't understand

why we had to move…
It wasn't very far.

I didn't know why everybody moved all the time. I didn't know why furniture was on the sidewalks. I didn't understand why women stood outside of Woolworth's and waited, hoping to clean the houses of strangers.

When we moved to the building on

Ogden Avenue

I rode up and down in a box with the man with the mustache and yellow spats to the 4th floor and back again to the marbled lobby to where I began my days at

P.S. 11

That first day of kindergarten, no, it was the second. It was the second, because the first was wonderful, and that was the day the teacher told us we'd need hangers. But the next day, my world came to an end…

Hangers…and they all knew, or their mothers knew to sew a strip inside their jackets to hang on the hooks in the long closet with the sliding doors.

I didn't know. I don't remember now if my mother didn't know or if I just did it on my own. But I brought a hanger, a wooden coat hanger, and they all laughed and I put my head down and cried…

Journey to Contentment

Evelyn Buretta

I sat all day, the shy, sad kid in school,
began each morn with pledge to God and flag.
The nun looked stern and said, "Obey the rule."
My strength was gone, I froze; I thought I'd gag.
Five desks in rows were nailed to planks of wood,
a scheme to keep the row of kids in place.
So scared to death I vowed I'd be so good.
With stick, the nun kept us in state of grace.
For those who dared to talk across the aisle,
eternal endless painful fire in Hell.
With head bowed down to desk, I dared not smile.
I sat with patience for the recess bell.
  Poor me, there were four boys to my dismay,
  no girls in class, I played alone each day.

And so it was for me the long eight years.
I stayed reserved. I lost ability
to gain the art of speaking well with peers
and hence could not enjoy frivolity.
My lack of skill in social groups became
my curse as I continued trying hard
to grow in poise and grace and yet my aim
seemed far away. I felt forever scarred
from childhood pain. Attempts to mix with folks
gave little joy so I became my own
best friend, the one to give me needed strokes,
and now I love my time alone.
  Was it, in fact, my school that formed my fate?
  Or was my providence prechalked on slate?

Goose Chase

Jan Rider Newman

In 1960 the world had started to change, but we lived in the middle of rice fields. Val and I didn't own a TV yet. We thought nothing would ever change, and one of us liked it that way.

The only thing Val knew was farming. His family never owned any land, so they sharecropped for others. Since the age of nineteen, Val had worked for Norman Fontenot. Norman owned a lot of land north of Bayou Nezpique, and he let it out to four sharecroppers, including Val. Spring and Summer were the busiest times, and during Winter there was livestock to tend, houses to repair and paint, equipment to get into shape for the Spring. There was also a lot of spare time for his tenants and their wives to sit in drafty frame houses with space heaters turned up all the way and windows rattling in the late January wind. It blew all Winter over flat, gray fields that not even sunshine cheered up. And when the men sat, they thought about Norman and his family in their pine-paneled den with the central heat on and the TV showing them the world.

So Norman always organized something when January got long and tiresome. One year he arranged a deer hunt, another year a catfish fry. The year after that, his daughter couldn't have picked a better month than January to get married, and we all went to the wedding. Nineteen sixty was the year of the goose hunt.

Norman pulled into our driveway just before dark one Tuesday in his new red Chevy truck. I lit the burner under the coffee pot and stepped out on the porch to invite him inside.

"No, thanks, Emmy. Is Val home?" He stood in the yard and hitched his jeans over his skinny hips.

I started to ask him couldn't he see Val's pickup right beside him. "He's milking," I said.

Norman headed around the house, and I went back to patting out biscuits. High above the roof, I heard geese honk. A flock had settled in a field close by, and at sunrise this morning they woke us up with their racket. Once the geese flew past, I kept listening. All I heard were the ticks the oven made as it heated up. Nothing else in the house made a sound. At this time of day, and especially this part of the year, I missed the noises of children. Val and I never had any. Now that we were in our late forties, I knew we never would. Val had his fields and his farming, and every other woman I knew had kids and grandkids to fuss over and brag about. I had Val and our house, which I painted inside every couple of years—yellow in the kitchen, blue in the bedrooms, white everywhere else—and kept the cabinets and furniture polished and the glass sparkling.

That day, just after I set the biscuits in the oven, I glanced out the back window and saw Norman and Val step out of the barn, heavy in talk. As more geese flew over, they pointed at them. Then Norman drove off, and Val carried in the milk pail.

"Norman says if we get us a good mess of geese by Friday, he'll throw a supper for everybody and buy all the beer and rice and stuff."

"Okay."

He took the strainer down from its hook on the wall and started pouring warm milk through it into the jugs I had scalded. We didn't talk for a few minutes. I turned the chicken frying on the stove, and Val got the milk into the refrigerator. He walked toward the bathroom, dropping the straps of his overalls and unbuttoning his shirt. "Damn, Emmy. You ain't got the heater on in here."

In the bathroom doorway I felt the contrast from the warmth in the kitchen. Not only did the air raise goose bumps, but my feet and ankles chilled from the wind blowing under the floor.

"I'm sorry. I was daydreaming." The paper from my brother's letter crackled in my apron pocket. "I heard from Ray today."

Val turned a handle at the sink and waited for the water to run warm. "They doing all right?"

"They're fine. Val, anytime you're ready, he can get you on at Conoco in Lake Charles."

"Emmy."

"We could have a brick house on a slab and a new Buick sedan every couple of years like my brother."

Val soaped his hands and wrists. "I'm not moving to Lake Charles, Emmy. I'm where I want to be." He yanked the towel off the nail next to the sink. "Why do you have to bring this up all the time? You know how I feel."

"What about how I feel? I want us to have something. Is that so wrong? Ray has a good retirement plan. On Social Security we'll never have better than what we got now, and you know it."

It was an argument I had never won, and that night was no different. Eventually, I did what I always had done. I gave up and waited for another day.

Early next morning Val took down his shotgun and went after geese, but they flew away like they had heard talk of the supper. He came in with two, and the other men didn't do any better. Only one of the men was worth a hang with a shotgun, and he was laid up with a broken ankle. Even so, he wanted to get up until his wife offered to give him another cracked bone. Fifteen people in all would be at the supper, and five geese wouldn't make the rounds. There was talk of Norman and Pam killing one of their turkeys or some hens.

Then, at sunset Friday, a big flock of snow geese glided into the fallow field half a mile behind the house. The blue-red sky was dotted with white. You could tell they were nervous, though, circling and circling, starting up at the least noise. Val and I stood on the back porch and watched them.

"You'll have a time getting some in the morning," I said. I wanted to get supper over with so I could get to my cousin's bridal shower. I also had one other thing on my mind. "Do you know what Bobby Comeaux told me when I was in Nezpique yesterday? He's selling his grocery store and wants three thousand down."

Val kept watching the geese. "Yeah, I heard that. I meant to tell you."

"You know, Val…he does a good business. He's going to live with his daughter because he's getting crippled with arthritis."

Val glanced at me. "Yeah."

"You've been with Norman thirty years, and we have good credit at the bank. We could get a loan for that down payment—"

"I thought that's where this was going."

"Why not? Come on, honey. This is our chance. If Bobby Comeaux can run a store on a ninth grade education—"

"And I got less than that."

"I have more. Val, the two of us can do it. Betty LeBleu works for Bobby a few days a week. She could help us get started. And the people around here know us. They'll buy from us. There's the house in the back. We'd have us a place of our own for the rest of our lives." I squeezed his arm. "And the best part is you could keep on farming. You'd have to, so we could make payments."

Val pushed his hat back and thought a minute, his age and weather wrinkles smoothing out as if he was stretching the idea in his mind to see it all.

"You farm as long as you want," I said, "and I'll run the store myself."

He shook his head. "We're too old to learn how to run a business, Emmy."

"We're not even fifty. Now, listen to me. You've had everything like you wanted it all these years. You want to farm, fine. I'm not asking you to quit this time. But my mind is made up about that store. I need something to keep me busy, too, and we don't have kids, so this is it."

This time, Val quit arguing, which wasn't the same as agreeing, but it was something new. I drove to the shower in Nezpique after supper and left as soon as I could because my mind stayed on the store. On the outskirts of town, I pulled over and looked at the source of my hopes, a white wooden building in need of paint, but solid, with a new roof. There was an overhang between the storefront and the two Phillips 66 gas pumps. Gravel and squashed soda pop caps covered the driveway under the overhang. I looked at the Coca-Cola thermometer, and the rubber gaskets hanging on each side of the double screen doors, and the heaped up tires, inner tubes, crates, feed sacks, and such that had piled up over the years. I saw Val and me cleaning up, painting, making the store ours. Owning it was right for us. I felt it like smooth cream in my mouth. Ours. Mine.

I shifted into first and took off for home, winding along the dark, narrow roads.

Val should have been waiting up for me, half asleep in his rocking chair. The lights were on, but he wasn't in the house. He didn't answer when I called for him outside.

While I was standing on the porch, a truck drove past. In the light from the yard lamp I saw wildlife patrol markings on the driver's door, and a thought hit me. I ran inside. A quick look on the bedroom wall where Val kept his shotgun told me what I needed to know.

The flashlight was missing, too, so I took off in the moonlight without changing out of my good black coat, best dress, new stockings, and Sunday pumps. I ran across the fields toward the place where we saw the geese settle. I stumbled and twisted my ankles in holes and tractor ruts and cut my legs and hands on dried grass stubble and barbed wire fences. All I could think of was getting to Val before he fired a shot.

Then I heard boom-boom, boom-boom. Two guns. What other fool was out there with Val? I screamed his name, but I might as well have saved my breath, what with the guns firing again and the racket from the geese that rose into the air all at once. As I got closer to the spot where the shooting came from, geese flew in a panic right over me. Then I saw flashlight beams, and a big, dark thing almost knocked me down. I caught it and hung on.

"Val?"

"I got no gun. Don't—I give up—what?"

"Norman?" I shook him by the front of his coat. "Where's Val?"

"Emmy?" All I saw were the whites of his eyes. "I got to get out of here. Let go—"

I hung on harder as he tried to run again. "Tell me where Val is."

"He ran the other way. Come on, Emmy, let go. I'm sorry. I—I'm sorry." He tore free of my hands and ran away.

"Sorry for what? Was this your idea?" I yelled after him.

I tried to decide whether to look for Val some more or go home, and that's when I saw another dark shape and heard steps crunch on the stubble. Before I could call Val's name, a game warden switched on his flashlight and shined it in my face.

"What are you doing out here?" He flipped his light up and down as if to get a good look at me. I guess he wanted to make sure I didn't have a gun, but I thought of my shredded stockings and muddy shoes and coat.

"A man ran this way," he said. "I heard you talking. Who was he? Where did he go?"

"A—a man? Uh, yeah, but I don't know who. I'm out here looking for my dog. She's a little bitty Chihuahua, and she's in heat, and—"

"You'd better go home, lady."

After the warden took off after Norman, I ran the other way to hunt for Val.

Splashes in the flooded part of the field and the moonlight shining on white, floating blobs led me to him. I called real low.

"Norman?" he answered. "Come help me."

"Fool, he's halfway home by now. It's me."

"Emmy? What the hell?"

"Let's get out of here. A game warden saw me and went after Norman. Get out of that water. Throw down those birds."

"I told you, they're gone. It'll be okay as long as we don't show no more lights." He handed me his shotgun and waded back out with his canvas sack. "We must've got a dozen."

Shivering in the wind, I thought I ought to leave him there. "You are going to pay me for this, Val."

Then a big, heavy hand landed on my shoulder. I hadn't heard anyone else coming. Slowly, I turned to face a second game warden.

"You'd better let me have that shotgun," he said.

"I wasn't—this isn't—" I handed it over.

"Here's another one," Val called. "Hoo, Emmy, look how big."

He turned toward me, holding up the goose. It was so big and so white with its wings spread out, I thought of angels. The warden switched on his flashlight. I saw a trickle of red on the breast feathers, and Val saw us. For a long time he didn't move or say anything, only stood there in the water. Then he waded over and set down the bag and the great big goose.

The other sharecroppers moved on to work other farms or get other jobs. Betty LeBleu bought the store, and I went to work for her. I made enough to pay our illegal hunting fines, Val's and mine. The game wardens never caught Norman. He gave me an old car for next to nothing so I could go back and forth to work, and I bought a TV and an antenna.

Val and I watched the televised marches on Selma and Washington. We saw John F. Kennedy assassinated in Dallas, Martin Luther King killed in Memphis, and students gunned down in Ohio. Images of women burning their bras and men their draft cards mixed with newsreel footage of the war in Vietnam. We listened as the Church changed from Latin to English and watched the first human beings leave footprints on the moon.

We stood still.

Origami

Judy Ray

Beside Mason jars bronzed with dust
and spare mantles for old lamps,
a small bright item beckons my reach
along a high shelf—red and gold paper

folded to form a box that fits into my palm.
Inside is another box, green and floral,
then another and another, nestled
in sequence, all the mitered corners tight.

Each unfolded paper I set down with care
as if I might reassemble the origami relics
of the family who left this old house
to its weathering and disrepair.

The weighty center of the tiniest box
is home to six cents, perhaps a treasure gift
between mother and daughter. But, impatient
from cleaning the debris of decades,

I sweep away the crumpled colors as if
they were no more than ash emptied
from wood stoves, together with the desiccated
bat found inside the iron grille.

Then news filters back from town
that the origami crafters have gone on to fashion
white cranes, more than four thousand now,
fastened to black boards bearing the names

of soldiers bidden to the opportunity
of their deaths, remembered by deft hands
that would transform a world to peace
with paper wings poised, straining into flight.

First Runner-up: Best Non-fiction Contest

A Child of the Fifties

Jo Wilkinson

I was twelve years old in 1959. My family rented the upstairs of a Spanish stucco duplex in the heart of the Jewish neighborhood on Crescent Heights Boulevard in Los Angeles. We had a television, black and white, and watched the usual programs: "Father Knows Best," "Leave It To Beaver," and, of course, "Davy Crockett" episodes on the Sunday evening Disney program. We were typical in that way, and in others: a mother, a father, two older brothers, and me, a shy girl usually hiding out in my bedroom, fantasizing all different kinds of stories and lifestyles, and listening to music, music, and more music. At about that time, Fabian appeared on the pop scene, and "77 Sunset Strip" arrived on TV, with Kookie Burns. I didn't like either phenomenon. I was listening to Pete Seeger, the Weavers, Paul Robeson, Rodgers and Hammerstein, Beethoven, and even Johnny Mathis. I also loved my older brother's record collection, with Little Richard, Fats Domino, the Platters, and the Drifters. My heart belonged to those sounds. Pete Seeger was my hero. I hoped I could be like him someday, leading people in song, striving to reach their hearts and minds with passionate melodies and lyrics. My girlfriends didn't have a clue what I was into. Being a "goyim" in the ninth grade of a predominantly Jewish junior high school, it was hard enough "collecting" a friend or two, so I wasn't about to reveal my musical tastes. I just smiled a lot when they giggled over Fabian and Kookie Burns.

I always felt different. In some ways my family was indeed very different from all the other families on the block, or anywhere else, for that matter. My parents seemed to have bigger ideas than most parents. Their ideas were not popular among my peers, so I learned at an early age to be very careful about what I revealed and what I kept a secret. The Fifties were more than drive-ins and colorful two-tone Chevies; there was also a thing called McCarthyism. Joe McCarthy was like the devil in my house. We were not religious people, but I had some Catholic friends who believed in the devil—and I could tell by the way my parents and their friends talked about Joe McCarthy that he was just as bad as the devil himself.

My father had been an employee of the City of Los Angeles in the Housing Authority before I was born. When I was a little girl, he was fired from the Housing Authority for trying to bring the first integrated public housing to Los Angeles. He had been called before a committee that investigated people's political beliefs, and he had refused to answer their questions. Around the same time my mother, who was a public school teacher, was also called before the committee. She was fired from teaching in the public school system because she also refused to answer their questions. The main question, of course, was "Are you now, or have you ever been, a member of the Communist Party!" At my age, I really didn't have a full grasp of what the Communist Party was. I knew a lot of fun people, though. My parents seemed to have the most interesting friends, and, sometimes, if I was lucky, those friends would have kids my age. We could talk about anything we wanted to, even Pete Seeger.

After my mother was fired, she got odd jobs tutoring wealthy people's children and teaching in a number of private schools. It was hard work and low pay. My father became an organizer with one mission: to abolish the House Un-American Activities Committee. He traveled all over the country, speaking to small groups and large, trying to get people to join together to fight back against the threats, fear, and destruction of lives that HUAC left in its wake. On one such trip to Atlanta, he was subpoenaed to go before the Congressional committee, who had come to Atlanta to try and bring fear and havoc to the burgeoning civil rights movement. Somehow, they knew his itinerary perfectly. As soon as he arrived in his hotel room, there was a knock at the door. When he opened it, two men in dark suits slapped a subpoena in his hand and walked away.

This was not the only time he had been subpoenaed. I remember when I was about ten years old, my father was in the hospital for knee surgery. While he was still under sedation, the "men in suits" came into his room and pinned a subpoena on his green hospital gown.

When asked to declare his political beliefs before HUAC, he refused, and was cited for Contempt of Congress. His case went all the way to the Supreme Court where, in a 5-4 decision, he lost and was sentenced to one year in federal prison. As a child, I knew these were scary times. I also believed my father to be a hero, but one that I couldn't openly speak about unless I was sure of the listener.

My father left home several months before he actually had to go to prison, in order to speak before as many people as possible to try and unite people to fight HUAC. He would eventually end his speaking tour in Atlanta where, after a farewell party held by Dr. Martin Luther King, Jr., he would surrender to the federal authorities.

One night at our apartment on Crescent Heights, when my father was no longer home, and my mother was at a meeting of the ACLU, only my older brother Tony and I were home. Oddly, the owners of the duplex, who were very kind and hard-working people, were not afraid of us. They had a little girl who was just a bit younger than I, and she and I often played together.

On this night, not only were my parents not home, but neither were hers. Her older sister was babysitting her, as my older brother was babysitting me. I was downstairs in her apartment, trying to get excited about playing with Barbie and Ken dolls, another phenomenon I never related to. Sometime around 8:30 PM, it was time for her to go to bed, and I went outside through their front door. There were Spanish tiled stairs going up to the second floor where we lived. I noticed a large tall bottle sitting in the middle of the third step. I remember looking at it and thinking it was something very out of place. It had a flat top with a round hole about the size of a silver dollar. Inside, there appeared to be a dark liquid of some kind. I nodded to myself after deciding that it was some form of fly catcher, a bottle full of poison, similar to something I had seen at a friend's house only a few weeks earlier. With that settled, I continued up the stairs, opened the big wooden front door, and went to bed.

I hadn't been in bed more than five minutes when I heard a very loud "bang."

"Tony, did you just drop a very big book?" That was the first thing that came out of my mouth. But our dog Flash was barking and clawing at the front door. My brother and I met in the hall. When we opened the front door, flames were shooting up from the ground all the way past us to the roof. Adults were all gathering on the front lawn, yelling at us to close the door and get out of the house through the back. We did. By the time we got around to the front, the fire department and police cars began to arrive.

Neighbors I had never seen before had their hoses on the fire. The physical damage wasn't too bad—a lot of black soot covered the front of the duplex, both downstairs and upstairs, and there was a lot of shattered glass. I looked over to the stairs and saw a stain in the shape of a circle the size of the bottle I had seen imprinted on the third step.

A police officer yelled into the crowd, "Who saw this? Who lives here?"

I walked up to him, shaking uncontrollably, and said, "I did. I live here."

He ordered me into the back seat of the police car. "Who would do this? Any friends of yours? What school do you go to?"

I don't recall answering those questions, but I did tell him what I had seen. "There was a tall bottle with a funny dark liquid in it, and a big hole in the top. It was sitting on the third step. I was playing with my friend downstairs, and I had to go around it on my way upstairs."

The officer looked stern and in some disbelief. "What kind of bottle? Did it have a rag in it?"

"No, sir, there was no rag in it. It was just like I told you."

"Well, it would have to have a rag in it to ignite the gasoline. That was gasoline that scorched the front of your place. Someone had to light it and throw it."

At that moment I realized that whoever firebombed our house had been interrupted when I came outside. He must have rushed into the bushes to hide, just a foot or so in front of me, until I went upstairs. I was so frightened, I felt like I was going to throw up. Why didn't this officer believe me, comfort me, tell me I'd be okay, figure out how to contact my mom? Instead, he just kept shaking his head at me.

"Who do you know who would do this?" he asked one more time.

I knew that no one would know exactly who did it, but I was sure it was because of my parents' politics that this had happened. After all, my father's office had been firebombed before. I was afraid to tell the police officer about my father's impending prison term, but I told him anyway. "There are people who don't like my father. He's going to prison because he refused to answer questions before HUAC."

I didn't need to explain anything further. At that time, police departments and police organizations were being indoctrinated by HUAC itself, which was distributing a film called "Operation Abolition," claiming that my father was a "well known international communist agitator." We had once called the police to our home because we'd gotten a telephone death threat against my father while he was speaking live on television. When the police officers saw his face on our TV, they turned around and raced down the stairs. They didn't care about the danger we were facing. They didn't want anything to do with my father or his family.

Now, still shaking, I began to cry. I looked out of the police car at the people on our lawn, hoping I'd see a friendly adult face. Instead, the neighbor who hated us and refused to let her children play with us came racing towards the car. I shuddered at her face.

"Excuse me, officer," she said. "What are you doing with that little girl? She's frightened! Leave her alone!"

The officer backed away, and the woman pulled me out of the car. She put her sweater around my shoulders and hugged me for a moment. "Where's your mother?" she asked. In one instant, my frame of reference about strangers was changed. The same woman who glared at us through her kitchen window was now my saving grace.

As the people began to disperse, my mother finally arrived, as did our landlord and his wife. I was sure this meant we'd have to move. But he said, "No! No one is running you out of this house." That night, many men came to stay. Some had shotguns; one had a machete. My mother tucked me into bed, assuring me that the men would keep us safe.

"Tomorrow, you leave for camp! You'll be off to the mountains and have a wonderful two weeks at Idyllwild. Sleep tight."

I didn't sleep tight. I didn't sleep at all. I trembled most of the night, fearing mostly the unknown man in the bushes and the young man in the living room with his machete.

In the morning, the people taking me to camp came by. I was packed and ready to go, but I didn't want to leave. What if something happened again? Where was Daddy? Wouldn't he come home now, before he went to jail? But my mother hugged and kissed me good-bye with a steady expression, and off I went to camp.

Two days later, someone came and painted a huge swastika in black paint on the front of the building. That was the one thing our landlord couldn't handle. He was very sad, but we would have to move. I found out from a post card my mother sent me.

Second Runner-up: Best Non-fiction Contest

The Ice Cream Man

Dolores Geuder

The neighborhood I grew up in was made up mostly of families from Ohio, Kentucky, and Tennessee. It was called "Hillbilly Haven," and our home was neatly nestled in the middle. Although we were the only Mexican family, the only difference I noticed as a child was the kind of food we ate. My playmates loved my mom's beans and tortillas, and I loved their cornbread and fried chicken.

Before refrigerators became a part of our life, we had to put up a sign in our window to show how much ice we needed for our icebox. Of course, the icebox didn't have a freezer, so when the ice cream man came pushing his cart and ringing his bell, we were overjoyed. We "hotfooted" home in our bare feet through the dirt to beg for a nickel or dime. As fast as we could, we ran back, crowded around his cart, and elbowed each other to be first.

He said we were in luck today: two for the price of one. He took the money from my friends and handed each of them two ice creams. I was the last one. I handed him my money, and he hesitated. "Two for the price of one is not for you, because you are a Mexican."

I was confused and bewildered. I didn't understand how being a Mexican could make a difference. I could see in his eyes that he wanted to humiliate me, and that hurt more than the words. Looking back, I really don't remember whether or not I got any ice cream at all.

My friends rushed to tell their mothers what happened, but I just went home. I didn't notice how hot the dirt felt under my feet, but as I passed their houses, I noticed their mothers shushing their children. I never told my mother because she would have talked about it over and over, and I didn't want to live through that moment again.

This was my first brush with the ugliness of prejudice.

Color Coordinated?

Helen Jones-Shepherd

Her Moreno eyes searched mine nervously,
As she reached for understanding.
"I'm not white like my mother or you,
My skin is brown," this frail child of twelve blurted out.

We were enjoying her favorite lunch, tacos, just the two of us.
I placed my food down slowly while ruminating, and finally
Reassured her, my skin, when sun-tanned, was darker than hers.
"No, grandma, it's not the same."

Isabel continued with, "My eyes are brown,
And my hair is raven, like the dark of night."
"Yes, that's true, like your father, Fred, and grandma Rosie."
"But momma's hair is blond and her eyes are like the ocean, so blue."

Her slight body shuddered, and she exclaimed,
"When we are together, people wonder."
"People wonder what?" I quickly queried.
With a pained expression and barely audible response, she murmured,
"If I belong to her?"

The Difference

Marilyn Hochheiser

Ever since I could remember, doctors had told me I had female problems that would keep me from having a baby. My fiancé, Sid, still chose to marry me. We had three glorious days together before the Navy took him, and he shipped out for a number of months.

Even though I didn't think I could get pregnant, wouldn't you know it, I got pregnant on our honeymoon.

I had a difficult pregnancy, and my doctor suggested I quit my job, as I had toxemia. During this time, I helped my sister by watching her two small boys, who were just young enough to get into everything. This convinced me that a baby was the last thing I wanted in the world.

Sid returned home at the end of my seventh month, and we had the normal adjustment problems. I needed a baby like a hole in the head.

Time ticked by, and it was finally my due-date. Yet nothing happened. Sid started feeding me castor oil, hoping to trigger my labor. It didn't work past keeping me in the bathroom a lot.

I started labor on Sid's birthday, December 31. I went into the hospital early that afternoon. I was prepared for delivery and practiced my breathing exercises for hours.

Finally, as my contractions intensified and became more frequent, I found myself screaming, while Sid gripped my hand. Or maybe it was the other way around? That part is a little vague now.

They wheeled me into the labor room at 9:00 PM on New Year's Eve. I was given a choice, so I refused the local anesthetic for the good of my baby.

Soon I heard, "The head is crowning," and then, "You have a beautiful baby girl." I heard my baby's bellow as the nurse told the doctor it was 9:31.

The doctor laid her on my stomach, and I saw her little red scrunched-up face as she continued to scream.

That night I couldn't sleep, because my spirit soared with happiness—not just because Glenda was born, but because the mother in me rose up with a capital M.

First Runner-up: Best Poetry Contest

Just So Story

Esther Brudo

when the baby was born
the mother named the birth an accident
a mistake
and threw the umbilical cord out of the window

she gave the baby room and board
the child grew in the cold dry climate
pale, unsure, off balance

the cord had fallen on the grass
was swept by the wind and
attached itself to a tree trunk
and a pile of acorns

then to a bird's nest where
it fastened onto an egg

the rain washed it down and
under the porch of the house
where it stayed many months
among the mice

gaining strength and purpose
it wiggled into the house
into the pocket of the woman's apron
the cord was warm and the woman
liked to feel it

one day the child saw it
dangling from the apron pocket
and reached up to touch it

the mother gave the child one end
while she held the other
and in that moment she saw
eyes just like her own

she might have been frightened
she might have turned away
but she moved closer
and that is how it began

Second Runner-up: Best Fiction Contest

In Her Mirror

Ronna Magy

When I am small, age five, and the cherrywood dresser in her bedroom is large, my mother stands in front of the oval mirror studying her face and hair. In one hand she holds the container, in the other, the puff. The round black metal contains the magic of film stars and beautiful women, a touch of Hollywood, the reddest of rouge. She presses the puff onto the cake of red dust and slowly, while looking in the mirror, pats rouge on her cheeks. Just above the hollow. On the right side, first, and then along the left. And, with careful fingers, she blends in the rouge. Across from her, in the oval mirror, a familiar face looks back. She lingers a moment; her dark eyes smile. A whisper of Claudette Colbert flits across the early morning spaces of her mind. A dance with Fred Astaire.

The two dabs reside as red circles painted on either side of the aquiline nose dividing her face. Two red dabs, below two dark eyes, below a mass of black hair. Wavy and wiry, with a few strokes of the brush her hair positions itself around the softness in her eyes and length of her face. A shake and spray and a second coat of hairspray hold it in place.

Red lipstick, a strong red to highlight the rouge, she presses along the top lip first, and then along the bottom. As she leans closer into the mirror, her fingers smoothe color to the corners, touching red to spaces where there is absence. Her lips press together, and when they open, with the air of the beautiful, she draws breath in through her nose.

Collar points of her blouse she straightens and smoothes. With fingers familiar with the touch, she slides bone buttons inside their holes. Her hands smooth over the hips of a brown tweed skirt and reach over to the bed to pull on her jacket. Turning into the mirror, she checks her seams.

Her oval mirror glistens above drawers with silver metal pulls. While she dresses, with small hands I slide open the top drawer. Enticed by the glint of gold and luster of pearls, I pick out a pair of golden earrings, pull straight brown hair back behind my ears and, in the mirror, while glancing at her above me, try them on.

"Look, Mom," I tell her.

"Let me see," she says as she hums a song and looks down. And as I turn and point my brown eyes and chin up to her, she smiles and says, "You look cute, honey. Do you like jewelry?"

"Yes," I say, "like you," and pull a pearl necklace over my head.

We like doing this together.

Sparkling earrings I place along the glass next to their matching necklaces. Rambling amongst silver and gold, I slide bracelets along my wrists. From a gold bracelet comes the story of Aunt Lillian's cruise to Spain on an ocean liner. From a blue ring box, the story of a garnet ring, the birthday gift of an adventuresome uncle moved far to the west, to Seattle, who ships a crate of Golden Delicious apples our way once a year. Each piece of jewelry I place along the dresser top near the rouge.

Wanting to try on her clothes, I pull out the black cinch-belt she wears tightly around her small waist and wrap it end-to-end, encircling my own. And while she watches, I dress up in her black high heels in front of the closet mirror. My feet move into a dance. Maybe I'll dance to Spanish music and wear a red dress and black veil. Twirling around, I hear her warm voice behind me saying, "You look nice, dear."

Initialed handkerchiefs hide in her top dresser drawer between flowered rose dividers. Curious, I finger their letters, tracing raised threads into the curls of the "E" for Esther, her name. Smelling my mother's handkerchiefs brings her close. From the cloth arises smells of perfume and smoke.

"Who gave you this, Mom?" I ask.

"Your father," she says, and smiles. "Last Mother's Day he gave it to me, remember?"

My mother wears pointy-toed high-heeled shoes and walks fast. These black shoes I trip forward in when I put them on, but not my mother. She moves quickly in heels and black skirt as we walk 'round the block and one street over to the five and ten to get her lipstick and rouge and things for me. Walking together, we pass shoe stores and toy stores and the exclusive clothing shops along Livernois, the Avenue of Fashion. I try to keep up. It is the early fifties, after the War. Rationing is over. Detroit streets are alive with the urgency of cars, and money in the pockets of those who can buy.

Up and down the rows of pins and buttons, underwear and bras, pajamas, oilcloth, stickers, and shirts, we walk through the dime store until we find the makeup aisle. She searches along the counters for her black pot of rouge and tube of lipstick, colored red. Then we go to the back of Kresge's, where I flip through pages of decals, deciding between a cornucopia of fruit and a basket of flowers to stick on the front of my school notebook. This time, I pick the fruit. Nearby, we find me a book of paper dolls I can dress up. Mom and I cut them out together at home while we talk.

That year, at five, Mom teaches me to read and write. At six, in school, I learn to add and subtract. At nine, I grow a bit taller and write poems. After I enter school, my mother begins work every day with my father. There are more times when she is not with me at home. More days when Mom is at the office when I arrive home. More days when it is Grandma who greets me at the door and not Mom.

Through my eyes, in front of the oval mirror, as I grow, my mother appears the same. Same woman, same face, same Revlon makeup, same hairbrush, same wiry hair. Same Tigress perfume bottle that sits on the glass over her cherrywood dresser from which she dabs a touch behind each ear before going out.

Once beautiful with her own darkness and youth, as I get older, she sees herself through a mother's eyes. Children, a husband, an aging mother, a house and job are hers to tend. Now, she has a mother's face, a face to make beautiful, but not linger upon. For her, makeup, beauty, and clothing become quicker thoughts, ones applied near the beginning of the day or evening, to be refreshed later on. Paint and fabric applied to bring back the fleeting glow of youth, a vision her oval mirror cannot reframe.

At First Light

Joanne Ellis

My eyes follow the squares of sunlight
as they cross the room. The sun falls
down the adjacent door
in shaded horizontal lines.
The bed reflects large splashes of sun
before the light crawls under the small
table dancing with wind-driven shadows
of the palo verde tree outside the window.

A doorway frames
yellow pansy faces
turning slowly
in my direction
as earth light shifts to the north.
The flowers shake in the wind
keeping a certain rhythm
with an ungainly tobacco tree that
grew as a weed in the moist summer,
its lighted tubular blossoms tempting hummingbirds.

The kitchen walls reflect a golden light
and later when that window sill holds the sun
like a small altar, I give myself to prayer
in that first light.

Bendemeer's Stream

J. R. Nakken

This is not a fish story. It is neither a Walden Pond philosophical essay nor an ecological exposé of yet another polluted body of water. This story is about a series of lovely coincidences that happened to a little family. Perhaps it's the story of a miracle. Why don't you decide?

I was the mother, recovered from alcoholism just a couple of years, growing up alongside my three teenagers. "To paraphrase Longfellow," I would say with a laugh, "I produced grave Marcus, smiling Douglas, and Dorcas with golden hair." Astrologically, we were all Leos except Douglas. He was the precise Virgo exception.

I wondered why they weren't all Aquarians, since water seemed to rule each of their lives. Marcus was seventeen, in hot water somewhere every day. Douglas, at the other end of the spectrum, was up to his ears in holy water, with a "call" to preach since he was twelve. At fifteen, he honored his mother religiously and considered her disintegrating atheism the personal cross he bore.

Dorcas Leigh got the dishwater. She of the golden hair and cornflower eyes grew quietly amid her noisy male siblings and irreverent, flamboyant mother. She grew. She grew and *grew*, until at thirteen she was taller and heavier than even my voluptuous self and was sick unto death of the phrase *baby fat*. "Baby sequoias, maybe," she once said, as she looked at her legs in the skirt the dress code decreed she wear to school. They were…well… unfortunate legs.

Those legs, on the 5'8" barely-teenager, were about six feet long. They began at her size nine shoes and went straight on up, with barely an indentation from ankle to thigh. Sturdy, they were, but sturdy is not the dream of any thirteen-year-old girl. This girl would interrupt a lively algebra discussion at the dinner table with plaintive remarks like "Oh, Mom. Why couldn't I have gotten your breasts instead of your nose?"

At home, we always sang. Our whole-family Christmas favorite was "The Twelve Days of Christmas." Douglas had a good tenor voice, down from the brilliant boy soprano he'd been, and Dorcas Leigh carried an adequate tune.

Marcus intoned his line—"three-ee tur-tle doves"—with baritone, off-key enthusiasm. Either Douglas or I played the piano, and we harmonized to all the old hymns I'd learned when I was a kid, and which the two younger siblings were now singing in church. Dorcas got a guitar that Christmas, and soon was chording away and singing with her brother at the piano. She needed approval, and I got out of myself enough to tell her often how beautiful and wonderful it was to hear her pick and sing, though she was nowhere near the vocalist that Douglas was, unless enthusiasm counted double.

She came home babbling, early in her freshman year, with sheet music the choir teacher had given her. "Mom, he asked me to sing a solo at the contest, and I didn't say yes until the last minute, so there weren't very many songs left, and here is mine: 'Bendemeer's Stream.'" She was tentative, beginning to suffer from buyer's remorse. I was no help.

"There weren't any songs better than this one? Dorcas, I sang this song twenty years ago. It was *old* in 1950. Plus, it's hard to sing. I only got a 'two' on it, and the accompaniment has to be just perfect or you lose the melody. Well, we'd better start practicing, if the contest's in three weeks."

We practiced. She sang bravely each night when I got home from work. In the second week, she reminded me that the contest was on Saturday, and the bus left from North Pines Junior High at 5:00 AM. On my sleeping-in morning!

Days ran away from us. Much of the time, she sounded fine on the hairy old ballad, and I acquired some hope that she might score well enough not to dash her spirits completely. I began to prepare her, anyway, with my "first time out is for experience" speech. The text could be altered to fit almost any situation, although I still hesitated to use it for sex education.

On Friday night, in between paydays, we were in the kitchen putting dinner on the table. "Now, Mom, you haven't forgotten?" she reminded me. "I have to be at the bus at five o'clock."

"Oh, dear, is that tomorrow? I thought it was next week. I wanted to get you a new dress."

"That would have been nice," she replied quietly.

How fortunate I was to hear the longing in her voice, so that I turned in time to see the lost hope in her budget-conscious eyes. I made a spot decision. "Okay, dear girl, let's see what's in the checkbook. Fourteen dollars. I have three bucks in cash, plenty of gas, and we could get by with just milk and bread until payday. Let's go out and see what we can do with fourteen bucks."

BENDEMEER'S STREAM

At the mall, we found we could do a great long dress with a tieback! The exact dancing blue of her eyes topped a flowing, flowered skirt. Her legs disappeared in the changing room, and it was on sale for $9.99. Adding a new pair of nylons for a buck, we whooped all the way home to clean up her old white sandals. Happiness was two females with a new dress!

She shook me awake at 4:30 AM. "Mom, get up now. I just have to put on my dress and brush my hair, and I made some coffee for you."

I sleepwalked to the kitchen in jeans with robe on top and poured a cup of coffee. Somehow, I found myself sitting and sipping on the piano bench, facing the bedroom hallway. A single bulb lit the hall sparingly as a golden girl came toward me, accessorized by shining hair and sparkling eyes. Shadows cast the planes of her elegant bones and granted a preview of the beautiful woman she was to become.

I stood up, staggered at the revelation. She giggled and made a joke about my not knowing whether I was "gettin' up or gettin' in," and I drove her the mile to the bus in silent awe. Kissed her good-bye, wished her luck, and said the first prayer of my life.

"C'mon, God. Please let her sing as beautifully as she looks."

Saturday passed. I stuck around the house, wanting to be there when they brought Dorcas home. She fairly flew in the front door, slammed her music and some other papers down on the orange couch, and screeched, "I got a TOP ONE, Mom! I was invited to sing at the evening concert, but no one else from Spokane was staying, so I couldn't get home. Look here, what one of the judges wrote on my score sheet!" There was the judge's comment in bold, black felt pen: *What is this marvelous voice doing hiding in contralto?*

She gushed on. "Oh, Mom, I was so scared. But just as the introduction finished, and I opened my mouth to sing, I got so calm, and *I knew it was going to be perfect.*" She hugged me and strutted down the daylit hallway to file her treasures away.

I suppose the golden girl was always a good vocalist. It could be said my self-involvement overlooked that fact. It's probably true that the choir teacher suspected Dorcas Leigh's potential. Logic led my life and leads it now, as I recount those probable actualities.

But, oh, I remember the five o'clock dark and the shiny girl dashing to the bus. I remember my very first prayer, and I believe. I believe.

Life Handed Me A Memoir

Diana Raab

My mother gave birth to me
on Mother's Day in the middle
of last century making me more than

half way to being an octogenarian
which is only years after
father found her a parakeet

she wanted instead of a kid,
but now that she's almost
a century old herself, she

realizes a girl bird couldn't care
for her aged needs—nursing care,
living accommodations and

flights across the country
to embrace the little woman
she never wanted, but I am

okay with all of that
because it's given me plenty
of fun fodder to write about, plus

my father is looking down
at me smiling at what
a blessing that day became.

Time Out

Louise Larsen

Sometimes I thought I just couldn't swallow another day of Mama and her infernal sayings.

> Early to bed and early to rise
> Makes a man healthy, wealthy, and wise.
>
> A stitch in time saves nine.
>
> A place for everything
> And everything in its place.
>
> He who hoots with the owls at midnight
> Can't fly with the eagles at dawn.

I was twelve years old and liked to do what I pleased, not be driven by a bunch of rules ruining my life. Then something wonderful happened. Mama was called to go to Springfield to take care of Aunt Lizzie while Aunt Sadie went to the State Fair to enter her lemon-blueberry cake in the contest. Aunt Lizzie often wandered away from home and had to have someone taking care of her. Mama would be gone three whole days. Mama had left lots of food for Daddy and me, even writing out complete menus for each day. She left clean clothes, too, in neat piles to wear each day. It made me seethe inside to be treated like a baby, so helpless.

Daddy took Mama to the train on Friday, and when he came back he was humming a song strange to me. He giggled and sort of danced. Then he told me he'd he gone for about two hours. When he came back, he smelled funny and was singing really loud and clapping his hands. I went up to bed and started putting red polish on my fingers and toes and just yelled goodnight through my bedroom door.

It was 10 o'clock when we got up Saturday morning. "Whoopee, she's left lemon pie," Daddy shouted. "We'll have that for breakfast."

I was horrified. Mama's menu said orange juice and cereal. But Daddy was in charge, and I loved lemon pie.

"Get on your overalls, Pickle," he added. "We're going into town."

Again, I knew we weren't following Mama's rules. We always had to put on second-best clothes when we went to town in case we met Pastor Brown or my teacher, Miss Eldridge, or Mayor Tucker. But Daddy was in charge.

The next thing that happened, I nearly fell over and honked the auto horn. Daddy took out some paper and a tobacco pouch and rolled a cigarette.

"I didn't know you smoked, Daddy, or even knew how to roll a cigarette." I managed to choke out the words.

"Smoked like a chimney when I was out on my horse on the range with the other bronc busters. That was when I was young and wild." He started singing "Get Along, Little Dogie" and sent curls of smoke rings up in the air. "I could roll the tightest darn cig of all those guys.

"You know, Pickle," he added, "we don't really need no supplies."

Daddy always called me Pickle when Mama wasn't around, because I loved those big green ones in the brine barrel so much. Now Daddy offered to get me one at Miss Eulee's Sundries and Eats, but I didn't hanker for one on top of my lemon pie.

"We'll just take this trusty old Model T out on the concrete strip to Route 66 and open her up. I might even pass a couple of slow cars doin' 20 miles per hour." He patted my knee. "Hang on tight, Pickle."

Suddenly, I felt faint and dizzy. I didn't know this wild new Daddy at all. What if he stayed like this and just loved being wild and woolly and didn't ever want to go back to the farm or read the newspaper at night and listen to the crystal set while Mama stitched? And what if he packed up a knapsack and took off for his home on the range and left Mama and me alone? I felt a tear in my eye and terror in my stomach, which was churning like a top.

"Daddy, do you like being footloose and fancy free and not loving your Pickle as much as those wild horses and roving the range?" I had to know.

I looked at Daddy with fearful eyes. Well, I thought, it really wouldn't make much difference, anyway. Mama always said that anyone who drove out on the strip was sure to get knocked clear off the road and would be dead and a goner. But I still had to know.

Daddy pulled out the throttle full force and careened wildly to 35 miles per hour, honking our horn with loud continuous blares. The cows and chickens scattered from the sides of the road. Then Daddy turned off and slowed down to 15 miles per hour, and I found I wasn't dead at all.

"To answer your question, Pickle…" Daddy took my hand. "Of course, I don't want to go back to my ravin' former life. That was all before I met your mother, the most beautiful girl in the world. And then an even greater miracle happened, and we had you, Lillian, my greatest joy in the world."

I was now so happy that I clapped my hands and reached over to kiss my daddy.

"Hey, Pickle," Daddy said, returning to his old wonderful self. "We've got to hurry home. I'm hours late feeding the animals, and you'll have to catch up on the watering, and then put out Mama's nutritional supper of roast chicken and squash and greens." He winked.

"Are we going to church tomorrow?" I asked.

"Of course, and you better get your hair washed and polish up your patent leather Sunday shoes. I'll polish my leather oxfords. We're back on schedule from now on—but it was fun being tipsy-turvy for a bit, wasn't it?"

"Yes, Daddy." I shivered with relief.

"But we need your Mama to keep things orderly and smooth. I even miss her rules, by golly."

"Me, too," I admitted.

"We'll get to bed on time tonight, so we stay healthy, wealthy, and wise," Daddy said and laughed with joy.

When In Doubt

Carole Kaliher

Buy milk and toilet paper.
Check the windows and door locks again.
Have the oil changed in your car.
Try a new food. How else would we discover the wonder of lobster?

Having a bad day? Smile at a stranger; they might be having one as well.
Think well of a neighbor, they may surprise you.
Think positively instead of negatively.
Give yourself a treat, like a massage, or a walk in the park.

Can't remember when last you called a loved one? Do it now.
Thank God for another gift of morning.
Finally, when in doubt…
Don't just love your neighbor as yourself,
but love yourself as you love your children,
for that's what God does!

My Little Red Wagon

William Speight

> "We move toward and become like the Stuff in our little red wagons."
> —Bill Sp8 Sr.

My mother will never know the gifts she gave to me as a child growing up down south in Northwest Florida. She had many sayings: "It's your little red wagon." "That is too much sugar for a dime." "That is like fatting frogs for snakes." "God does not like ugly, and He is not that crazy about pretty."

All of these refer to day-to-day living, behaviors, or actions to be taken or not taken. There are many more of her sayings that are indelibly etched into my memory. Thank you, Mama.

The older I get, the more I understand what she was saying to me. She was a person of intellect with deep insight into living. She gave me a firm foundation to operate from on how to get along with people. I still can hear her saying to me, "Junior, that's your little red wagon. You can pull it, push it, tow it, or do whatever you want to do with it." My mother talked so much about my little wagon that it became a metaphor for living. This story is about some of the negative "Stuff" in my wagon that has caused me the most anxiety.

I pull my little red wagon around with all of my Stuff in it, the positive and the negative. As an adult, it seems to be a habit, always exploring the Stuff in my little red wagon, just to make sure it is all still there. During a wagon search, rarely do I delete anything from my wagon, thinking that, some day, I might need this Stuff.[1]

For years, I placed Stuff in my wagon, then blamed others for putting it there. I now know and understand that no one can put anything into my wagon unless I allow them, and the Stuff in one's wagon can make or break

---

[1] "Stuff" is used throughout this story to represent everything good or bad, right or wrong, real or imagined that is a part of current reality.

relationships, make you happy or sad, rich or poor. Some of us live a lifetime hoping, wishing, and praying about our wagons, living and dying, never fully understanding how our wagons became filled with all that Stuff. It is imperative we know what is in our wagons at all times, because our little red wagons can determine our attitude, and our attitude determines our altitude in life. Where are you headed?

Think of each of us having a little red wagon (sometimes, the older we are the more Stuff we have in it) that includes our genetics, our "Social Heredity" (all that we have socially encountered since birth until this moment), and our "Book of Rules" (how we feel the world should work). All that we see, eat, smell, hear, taste, and experience from the moment we are born until this present moment of our lives is connected to the Stuff in our little red wagons. Remember, other people can only put into your wagon those things that you authorize. For example, I allowed my mother to put into my little red wagon the thought about the little red wagon. Do you know what is in your wagon?

We are continually putting Stuff into and taking Stuff out of our wagons. Some of the Stuff we place in our wagons during our younger years stays with us for a lifetime. What we put in or take out of our wagons is connected to consequences, most of which are not noticed until they are fully developed into events / situations / problems in our lives. This development is hidden from view until we bump up against what I call a "stop" that will no longer allow business as usual. These "stops" are by-products of our thinking, feeling, thoughts, actions, or lack of actions. Is your little red wagon too heavy to pull?

At home, work, or play, the results are the same when parties in a relationship do not understand the possibilities of unintended consequences eroding the foundation of their communication or relationships. Some of the secondary behaviors / emotions / by-products of the negative Stuff in our wagons are:

- *Anger*
- *Blame*
- *Defensiveness*
- *Ambiguous Communication*

MY LITTLE RED WAGON

Exploration

There was so much Stuff in my wagon that a wheel came off. This forced me to take all of my Stuff out of the wagon in order to repair the wheel. What a mess! I found Stuff that had been there for years. As I started to put it all back in the wagon, I thought I should eliminate Stuff that I no longer shared with others or that was of little or no use / value to me. I asked myself the following questions:

1. If I stop using this, what will happen or not happen?

2. What is this connected to? (This question enabled me to see how my thoughts, actions, or non-action relating to everyday living help to create my current reality.)

3. Will using this move me closer to my goals? (This question helped me to clean out old Stuff and add new Stuff that was more current to my situation. I am no longer trying to solve 2008 problems with 1950 solutions.)

My wagon is neither good nor bad. However, it is clear to me that social heredity can be stronger than my gene pool. And, if I continually assess the Stuff in my wagon, I can efficiently use it to be successful and maintain balance in all areas of my life.

It Will Not Last Long

Kathleen A. O'Brien

Lie down.
Stretch out.
Basket-weave your fingers behind your head
    and flare out your arms like wings.
Cross your legs at the ankles.
Let your pressing thoughts hover,
Tell the world to leave you alone;
    you haven't the time for its madness,
It's a summer rain on the roof—
    soft and tuneful—
it will not last long.
Stop what you're doing
    and listen to the cleansing of the day.

The Chase for Somebody

Ruth Hohberg

When I was ten we were living in a remote village in central Asia. It was my birthday, and I was recuperating from a long illness. My dad and I were taking a walk on this unusually lovely day in March. We were chatting away about many things, including what to be when I grew up. I don't remember anything of what was said, except the phrase: "You have to be somebody."

Later, when I was fifteen and a world away in New York City, we were walking along Riverside Drive and talked more seriously on the subject.

"Times have changed," my dad said. "When you're ready, you'll have to be independent, you'll have to have your own profession. A girl won't be able to count on marrying and being taken care of. She'll probably have to have a Ph.D. to earn a good living."

I accepted it as Truth, like most things my father said. I didn't visualize in what field that Ph.D. would be, but it sounded like something I'd want to do. I thought that, when the time came, I would be tall, blonde, and beautiful, with blue eyes…you get the idea. I would feel important when I became "Somebody." I didn't know what it would take, but I was willing to strive and work for it.

After high school, I felt that I was on my way when I was accepted to a prestigious college-level art school. Fantasies of seeing my paintings on the walls of important galleries, eventually maybe in a museum, fogged my imagination. That kind of achievement would surely make me feel that I was a "Somebody." But as the three years of art school came to a close, I felt more like a "nobody" than I ever had before. It was time to find my first job in the real world. I hoped that "Out There" in the advertising world, someone would sense my potential and offer me a place in a studio.

My portfolio open on the table, I quaked with insecurity in my soul, while the nattily dressed young man turned the pages slowly, emitting an occasional "Hmmm…" I felt positively naked, and far from the goal of having arrived. When he said, "Thank you for coming in, we'll call you," I actually thought they would. I was so trusting. I didn't understand the concept of calling back to "follow up," not letting them forget about me.

On graduation night, walking up the aisle to receive my Certificate of successful completion of the prescribed course of study, I secretly expected the morrow to bring the sought after feeling: "I'll be a graduate of The Cooper Union tomorrow. I'll really be 'Somebody'."

Tomorrow became today; when I awoke and looked around my room, my sense of self hadn't changed. I got out of bed and appraised myself in the mirror. I was twenty years old, I hadn't grown taller than the 5′ I was yesterday, my eyes weren't blue, nor my hair blond. There was nowhere to hide from myself. Real life was here and now.

I began to think that maybe earning a real college degree in addition to the art school certificate would give me the sense of importance and entitlement I considered a prerequisite to speak with a sense of authority and render opinions like some of my college graduate friends did. People who had Master's degrees bowled me over. I thought these folks must be highly learned and brilliant. Surely, they possessed the feeling of being "Somebody" that I was hankering after. Maybe going to a four-year college was really The Answer.

I spent years attending night college, slowly, laboriously building up credits while my children were little, working my way to the promise of "Somebodihood." After many years of concentrated effort, with Bachelor's degree in hand, I looked in the mirror once more. There I was, my hair and eyes still chestnut brown, and my height unchanged.

Art teachers were being 'excessed'—laid off. After all these years and toil, I couldn't even get a job in my field. I didn't feel anywhere near the way I had expected to feel as a college graduate, a "Somebody."

I was disappointed. My goal was elusive. Was I in the wrong field? Perhaps a Master's degree was the magic ingredient. I struggled through more night school, earned a Master's degree and still couldn't get a job; the interviewers wanted someone more experienced. I began to despair of ever being the "Somebody" my dad had inspired me to want to be.

I had a fleeting moment of exultation when, after an interview with an agency that helped the retarded, the director said, "You have great qualifications. We'd love to have you work for us, but can you afford to? We pay very little, you know."

THE CHASE FOR SOMEBODY

In a split second the elation that someone thought me a "Somebody" lifted my self-esteem, and just as quickly devalued it when she mentioned the inadequacy of the pay. I accepted the offer, thinking I would change this little piece of the world for the better.

It was hard to win; I heard someone remark offhandedly that people who work for agencies are lazy and don't know what it is to really work, another dampening slant on my quest to be "Somebody." I pushed that to the back of my mind. In the meantime, I was thrilled. I had a job, someone wanted me, and I would be in a position to help to improve the lives of less fortunate people. Full of enthusiasm and energy, I started work at the agency in the capacity of head of the Ceramics department, a one-person operation. It didn't matter; I had a "handle" that made me "head" of something, and I was expected to be there and produce.

As time passed at the agency, I felt less and less like "Somebody." I recognized that the promise and effort of the CEO and the director added to mine were not enough to put the ceramics operation onto a viable commercial footing. Making each piece by hand and buying the materials at retail prices, we couldn't begin to compete with Japanese planters, cups, and spoon rests. Even the electrified Christmas trees festooned with colorful lights simply couldn't put us on a basis of "breaking even."

I struggled through yet another Master's degree, still chasing the elusive fantasy of being "Somebody," this time in Social Work. It was promising. I started from the bottom, helping in the resettlement of Cambodians, Russians, Iranians, and whoever was the "Refugee Group of the Year." It was exciting and rewarding. I felt I was making a clear difference in people's lives. I felt good and, yes, important in the scheme of the agency's mission. And yet…

Assuming that, in order to count as "Somebody," a person had to be a significant player on the World Stage, and being on the other side of middle age, I realized that I needed to re-evaluate the definition and come to terms with my existing life and accomplishments, or be chasing the "Somebody" phantom for the rest of my days.

A friend and I were talking one day about what constitutes being a worthwhile person or "Somebody." He defined it according to his view:

"To me," he said with confidence, "it means having a trade—like being a plumber, a carpenter, a teacher, or doctor. It doesn't matter what it is, just so long as it's productive, pays one's bills, and makes one feel independent.

When one sleeps well at night knowing that one is taking care of one's own life."

When I was ten, I had not asked my father to explain what he meant by the phrase he uttered that had haunted me for most of my life. Now the lights went on in my brain.

Perhaps my father had been trying to tell me what my friend had just said, and I misunderstood. Perhaps I was "Somebody" all along and didn't know it!

So I don't have a Ph.D., my artwork is not in a permanent museum collection. I have been a daughter, mother, friend, lover, and wife. I have sold my work, participated in exhibitions in small museums, won prizes, have had a book published. I came to realize that, like so many other intangible things, the "Somebody" issue is one of self-perception. I am "Somebody."

Authentic Self

Lolene McFall

Do not say of me
She is this or that, thus or so.
None of your musings count now
Or ever did. I am what I have become.
Whether due to fate, choice, circumstance,
Or conditioning, it's of no moment now,
Least of all to you who judge and chat about me
And comment upon when you knew me,
With chuckles and whispers and idle musings.

I've re-birthed myself and grown
And you know nothing of it.
Nor did you know me in that prior time,
So still your voice.

See me now, but not with past perception.
Don't watch my lips; I *show* you the truth of me.
Behold me *now.* I am someone we never knew.
I am what I have become, no more, no less.
I have become that which I am—*authentic.*

At the Gazebo in Larchmont

Sandra Sturtz Hauss

I'm watching a man who reminds me of you,
Whose voice and movements conjure up an image
That makes me wish you were here with me now
So we could sit together and write;
Grandpa, I'm speaking with this man
Whose voice is so like yours
That tears are falling from my eyes
And my own voice becomes inaudible,
So hard is it for me to speak
For memories are flooding my brain
And my heart wants to reach out to him
To be closer to you;
He tells me he sits on this park bench each day,
Just watching the movement and reflecting on life,
The way you would if you were still here;
He speaks with an accent so familiar to me
For my childhood was spent hearing that warm
    inflection
And his eyes are warm recollecting his love
From a wife now long gone and his children,
    both living,
He wears a fur coat to be shielded from winter,
And sits on a pillow for his bones are now aged,
He walks with a cane though his steps are still steady;
Grandpa, when we spoke, I swear I was with you
And felt it was fate to have met him
Just when I was missing you most.

My Dad

Janet Kreitz

I miss my dad. I miss his warm easy smile. I miss him at the Sunday dinner table. I miss his unconditional "I love you." I miss saying "Dad." He left too soon. He left before I had the wisdom to say thank you.

Dad gave me many gifts during our time together. At bedtime, I nestled in the bend of his arm while he read me fairy tales in his deep voice. When I was older, we walked up the library steps. The library, he said, held an unlimited world of enjoyment, knowledge, and adventure. Though his own reading hours were replaced with family needs and work, he waited patiently in the car every two weeks while I browsed the library shelves. His gift continues to his grandchildren, who cherish reading.

His love of reading evolved as an escape from his tension-filled childhood home. His voice warmed when he spoke of reading *Treasure Island*, *Robinson Crusoe*, and *Tom Sawyer*, but cracked remembering his parent's daily arguments. He loved his mother and father, but thought it was difficult for the Irish-German temperaments to mesh for a calm, peaceful marriage.

I am grateful he lived the role of a good man. A short, lean man of Irish-German descent, he worked five days a week, year upon year. His rewards were a well cared for family and two weeks yearly vacation. I think the only money he spent on himself was to buy cigarettes, the weekend newspaper, and a Saturday night beer. He mowed the grass, painted the house, hung the storm windows, washed the car, and daily praised my mom on her cooking. He was the man who drove his family in a heat-soaked car across Kentucky, Tennessee, and Georgia, so we could see the ocean in Florida. He was the man who lay on a snow-packed driveway, coaxing his stiff fingers to thread stubborn chains onto the tires so he could get to work. He said Buffalo, New York had real snow, where it was measured in feet, not inches. Dad graduated from high school when the Depression was roaring across America. He lived with cousins in Buffalo while he worked at the Pierce Arrow auto plant until its demise in 1938. For the harsh discipline of his childhood, he substituted firm loving guidance to elicit my good behavior.

He sprinkled conversations with nuggets of his boyhood in Quincy, Illinois. He helped me see beyond his lined face and gnarled knuckles to a skinny-legged boy. Dad and his friends suffered bruised knuckles and bloodied noses during after-school retaliations against the hurlers of "mackerel snapper" and "papist". The Mississippi River was his swimming pool. His adventure was walking the train trestle to Hannibal. His challenge was to white-knuckle grip the trestle sides, waiting for the roaring monster to pass. He earned spending money from his paper route. He was an altar boy, but missed seeing his grandson perform that unchanged ritual.

He spent some summer weeks with his grandfather in Galesburg, Illinois, where he learned and never lost the fierce pride for his Irish heritage. His grandfather's brogue-laden voice told Dad the family story of the flight from Ireland during the potato famine, surviving a horrendous sea voyage on a coffin ship, and struggling years against Irish-Catholic bias. Dad was a teenager when he witnessed the Irish wake for his grandfather. "Ah," Dad said, "the Irish believe this life is a brief interlude to a better life and cause for celebration when someone dies." The Carroll men and friends celebrated deep into the night and included the corpse in a round of whiskey and a cigar. Dad said this act created a volcanic fury in the morning from the women, a fury that lasted long into the day.

I have the stained, yellowed map Dad used to follow the American military across Europe in World War II. The selective service rejected him because his heart had been damaged during a bout of rheumatic fever he suffered as a boy. His concern was as deep as my mother's for her brother, who crossed the English Channel twenty-nine times.

Dad loved to laugh, tell jokes, and talk. Stranger was not a word in his vocabulary. He talked with anyone. An errand to the grocery store, the gas station, or buying the weekend newspaper was never done quickly. Always, time was taken for conversation while I waited by his side, balancing from one foot to the other.

Dad valued his family, his church, and his country. He was a life-long Democrat who today would wear the liberal label. He lived women's liberation, racial equality, and railed against a war in faraway Vietnam before these were everyday topics in American conversations. He and I catnapped through election returns on a long November night in 1960. Three years later, for the first time, I saw my dad cry.

MY DAD

I am gifted by Dad's love and value of me. There was no question, when I graduated from high school, that I would attend college. Dad believed the family was a link in a chain of generations, and each generation held a responsibility to better itself for the future generation. My mother questioned the value of educating a woman, "as her husband will take care of her." Dad was irate. "A woman needs to be able to take care of herself. Maybe she won't marry. Her husband may die." Years later, after fifteen years of a tension-filled marriage, I divorced. Daily, I thanked Dad for my education. My education fed, clothed, housed, and educated his three grandchildren. I missed him at their college graduations.

I am a senior citizen who has lived longer than my father. Yet I have stopped writing this countless times because it is difficult to see the keyboard through my tears. I miss Dad. I mourn the Sundays, birthdays, holidays, marriages, births, all the days and years not shared with him. I am grateful for the caliber of man he was. Thank you, Dad.

Harvey Levi
(August 7, 1897 – February 19, 1971)

Jolly Ann Maddox

My Daddy was a gambler who
    had a third-grade education
    taught me to count using the spots on a deck of cards
    to play gin rummy before I was six
    showed me off—all those golden curls, those baby blues—
    lifting me on tables to tap dance in bars
    bought that Philco phonograph
    the one you pulled down the door and
    slipped the 78s in—and I tapped and twirled
    smashed up that Philco and other odds and ends—
    I was whisked off to my aunt's—
    I wondered what had happened
    gave my play house to the milkman to pay the bill.
My Daddy was a gambler who
    went to France before he was 18
    sent his doughboy's earnings to his mother
    saw death, suffering, horrors unimaginable
    never talked about the Great War.
My Daddy was a gambler who
    practiced with a broom handle long before he held a cue stick
    had a crease in his slacks
    starch in his shirt
    shine on his shoes
    cocked his hat, ever so slightly—somewhat rakishly
    lifted his little finger—the one with the ring—
    just before he sent the ball into its designated hole
My Daddy was a paradox
    A gentleman who was loving and fun
    when not angry and depressed
    Who
    loved my mother but couldn't stand
    the responsibility of a family
    took pride in his family
    but took his frustrations out on them.

My Daddy was a brilliant man who
    played the horses until the Rangers shut him down
    sent my 13 year old sister on the bus to SA with scratch sheets
    could not find his niche
    could not fight off the demons in his soul.
He was Blackjack.

A Congenital Liar

Elisa Drachenberg

If I had to describe my grandfather with just one word, I could pretend to agonize over the choice between womanizer, alcoholic, or liar, as if I were not absolutely certain that what he did most, and perhaps best, was lie. His lying seemed necessary for various reasons. Mostly, because the truth simply would not do when it came to hiding his extramarital trysts from my grandmother.

Truth would not have served him well, either, if he had admitted to spending his mornings in his favorite village bar while she thought him repairing watches in the jewelry shop she had inherited from her father. She wanted him to "make an effort"; he wanted to escape the drudgery of working and preferred, like all alcoholics worth their label, to drink. First, he just drank after dinner; then, with lunch; then, with—or mostly instead of—breakfast.

If my grandfather had tried to explain to his wife that putting minuscule coils and screws in appropriate places required at least a couple of beers to keep his hands from shaking, and a few more to steady them for the rest of the morning, she would have screamed. Early in their marriage she would throw her head back, purse her lips and let out a grieving shriek that slowly turned into a wail. Later—more than three decades later—she just stopped talking altogether, as if wanting to punish the rest of the world for the deal that did not work out in her favor, a deal with a man whom she blamed for not living up to the potential that she and her family had chosen to detect in him. In those thirty-some years Sophie, my grandmother, came to recognize that he actually had lived up to his potential, just not what she had opted to see. By that time, she had accepted that her family's money had not been able to buy a caring husband, much less a loving one. And by that time, most of her inheritance was lost.

Through their marriage, Ferdie, her husband, had been elevated from a lowly employee in her father's jewelry business to proprietor of his own thriving store. He had moved from a cheap rented room to one of the most exclusive villas in Coburg. Her great-grandfather had once sold the finest jewelry to the Queen of England. Sophie had grown up hearing that Queen Victoria and Prince Albert, the handsome prince of Sachsen-Coburg-Gotha, had been regular customers in one of the very stores still owned by her father and that the royal couple, vacationing in Prince Albert's castle, would regularly stop in to buy souvenirs for their children.

"Imagine, Queen Victoria in our store at the Marktplatz. Judging from the photos, she wasn't much to look at, I guess. Especially next to Prince Albert, she looked rather plain. He was such a striking man. Yet he loved her." Sophie's mother never seemed to tire of talking about that remarkable affair of Coburg's prince who had married his first cousin, the Queen of England. "Against all odds, he came to love her. And, of course, she absolutely worshiped him. So, when he died of typhoid fever, she was utterly grief-stricken. He was only forty-two at the time."

Sophie loved that story for various reasons. She was a romantic, a starry-eyed only child, protected and privileged. But she was neither naive nor dim-witted. Had she not stood often in front of the mirror, staring at her image, at her flat chest and large teeth, her thin hair and fat ankles? Still, somehow she had come to believe she would encounter her Albert. If an attractive prince could love a dowdy-looking queen, why, then, couldn't she be part of a similar fairy tale?

At dinner, she would often gaze at her father's face, much homelier than hers, and pretend she had inherited her mother's entire loveliness. And when the mirror kept reminding her otherwise, she decided to compensate by preparing to be a more than perfect wife to a husband who would have as much integrity and devotion as Prince Albert.

At seventeen, she thought to glimpse that man in her father's store: dressed rather shabbily, wearing an inexpensive suit, a size too small for his muscular body, but there was something regal in his posture, in the way he stood and crossed the room to greet her. If she had not known better, she could have believed that it was Ferdie who owned the store. Dazzling Ferdie, the town playboy, the one who could have had any woman in town, stood in front of her and smiled. She had never seen anyone smile like that, so warm, so engaging, and, oh, so tempting. He bowed and kissed her hand. The instant his lips touched her skin, she grasped that he was the one. The top of her hand tingled, and the fire spread through her arm and down her body. It settled between her thighs. And still he smiled. At her. She would be his Victoria. And he would love her until death.

She knew her father would have been horrified, had he been able to guess her thoughts.

"Ferdie is a *luftikus*; he'll never amount to anything. But you can't find any decent help now, with all the young men wanting to earn more," he remarked that night during dinner, eyeing his only daughter, whom he had observed eyeing his least worthy employee. It troubled him that Sophie seemed smitten by a young man who so clearly had nothing to offer her. Sure, Ferdie had a gift. With his winning demeanor, he could mesmerize customers, training his smile especially on widowed women: women, often old enough to be his mother, lonely women, who began to giggle shamelessly, who came to the store with no intention of buying anything, but did. He had seen Ferdie's charm at work, and, yes, he had profited from it. But what was good for business was not good for his daughter. He watched Sophie putting down her fork. She had barely touched her food. Damn that Ferdie. Only the thought that she would soon go off to college could calm him.

Sophie was eighteen when her first son was born; Ferdie was twenty-nine. Unlike Sophie's parents, the young couple had looked joyful, even jubilant in their wedding pictures; the loose-fitting dress and the white roses clutched closely to her stomach had hidden the early pregnancy so well that many people had been inclined to believe she had actually given birth to a premature baby less than six months later.

Sophie never knew about the deal between Ferdie and her parents. Ferdie never mentioned it; neither did her parents, leaving her room enough to believe that he was the man she needed, a man whose word could be trusted, a man who would take care of her just like her father had done before.

In return for a substantial amount of money, a share in the business, and the touch of sophistication that only old money can bring, her parents felt it only fair to expect his focused dedication to their business and an equally focused commitment to Sophie, their only daughter. And yes, to be fair, Ferdie tried. For a few months, he went to the store, now not merely looking the part of proprietor. Afterwards, he came home to his elegant new house, where big-bellied Sophie had prepared a delicious meal despite feeling nauseated. He drank his beer—he never did acquire a taste for wine—

and smoked his cigar; he even lifted her nightgown high up above her waist in those nights that he could bear to see her nakedness.

Within a year, Sophie had given birth to Uli and was pregnant with her second child. Ferdie could no longer bring himself to touch her ballooned body without drinking. He had always loved to fondle women, just not women who looked like Sophie. Besides, he had never been able to stay around for too long. And so it was not really surprising to anyone but Sophie that Ferdie—relishing in his newfound wealth, but feeling trapped by the way he had to qualify for it—returned to his old routine of wine—or, in his case, beer—women, and stories.

Ah, the stories. There were the innocent ones, in which he enhanced and embellished events, when, with every new version, the trout he claimed to have caught with his bare hands in the stream behind the restaurant grew by at least five inches. Everyone knew he had an aversion to water. He would not drink the stuff, let alone wet his feet to fish in it. Everyone knew that the deals with his big-shot male clients, whom he claimed to charm into significant purchases—just as he had done with the widows before—were a figment of his imagination. As his drinking increased, his clientele diminished. But those were the stories that did not harm anyone; actually, they seemed to benefit all concerned: the storyteller, who harvested laughs or feigned admiration; the listeners, who were rewarded rounds of free beer; and the innkeeper, who made his money keeping their glasses filled with amber brew.

The other stories, the ones Ferdie needed to cover up his affairs, were, of course, much less innocent. Still, in the fall of 1951 at the sagacious age of four, I quickly came to understand his reasons for not telling the truth. I was spending a couple of weeks in Coburg in my grandparent's house of faded glory when I learned that a lie was neither immoral nor bad if it kept the truth away from the person who would surely be most hurt by it. And if, simultaneously, this lie prevented punishment for sins committed, then at least two people would be happy. Lies worked, if you were clever enough, if you told people the things they needed to hear and, most important, if you had a perfect memory to recall what you had said and to whom. Lies didn't have short legs as my mother claimed; well-delivered lies made people adore you.

It was at my grandparent's house that the foundation for these beliefs was formed. I was still an only child then, pampered by my parents, and certain that my grandparents would not treat me otherwise.

"Promise to be a good girl," my mother whispered in my ear, as if she had not been telling me the exact same thing during the three-hour trip down south.

"I promise," I whispered back, not realizing the full extent of that promise.

"It's only until the baby is born. Then Daddy will pick you up."

"Always the baby. I don't want the silly baby."

"You don't mean that," my mother said, rummaging through my suitcase. "Here, princess." She held up my favorite doll. "To keep you company."

From the very beginning, I disliked grandmother Sophie.

"You are not a princess. The sooner you know, the better," she said after my mother had left. She began barking orders and demanded that I help her set the dinner table. I was scolded for speaking with a full mouth, for gulping my grape juice, for burping, for eating with my fingers and for not using my napkin. She corrected my grammar and bemoaned my posture. She insisted I curtsy when the neighbors came to visit. And, worst of all, the very first evening she asked me to help her with the dishes.

"You can dry the cutlery," she said. "Make sure you wipe them completely dry. I don't want to see any spots." The heavy silver knives and forks and spoons felt more like weights than eating utensils and drying them was a grueling, seemingly never-ending task.

"I have to go to the bathroom," I wailed.

"Go ahead, but don't think I'll do your work for you." And she didn't.

After having spent close to ten minutes sitting idly on the toilet, I returned. With a big sigh, I picked up a knife and began sawing through the dishtowel.

"No, no, no. Didn't your mother teach you anything?" She removed her hands from the suds, took the towel from me and demonstrated how she wanted me to dry her knives. "See, you wipe the blade like this, from the back."

"Good job, Omi," I said, clapping my hands. "Can you show me again?"

Instead she handed me the dishtowel. "You must learn these things."

"Mom never polishes the silver."

"I know." She sighed.

"Mom says, when you don't polish it, it turns into gold."

"Nonsense."

"It's true, Omi. It looks golden."

"It looks like tarnished silver. Any self-respecting wife would take the time…" She stopped, picked up the linen dishtowel that was reserved for "crystal and crystal only" and shoved it into a wineglass. "You have to learn early to be a *good* wife."

"Are you a good wife, Omi?"

"Certainly. Can't you tell?" She made a sweeping gesture over the sparkling crystal glasses, the blinking pots and shiny cutlery.

"Mommy says you had a maid once. Can't you get another one? Then she can do the dishes."

For a moment she seemed stunned. "We can choose what we want, but we can't choose what we get. Remember that, young lady." The down-turned corners of her mouth quivered. When she went on, she seemed to be talking to herself. "A maid, indeed. The answer to everything."

The next morning, my grandfather did not come down for breakfast and, when he finally did show up, his breath smelled sour, and his hands shivered as if he were cold.

"Why don't you take her with you? Take a nice walk to the store?" my grandmother said, and then, looking at me but somehow also looking at him, she added, "Grandfather no longer drives."

If my grandfather flinched, I did not notice. He turned to me with a smile so endearing that I quickly forgot about the long walk down to the village, which to my surprise turned out to be much shorter than anticipated, mostly because we first stopped in a bar. It must have been about ten in the morning, but the bar was filled with seven or eight men sitting around a huge wooden table, telling jokes, teasing each other, discussing politics, rumors, and the weather.

"And who is that lovely little girl?" a fat man with three golden front teeth wanted to know.

"Isn't she a bit young for you?" a bald man asked before taking a gulp of his beer.

"So the wife is keeping tabs on you?" said a thin man, rubbing his stubbly beard.

"Meet my granddaughter, Christine, Uli's kid. He's a big-shot director now at Bayer in Leverkusen. Remember, I told you about him, how well he's doing? Ah, such a sharp kid. Turned out to be a very important person. Must have gotten it from me." He looked around at the men, who were simultaneously raising their glasses to him and didn't put them down until they were empty. "Kiki here is staying with us," he said, giving me his wonderful smile again. He ordered a round of beer for the Stammtisch and sat down next to me. "Tell them, Kiki, where does Daddy work?"

"At the spirin place," I said, just as we had practiced on our way down to the bar.

"Aspirin."

"Yeah. At the a spirin place."

The men roared. I climbed onto my grandfather's lap, thrilled to have caused their laughter with a bogus story. We lived in Frankfurt, and Daddy, I knew for a fact, worked for the city. But that no longer mattered. I had fallen under the spell of granddad Ferdie's smile.

A blond woman with shiny red lips put a glass filled with amber liquid in front of me. "An apple juice for Ferdie's adorable little sunshine, and a *weizenbier* for her granddad and the rest of the gang." She pinched my cheeks a little too hard. Grandpa patted her back as she marked his beer coaster with straight and horizontal lines. She winked at me before leaving for the kitchen. When she returned, she carried an enormous tray heaped with salty pretzels larger than my hand. "These are on the house."

Later, there was strawberry ice cream brought by Wanda, the same woman with the shiny lips and the large breasts that bounced up and down when she giggled at something my grandfather told her. The longer we stayed, the more she giggled. One by one, the other men finished their beers and left, wishing us a good day, and every time the blonde behind the bar waved at them.

"See you tomorrow," she sang in her husky voice, and when the last man had closed the door behind him, she went to lock the front door, came over to our table, and sat down. The same hand that had waved goodbye to her customers now fluttered up to her hair and raked through her curls, as if they needed combing. Her other hand kept fiddling with the top button of her white blouse that already showed more cleavage than I had ever seen before.

"Ferdie," she said, her voice even lower than before, "how long will the little sunshine stay?"

"Omi makes me help her all the time," I complained. "I really want to go home, but I can't. The baby, Mom's having a baby."

My grandfather was finishing his beer in one last big gulp.

"How long, Ferdie?" Wanda raised one finger to trace his mustache, gently removing the foam, all the while licking her lips into even more shininess. She leaned her spectacular breasts into my grandfather's shoulder. She smelled of lilacs and cigarettes. "There is some chocolate on the kitchen table," she said to me without taking her eyes off my grandfather. She gently nudged me off his lap. I had never seen him in a better mood. He had smiled more in the last few minutes with Wanda than he had in an entire evening with my grandmother. "Chocolate," she repeated, beginning to stroke his thigh.

Wanda was so much nicer than grandma Sophie, so soft, so sweet, so kind. When I returned from the kitchen, Wanda had taken my place on grandpa's lap. Without being told, I stayed behind the counter, pushing one square piece of milk chocolate into my mouth after another. I chewed thoroughly and slowly. I was four, but I knew that, if I wanted to keep getting juice and pretzels and ice cream, I needed to forget what I saw. With every piece of mouth-watering chocolate, it was easier to ignore them.

It was not that I failed to remember my grandmother or the fact that my grandfather was clearly married to her and not to Wanda, but I favored him, anyway. Given a choice, I would always pick grandpa Ferdie.

Two years later my loyalties would shift.

It was on a sunny Sunday in June of 1953—by then I was six years old—when my father and I walked thirteen times to the bus stop half a mile up the road, waited impatiently for every invariably late after-war bus to arrive, clutching our ever more wilting carnations while eagerly watching passengers getting off, one by one, craning our necks, praying for two more people to step out and willing one of them to be my grandfather. Finally, we sauntered back home. We pointed out every bird. We stopped to pet every dog. We admired every baby in a stroller or front yard, stretching time.

My mother had opened the front door before my father could get out his keys. "So he did not show," she hissed. "How odd, how very peculiar for a man who is so reliable and dependable and trustworthy and…" She saw him close his eyes, a sure sign he would not fight back, and pushed on. "I wouldn't even let that cheating, lying son-of-a-gun back into our house if it were not for Erwin." Later, when she realized we were considering yet another trip to the bus stop, she treated us with the same contempt that she reserved for my grandfather.

"Is Wanda coming, too?" I asked, knowing full well that my mother had never called her by that name. After my grandmother had suddenly died and my grandfather had moved in with Wanda, my mother referred to her as "that gold-digging tart," even though she admitted there wasn't any gold left to dig for.

She threw me one of her famous killer looks. Suddenly, seemingly less sure of herself, but angrier than before, she jammed the wilting carnations into a vase. "He would not dare bring that…that…floozy. Or would he?" she asked.

My father shrugged.

"Floozy, floozy," I sang. I liked the sound of the word; it rhymed with oozy, something icky and slimy, but mostly I liked it because it sounded like something I was not supposed to repeat. "Floozy, floozy, floozy," I kept singing even louder, picking up my lazy little brother, who after almost two years still refused to speak, despite my mother's constant coaching. With his chubby fist he reached for my nose. The boy, who had only been willing to utter *nana*—bananas were his favorite food—and *Mama, Dada,* and *Kiki* to rally us to get him whatever he pointed to, started to grin. "Kiki," he crooned, clearly pleased with himself, and then he added, this time without any motherly coaching, a fifth word to his vocabulary. "Foozie," he said.

He clapped his hands, as if to applaud himself and repeated, "Foozie? Foozie?" until my mother took him away from me.

"Look what you've done," she said, and the sound of her voice made me stop singing. Under different circumstances, we all would have laughed; today was not a day for laughter. Today, my mother mocked my dad for believing his father had, for once, been honest.

"He would not lie about this, not about this. There must be a misunderstanding. Perhaps they missed the bus," my father said. He removed the limp flowers from the vase, and water dripped on the floor as he again headed for the front door.

"He made it all up, mark my words. It's all because he needed the—" She bit her lip and went on feeding my brother his favorite *nana* to keep him from repeating his newly learned word.

~

We walked up the hill twelve more times. Every time we spotted a new bus in the distance, our hearts began racing.

"Maybe, Daddy, maybe this time?" I said, by the fifth time no longer believing my grandfather would actually get off the bus.

"Maybe," my father said, nodding his head. "You never know."

But we knew. And, because we knew, we needed to appear cheerful. He waved the drooping carnations after every departing bus, pretending the bus drivers—who by now knew why we were there—had become steadfast friends. As soon as the last bus of the day had disappeared around the corner, my father stopped talking. Silently, he shoved the flowers into a trashcan, their red blooms dangling over the edge like weary heads. Silently, we walked home, and the closer we came, the tighter he squeezed my hand. I could see his knuckles turn white and feel my fingers go numb, but I never let him know.

At home, he only nodded to my mother, his face pale, his jaws clenched, the veins in his temples throbbing. He looked around the living room, as if seeing it for the first time. He still did not speak. His eyes wandered to me, to my mother, to my baby brother, whom they had named after my uncle because, unlike my father, his brother Erwin had never come back from the war that he was too young to fight, but not too young to go missing in.

Missing, an ambiguous word. While causing anguish and despair for not knowing his brother's fate, it also left my father plenty of room for wishful thinking. True, Uncle Erwin had never returned home. The war had ended eight years earlier, and people were busy forgetting their traumas by rebuilding their lives. My father clung to hope. For him, Erwin was alive, perhaps in a prison camp, but alive. Until now, neither the Red Cross, nor the Bureau for Missing Persons, nor any of the other agencies had been able to find him. But neither had they confirmed his death. Surely, a boy as strapping and spirited as Erwin could not have vanished without a trace. Someday, his brother would return home. My father willed his truth to be a fact.

And then, on June 8, 1953, on the precise day that Uncle Erwin, wherever he was, turned twenty-three, my grandfather's telegram arrived: *Red Cross located Erwin—Both coming Sunday—Arrive 2 PM at bus stop Kaiser—Need money for transportation etc. etc.—Momentarily short on cash—PLEASE send 250 DM—Father.*

And that Monday my father, who was not the hugging kind, not only hugged, but kissed all of us, especially little Erwin. For one whole week, he did not seem to suffer from migraines caused by his war injuries; for one whole week, he went to work humming. My mother's raised eyebrows regarding the money transfer would not deter him from nearly emptying their bank account.

But now it was Sunday evening. And there he stood in our living room, staring at us, shaking his head. I would have gone to the bus stop with him for a fourteenth time, despite my aching feet, despite my mother's mumblings, and despite the fact that I did not really care about this unknown uncle for whom she had baked the scrumptious cake that we were not allowed to touch until he arrived. But I knew the busses stopped running after eight o'clock.

My mother cut the chocolate-almond cake and gave me an extra large piece. "You deserve this," she said, and when she cut another piece for my father, she set it down gently.

"You were right," he said in a nearly inaudible voice.

"I am sorry, Uli," she whispered and put her arm around him.

And so the blond little girl ate her cake. With every bite she glanced at her parents, who had quarreled because her mother had been right—right in predicting that her father-in-law was "a congenital liar, unconscionable, impervious to correction, and this time there is no possible excuse." She had been furious with her husband for still defending "this man and his *vivid imagination*," in front of his only daughter, Christine, who, they both agreed, needed to be taught the ethical values of telling the truth and nothing but the truth.

"I wanted to believe him," the girl's father said after a while. He had not touched his cake.

"I know. We all did, but you more than anyone." The mother no longer looked angry. She smiled as she reached for her husband's hand.

"Nothing but a ruse," he said. "To think my own father…"

They didn't pay attention to the girl, who had finished her cake and now sat quietly, studying the pattern on her plate.

When Erwin, the girl's baby brother, stirred on the couch, her mother picked him up. "He's dead tired, but he refused to sleep in his bed. Must have sensed the excitement." She hugged him. "Anything we can do for you, young man?"

"Foozie?" he asked, rubbing his eyes.

"We're fresh out of those. All gone. How about cake?" the mother offered, and the baby boy nodded.

That Sunday, Christine vowed to become a pathological truth-teller. Like her father, who had chosen never to touch one drop of alcohol, not even to celebrate the birth of his son, she promised herself to stay away from her own addiction: the lies that came to her so easily, the illusory worlds that lured and tempted.

She did not understand it on that Sunday, but looking back, decades later, she could clearly see that both she and her father had been terrified all their lives. The same demons haunted them: What if their DNA predestined them to be no better than Ferdie? What if they had inherited, along with his genes, his vices, as well? Her father, scared of becoming an alcoholic, drew on his immense willpower. That, and the fact that his migraines made him unbearably sick every time he merely detected alcohol on the breath of others, helped save him. He never once drank, knew that he should not tempt the gods or himself

You can refuse alcohol, ban it from your house, from your environment, but how do you ban words and ideas from forming in your brain? The girl did try. Honestly. But, like any good addict, she simply could not wean herself off the substance. Ultimately, she failed. Unable to control her hereditary vivid imagination, unable to stop inventing stories, she abandoned the promise she had made.

She realized that nothing could ever save her. Just like Ferdie, she continued to make up tales she clearly knew to be totally, utterly untrue. Just like Ferdie, she could not keep herself from spinning yarns, from concocting worlds, from fabricating places and creating characters, not merely for the kick or the rush of adrenalin—although the memory of the highs kept her going when the lows invariably set in—but because she had to, because otherwise she would surely die or, worse, go insane.

Just like Ferdie, she lied. There was no doubt that lying was in her blood. With time and practise she improved, actually turning into one of the most skillful liars.

But, unlike Ferdie, she never harmed anyone with her lies. On the contrary, people came to admire her style. Last year, she even won the Writer's Guild Award for Best Fiction.

Capsized

Mimi Moriarty

This poem is not about my father,
it is about another man, an alcoholic
found floating next to his capsized boat.

This man drowned; in a way
so did my father, but this poem
is not about my father, it's about
the dead man in the Chesapeake Bay.

Pages of a manuscript floated
nearby. He must have been
writing in the failing light,
a gust of wind should have
warned him. The storm fussed
its way toward him, but he did
not notice the sturdy rise of waves.

I expect it was a swift end, not like
my father's week of seizures, though
both men's lungs filled quickly, but
this poem is not about my father.

The drunk, Alfred T. Bascomb,
scribbled his first drafts longhand.
That is how they found him,
horizontal in the water, face down
amid the lined sheets. His clever tales
lie beneath the Chesapeake, his last words
lost in the deepest hollows of the bay.

Not like my father's last words which
he mouthed to me. I adjusted his sheet
around his neck, he nodded, then fell
into the greenest sea where he breathed
and breathed and breathed.

Serendipity

Helena Frey

We are sitting aft of the pilothouse toasting our new venture. I've prepared dinner on the electric stove beside the companionway that leads out of our snug cabin onto the deck of the 'Most distinctive boat on St. Clair.' That's how the ad described the ship rocking beneath us. We are in a berth at Gregory's Marina on Detroit's Eastside. It's the tag end of the boating season as Ernie and I celebrate our purchase of the Serendipity with the former owner, Leonard.

Leonard leans back and breathes deeply. He is an elegant man with long slender fingers. He told us he could have been a concert pianist, and he has the intensity of an artist. In appearance, Leonard is an older version of my husband, Ernie. His fine angular cheekbones and the curve to his hazel eyes suggest a hint of Asian ancestry. "I envy you," Leonard says, looking across the table at both of us. "I wish I were your age and ready to take on the world again." *Is that what we're doing?*

Leonard has sold us his 38′ yacht at the end of the boating season when 38′ yachts are not easy to sell. Leonard leveled some of the financial hurdles for us. We will pay Leonard directly. He will carry the loan and pay the bank. "This has been a different experience for me," he says. Ernie beams at the man as if Leonard were his mentor. "I like a business transaction where all the parties are pleased with the outcome," Leonard adds.

Whenever Leonard stood at the helm of the Serendipity for a jaunt down the Detroit River, admiring glances would come his way. He is high class. He projects money—the suburban home, children in good schools, several cars in his garages, and other boats to tool around in—whereas Ernie is stretching his paycheck to cover his dream. Ernie and I, both in our thirties, are sitting just feet away from our six-month-old son, Lewis, asleep in his playpen.

The soft breath of the sleeping child, the warmth of a September evening, the gentle pull of the undertow truly christen our pleasure at living aboard our new boat. "Serendipity, it suits you both," says Leonard. "You'll like this ship. The hull's aluminum, and you'll have no trouble freezing in this winter at dockside." Ernie's glance travels upward to the pilothouse and catches a glimpse of the mast on the sailing vessel berthed in the slip beside us. Leonard's face follows his glance, but his eyes don't light up like Ernie's. His eyes have a look of farewell. "You'll have to drive out to Grosse Pointe Farms and meet my wife. Like you, Helena," he says, "she's an accomplished cook, too. We will have you both over for dinner. Let's plan it soon. I want to hear how the ship treats you; I know you'll treat her right."

We climb to the pilothouse. Lights from the parking lot at the end of the wharf brighten our pier as we walk Leonard to his car. Our ship is berthed in a large marina facing on Jefferson Avenue, not too far removed from downtown Detroit. We watch Leonard go as he travels a dirt road, passes the marina's store, and skirts several maintenance sheds. We wave our goodbyes to him and turn, hand in hand, to look at our new home. The gray aluminum hull gleams silver in the moonlight. Forward in the cuddy cabin under the pilothouse, Roberta, seven, and Eric, four, are both asleep in their bunks.

Well, it has begun—our venture.

A large cabin aft serves as our living room, master bedroom, and galley. Forward, there is a small cabin that has two bunks and a head. In an apartment we would feel sealed in, but vistas abound on a ship. The eye ranges over an expanse of water that reflects the sun's rising and falling.

The kids sit out on deck and watch the spectacle of the weekend boaters hauling in sails, lines, and bumpers to prepare their boats for winter storage. Other boats are lined up waiting for a boat hoist that wheels down a pier and lifts a boat out of the water to go into dry-dock. The passageways and piers are pulled from their moorings, broken down, and moved to sheds or covered over with tarps for the winter. We, too, move our boat to a pier, where ropes and chains secure us to cleats on a solid dock. The boating season has come to an end.

At winter's approach, the boat protests with grinding sounds and muffled creaking as ice thickens under our hull. Leonard told us we'd have no trouble freezing in, but he didn't take into consideration the fluctuation of the water level. The three Great Lakes to our north are subject to evaporation and precipitation, which either raises or lowers the water level by as much as three feet in any given month. We are on the Detroit River, fed by

SERENDIPITY

Lake St. Clair and Lake Huron. The ice encircling our hull gives us the illusion of solid footing, but when the water level drops, our boat drops. There's no adjusting to this free-fall. It's a drop of a foot, and we aren't hurt (yet), but we can't continually await this unpredictable loss of footing. We opt for another method to take us through the winter: bubletting. A hose will encircle our hull releasing air bubbles into the water, which then prevents the water from freezing.

The only other person in the marina living on his boat through the winter is Carl Breckenridge. He and Ernie become friends. They are that breed of men who have read *Wind in the Willows* and, like Rat, *nothing* compares to "messing about in boats." Both of them are always working on something and, when that is done, there is always something else to do. And, like Rat, they prefer it that way.

The kids don't find it odd that their dad opens up the deck and descends into the ship's depths. Roberta sits snugly on her bunk and reads about life on the prairie. Eric entertains himself without television, and Lewis crawls everywhere. On one occasion, he joins his dad in the bilge water. I hear the piercing cry and rush from the galley to the cuddy cabin as Ernie lifts a cold, wet baby out of the hold. He's not hurt, just indignant. I wrap Lewis in a towel and cart him aft. He's none the worse for wear.

When the ice thaws, Carl, our marina neighbor, invites all of us aboard his relic from the past. Built in the twenties, his sailing yacht is elegant with a long, graceful hull. We descend the curving wooden steps into an eclectic lifestyle. Overstuffed, man-sized couches are comfortably strewn with pillows. The dining room table is banked by built-in, leather-covered benches and backed by built-in bookcases. Daylight streams in through the portholes lining both sides of the saloon. We pass through three separate saloons, each with its own fireplace. Persian carpets cover the teak floors. It is shabby chic. If a woman had a hand in it, the interior would be remodeled and brought into the '60s, but no woman's hand touches the faded grandeur of his cabins. No woman's hand touches Carl Breckenridge. He is comfortable in the company of men; women are another story.

Late spring finds us moved from our winter mooring and again berthed beside sailboats and seaworthy vessels in slips to our port and starboard. Not much activity on the dock today, but that will change as the day lengthens and the weekend boaters arrive at their berths. Ernie is in New York City for the weekend with a friend and has left me the car. It's a perfect day for taking to the highway. Our first stop will be Roberta and Eric's swimming lessons at the local "Y". From there, we will head for the freeway out to Livonia and visit my friend Mary and her two girls.

"Danger. Danger." I hear it distinctly. And then again, "Danger." I look around. No one in sight. Danger, but from whom or what? Fire is always a concern living on a ship with the capacity to carry 200 gallons of gasoline. What does it mean, this repetition of 'danger'? Am I to grab the kids, run down the pier, jump in the car, and leave the marina? This doesn't make sense. If I am being guided or given a verbal clue, and the danger is already upon us, the warning is meaningless. I pause in what I am doing and sit quietly in the pilothouse, trying to decipher the message.

What is Mr. Breckenridge doing at the end of our pier? Carl isn't quite a recluse, but he rarely visits anyone in the marina.

I slide open the pilothouse door and step out onto the walkway. Carl is a big man with a broad face. At sixty he is still a good-looking man. If he has added weight over the years, he carries it well. His ample hair is battened-down under a captain's cap. He is dressed in jeans and a gray t-shirt. Nothing pretentious about the man.

"Hello," I say.

"Is Ernie around?' he asks.

"No, he's in New York City for the weekend."

He pauses and stays put. It is rumored that his wife either left him penniless, or for another man. In either case, he doesn't want to repeat the experience, and he keeps his distance from women. He is keeping his distance now. "Do you expect him Sunday evening?" he asks.

"Maybe Monday morning," I reply. I expect this man to bolt down the pier at any moment.

He surprises me by asking, "Can you call him?"

"I have no way to reach him," I reply.

He hesitates. I wait.

"My son," he begins, "was visiting a friend of his at a local bank. They were in the manager's office, and they began to talk about your ship, The Serendipity. The manager and several men were laughing so hard the tears were running down their cheeks. They couldn't restrain themselves as they told my son the fun they were going to have with this ship."

I stand very still listening to his every word. I can't help but admire this man who is sharing something with me in spite of his disinclination to do so.

"They've hired an outside agency to board The Serendipity and jimmy the engine. They'll pilot it to some other location near St. Clair Shores. It's to be sold at auction, and no matter what they get for it at auction, Ernie will still be liable for the loan." He hangs back from the words, and his voice tightens. "It seems your ship is in arrears," he says.

This man standing by my dock and keeping his distance loves boats. Ernie shares that love. It isn't his friendship with Ernie that led him to stand in great discomfort at the dock's edge to speak to me. It is the arrogance of the men at the bank, bankers with little love for ships or the feelings that attract men to ships. They will vandalize her, commandeer her, and sell her out from under us.

"Have they been sitting on the dock waiting for me and the children to leave?" I ask.

"There are a couple of men I've never seen before sitting in a car by the sheds," he replies.

My chest tightens. Should I ask him what I should do? I think better of it. He has already done us a great favor. "It is very kind of you to tell us what's going on, Mr. Breckenridge. Thank you very much."

He nods and abruptly turns away.

The danger does have a face.

In the fifteen minutes it takes Carl to reach his gangplank, I formulate a plan. In my days before college, I worked for Pinkerton ever so briefly. Banks were their big customers. Banks hire detectives to discover: Who is taking from the till? Nothing was to go public. The face the bank showed the world was serene. Publicity was never to besmirch the gentility of the banking world.

It amuses me to think about the men on the dock. They must have felt some excitement this morning when they saw me on the pier. I carried out the trash. How long have they been sitting on the dock? I imagine their irritated exchange. "Damn it, why doesn't she go somewhere! You'd think she'd have somewhere to go and something to do. Does she keep those kids cooped up on that boat all day!" *The indignation of men whose plans have gone awry.* They have nothing to report to the bank. I am almost positive that they are under orders not to board the ship while we are on board. The bankers laughed because it was such a simple undertaking.

Our refrigerator is full. Roberta has plenty of library books, and Eric always keeps himself occupied with blocks or toys. I make no attempt to call Leonard, the former owner, because I suspect he is the problem and not the solution. While the children are pleasantly oblivious to our plight, my anxiety mounts.

A ship is easy to secure and hard to penetrate (unless mayhem is the means of boarding). If a sheriff attempts to board our boat, I'll call the papers: "Bank Attempts to Steal Boat from under Mother and Children." Front Page! I won't hesitate to pursue such an action. There is a gun on board, but I'm not going to sit in the pilothouse with a rifle across my knees. However, I sit wide-awake in the darkness watching the pier.

It's four in the morning when I slide open the entryway and Ernie steps into the pilothouse. I immediately pepper him with all my anxious fears. "I'm so glad you're home, and the boat is still here and not Down River. Leonard hasn't paid the bank! Men plan to board our boat and sell it at auction because the loan is in arrears."

Ernie has to sit down. "*Not pay the loan?*" says Ernie. "That doesn't sound like Leonard."

I am so relieved to be talking to Ernie. I calm down and repeat Mr. Breckenridge's story. When I conclude, Ernie says, "I have no recourse but to call Leonard, even at this hour."

As Ernie cradles the phone in its receiver, he says, "The loan is *not* in arrears. The men at the bank did not tell Carl's son the truth. Leonard's sorry it has come to this. He will call the bank at 10:00 this morning."

"If we aren't in arrears," I ask, "*why* did the bank hire those men?"

"I asked Leonard that same question," Ernie replies. "The men at the bank felt they had a score to settle with Leonard because he didn't go through the bank when he sold us the boat. They were laughing, not at us, but at what they planned to do to Leonard."

"Did they call Leonard?" I ask.

"No, he was to be punished for circumventing the system."

My voice is now shrill. "You mean," I shout, "they'd leave us stranded on the dock because they wanted to get even with Leonard?"

"Yes," Ernie replies, "it was Leonard they were after. They never gave us a second thought."

Leonard calls to tell us the bank wants the loan paid in full by noon or else.

"Can Leonard pay the loan?" I ask.

"Yes, I'm to meet him, and we'll secure a loan through another bank."

Ernie reaches the end of the pier and turns and waves to me. I linger a moment after he is out of sight and turn my full gaze on the dock, where all of us could have been stranded. Blessings on the reticent Mr. Breckenridge; he saved our dream.

On the High Seas

Carole Ann Moleti

The ship pitched, tossing us side to side in the labyrinthine corridor leading to our staterooms. My thirteen-year-old son swiped the same "sea card" that got him unlimited food and drinks to open his cabin door. I heard him retching in the bathroom.

My niece, tension etched on a freckled face, her complexion the ultimate in redheaded pallor, and even my fifteen-year-old, "Mr. Macho," decided to stay in for the night. I doled out Benadryl and reassured them a ship big enough to carry more than three thousand passengers and crew was well equipped to handle a bit of rough sea.

After all, the night before, at a party hosted by Captain Per Kjonso, we sat bedecked in our formal wear as he crooned to us in his lovely Norwegian accent that there were "planty of staabeelizers" to keep us comfortable on his luxurious Royal Caribbean cruise ship, *Enchantment of the Seas*.

I was ready to go up to the pool deck for the dance party and midnight buffet, but, by the time I got to my cabin, my three-year-old daughter was sound asleep. My husband complained of being lightheaded and ruined my romantic aspirations of dancing the night away by falling asleep in his clothes. My brother-in-law and nephew hit the casino; my sisters and parents disappeared. I gave up and was rocked to sleep by the motion of the ship.

Such sweet dreams! My new agent loved the novel and was sure she could sell it. I was comfy and cozy, snuggled up to my swashbuckling sailor. Light was just peeking through the portholes when the public address system squealed, and the distinguished voice of the Captain intruded on my moment.

"Ladies and Gentlemen, Captain Per here. I am so sorry to disturb you at this early time, but it seems we have happened upon some Cuban rafters and will be stopping the ship to effect a rescue."

My husband and I leaped to our feet and, for a change, woke our daughter up. It took no time to dress; bathing suits and bare feet were *de rigueur*. She protested loudly as we ran down the hall along with several shipmates, cameras in hand.

A woman who didn't speak English stood in the hall, dripping wet from her morning shower, clad only in a bath towel, her eyes wide in fear. I ran past, smiled and mouthed, "It's okay," trying to reassure her we weren't sinking, even though the groan of the engines slowing and reversing caused the ship to rattle like the shakers they used to mix all those incredible drinks at the pool bar.

Our fellow passengers lined the gunwales, the vast majority Americans like us, clad in tee shirts with tasteless pronouncements, garish flowered shirts, and see-through cover-ups. Beer bellies, love handles, sagging breasts, and cellulite peeked out from clothes we normally wouldn't consider wearing to breakfast in a restaurant. The behemoth of a ship stopped next to a lime green rubber raft about the size of a bathtub, loaded with rusty cans and seven men. The torn sail hung off what looked like a broomstick.

Six of them, burnt black by the sun, sat upright in rags. The seventh didn't look much older than my teenagers. Pale as the moon, he lay sprawled in the front of the raft, unable to climb the tiny rope ladder the crew dropped out of a hatch near the water line. His comrades picked him up, and he struggled, pushed from below and pulled from above, to safety. Two men, sitting at the makeshift tiller in the stern, would not leave the raft. An orange tender from the ship, manned by three crew members in helmets and orange vests, probably toting weapons, convinced them with firm gestures they better get moving. Barefoot, clutching baseball caps and filthy canvas bags, they reluctantly did so.

"They should have just left them there," said one woman, a pareo barely covering her ample, bikini-clad butt as she sashayed off, high heels clicking like knives. She didn't acknowledge the man that called out to her.

"How could you say that? They could have died." He then resumed a conversation with his teenage son, taking advantage of the "teachable moment."

I looked at him, and we smiled at each other. Most of the others wandered off now that the show was over. The sun shone, calypso music started up, and the pool opened for the day.

"I want my ba-ba," my daughter wailed. Dressed in a tee shirt that proclaimed, "I didn't ask to be a princess, but if the tiara fits…," the tiny Guatemalan orphan we adopted was blissfully unaware that, except for divine intervention, she might he rummaging in a garbage dump for food, one step away from the desperation we had just witnessed. She wanted her "ba-ba"—right now.

"Maybe I should go down to the infirmary. They have seven ill people down there and might need help." Always the nurse, sometimes the missionary, I found it hard to gorge myself on the first of endless, sumptuous meals.

"You're on vacation," said my husband. "Let's go eat."

"I'm staying here," I said.

Hoisting the raft onto the deck was an impressive operation. The crew members in the tender secured its contents. Three Hispanic men in one-piece uniforms operated the crane. The Captain and his first and second in command stood on a side bridge, surveying.

"For God's sake," said another passenger. "All this fanfare, for what? They even have the Captain out here overseeing. We're going to be late getting back to Florida, and I'll miss my flight." He stomped off, probably to the bar for a Mimosa or Bloody Mary.

"Come on, they're safe," said my husband over my daughter's moaning.

"I have to write about this."

"You're out of your mind!" He lost it and carried our bereft child off to the dining room.

I watched and sweated with the other silent die-hards under the blazing sun, approximately 200 nautical miles off the coast of Cozumel. The rubber raft, to be held as "evidence," was secured on the foredeck, almost unnoticeable amidst a jumble of mechanical equipment. The ship powered up, and we resumed the final portion of our sail to Fort Lauderdale.

Of course, I needed to chronicle the absurdity of a Norwegian luxury liner, registered in Nassau, The Bahamas and carrying a bunch of middle class wannabes, rescuing seven half-dead men from a raft. We were born by a stroke of luck into a country that gives everyone a fair chance.

The staff attending to us didn't look much different from the Cubans, except for being cleaner, better hydrated, and well-fed. White-uniformed waiters balanced Bahama Mamas in brightly colored glasses on tiny trays, slithering in between the deck chairs so quickly we didn't notice the refill until they asked for our "sea card." Porters cleaned staterooms and fashioned monkeys and chickens out of towels to amuse the kids. Besides entertaining us with Conga lines and flag-waving revues on deck and in the dining room, they prepared food native to their countries and carved melons into likenesses of tropical fish. We got whatever we asked for, with a smile. Well drilled in customer service, there was a standard line:

"Yes, sir."

"A pleasure, madame."

I tried not to feel guilty. After all, in hurricane-ravaged Cozumel, I and the rest of my shipmates spent a lot of money on cheap souvenirs hawked by Mexicans desperate to make up for American dollars lost when the cruise ships couldn't come into the ruined docks.

I gave a generous tip to Carlos, Enrique, José, and Miguel, who took us out snorkeling to Palancar and Columbia Reefs. After our expedition, they danced around a huge Mexican hat, plied us with rum punch, Margaritas, and tequila shots before dropping us off at the pier that still looked like a giant had chewed up and spit out chunks of concrete and rusty metal along the shore.

The kids finally awoke from their sedated stupor around lunchtime, saw the digital photos, and recalled how rough it had been the night before in an 81,000-ton ship, let alone a rubber raft. I ignored the bad jokes about there being seven more waiters for the buffet that night. Captain Per had assured us they were all in good condition, despite having been afloat for seven days, the last three without food and water. He advised us the U.S. Coast Guard would retrieve them later that afternoon from the hospital wing.

Sometime after the men's lovely legs contest, but before the high-stakes Bingo, while the Jamaican steel band played, kids splashed in the sprinkler pool, and adults guzzled Coco Locos, the ship again slowed. The Coast Guard cutter materialized in the distance. A small boat maneuvered next to the cruise ship. The rope ladder again dropped down and seven men, dressed in white overalls and Adidas sandals, descended, clutching clear plastic bags containing all their worldly possessions. The Coast Guard crew, wearing helmets, vests, and no doubt carrying weapons, guided them into their seats.

The Cubans waved to the passengers hanging over the rails, and we waved back. One crew member, wearing rubber gloves to ward off the contamination of poverty, pushed them down and made it perfectly clear they were to shut up and stay put.

Now, I lost it. "¡*Suerte, amigos! ¡Suerte!*" I yelled in my most authoritative, revolutionary tone. The Cubans waved again, and several other passengers called out encouragement in Spanish. The boat sped them off to the cutter and an unidentified destination. Maybe back to Cuban authorities for torture and punishment, or perhaps Guantánamo Bay for detention. They were lucky to be alive, but, rescued in international waters, had no right to stay in any country.

Captain Per spoke again. "Ladies and Gentlemen, I don't know their fate, but we saved their lives. I'm so sorry for the inconvenience. Please, enjoy your final evening aboard the *Enchantment of the Seas*."

The ship powered up again. Bands played on. Glasses tinkled. Jugglers and comedians entertained. People laughed.

At the midnight buffet, a chocolate pirate ship almost as big as the lime green raft rode the swells over a sea of pastries and fruity fish. I felt nauseated, and it had nothing to do with the waves.

Near Point Lobos

Claire Livesey

The sea snarls
in yellow froth
that drifts
over the rocks
the fishermen
stand upon,
themselves like
outcrops from
an ancient time,
an oriental land.
Flimsy poles,
invisible lines,
they wrest food
from the sea,
pry off mussels
welded to stone,
scrape out food
to last the day.
They huddle
together in the
bitter wind,
flying spume.
Their ancestors
live in them.
In their hunched
shoulders, worn
hands, clever eyes.
Stolid against
the ever-changing
sea, they fill me
with delight.

Cloak of Fire

Marilyn J. Morgan

Skeleton woman dragged a nondescript mass from the bottom of the sea. Pausing upon the rugged shore, She dropped the sodden cloth in the burning sand. Slowly, She rotated Her head 360 degrees to make sure that Her actions were observed by all who hovered in shocked stillness nearby. Chuckling softly to Herself, Skeleton Woman stepped back into the sea and sank beneath the inky, frothy waves.

Released from Her mesmerizing presence, the observers on the beach shook their heads and moved cautiously toward the lumpy object left for them to find. They knew that, whenever Skeleton Woman made an appearance, something of an ethereal, mysterious nature was about to unfold in their lives.

What now? they each pondered in their individual thoughts. Was this to be a singular experience related only to their particular lives, or one that would entangle them together in Skeleton Woman's net?

One brave soul slowly approached the lump in the sand, gently poking it to see what it could possibly be. Nothing happened. Feeling somewhat reassured and braver, she knelt on one knee to look closely at the object. Her eyes registered that it was a cloth with strange lines and knots woven into the fabric. Upon closer inspection, Brave One saw that the cloth was folded with the inside out, and that the pattern was stitching that held something to the other side.

Her curiosity overcame her slight feeling of dread regarding any of Skeleton Woman's gifts. Gingerly grasping the corner of the cloth, Brave One began to unfold the mysterious cloth. On the other side, she found the cloth covered in beautiful, luminous feathers. At the upper edge was an intricate frog clasp. Brave One realized that this was a cloak. Never before had she seen an object of such rare beauty.

"Why would Skeleton Woman bring such a gift to the surface of the ocean and drop it so carelessly on the sand of this shore?" wondered Brave One.

She looked around and saw that the others who had been there were now gone. She was alone on the beach with this wondrous gift. She walked with measured steps around the cloak to look at it from every angle. She sat down in the sand and studied the mysterious feathers. What kind of bird had feathers of such luminosity and beauty? She could only think of the legendary Phoenix Bird, which sported feathers of scarlet and gold. She knew the story from days of old and regarded it as a myth that held little meaning today. Perhaps she had been wrong about this.

As Brave One sat cross-legged next to the Cloak, her head bobbed down to her chest, and she drifted into a reverie about these remarkable feathers. She felt herself lifted and rapidly transported to the nest of the Phoenix. She shivered as she remembered that, when the Sun beat fiercely upon the nest, it burst into flame and consumed the Phoenix until it was nothing more than a pile of ashes.

Brave One looked around and saw an ordinary looking egg nestled in the twigs and sticks of the enormous nest. Suddenly, a crack appeared across the face of the egg and chirping seeped out of the crack. The chick broke free of the egg and quickly grew to the size of a full-grown Eagle, but covered with scarlet and gold feathers. Brave One stared in disbelief. She couldn't understand how she had landed in the nest of a Phoenix Bird.

The powerful bird gazed down at her with glittering, liquid, unknowable eyes that held the wisdom of the Universe deep within.

Brave One sat speechless in the presence of this legendary bird. *What am I doing here?* she thought to herself.

You are here because you wanted to know about the Feathered Cloth, Little One, she heard in her mind in answer to her question.

You are real, and I am really with you? Brave One thought with awe.

"Yes. I am ready to fly away to my new home, so please do not waste my time. What is it you would like to know?" the Phoenix replied.

Brave One hastily collected her thoughts. "Why has Skeleton Woman brought this cloak to me, and what does it mean?" she quietly asked.

The Phoenix chuckled. "My sister, Skeleton Woman, has a unique way of getting attention," he said. "She has noticed that you have been approaching the borders between the worlds for some time now as you struggle to understand the ways of the dance of life and death. I live, die, and am reborn every 500 years. I carry the hope of peace. There are many kinds of peace

CLOAK OF FIRE

and many ways to see it. You know that the Dance of Life and the Dance of Death are inextricably entwined. You know this in your head, but your heart shies away from knowledge. However, it is time for your heart knowledge to be awakened as you call forth the wisdom of the Elder. It is time for you, now, to put on the cloak. It is a cloak of fire that burns away that which is no longer necessary, but it does not destroy your essence. It will become your way of standing in the doorways in order to look forward and backward at the same time. It will protect you as you dance with Death on behalf of the journeys of others. It will enable you to know more than you wish. It will free your tears for healing of yourself, others, and the planet. You will know when to put it on. Care for it with your wisdom, and protect it with your heart."

The Phoenix flew swiftly into the new world into which it had been born. Brave One slowly opened her eyes and found herself still seated next to the cloak on the sands of the North. Reverently, she picked up the cloak and carefully tucked it under her arm as she turned to go home. She felt wonder at the ways of the Universe in leading her to that which she needed to learn. She had just received the first lesson of the Cloak of Fire that was to initiate her into Elder-hood.

Celilo

J. R. Nakken

Twice a year, they gather here
At the edge of the desert
In the place where the falls are no longer.
Sober men, women, children,
Silent dogs sensing Old Ones;
Celilo, where our spirits are strong.

Soul of A Warrior greets the dawning,
Drums a prayer with the moon's light.
No night terror or madness dares linger
In the lodges and tents
On the shackled Columbia;
Celilo, where our hearts long to sing.

"I want to go to the river,"
A child speaks from the grass.
The camp says I must take the young swimmer
And an eagle is there,
Still ruling his blue world.
Celilo, where obsession grows dim.

Art has gone to his Grandfathers.
The circle is without him.
Drums call a titian-haired, toddler dancer.
Elder brother shows him the steps
And our loss is abated.
Celilo, where grief goes at a glance.

Young warriors load pickups
While the grandmothers hug.
First-time couples fuss; not touched by the fervor.
But their children hold prayer ties
And will bring them again.
To Celilo, where each heart learns to serve.

Dawn in the West

Andrew J. Hogan

The clunky engine sputtered to a stop in front of Frank Tombe's house. He raised his head from the armrest of the sofa where he had been sleeping off last night's hangover. Frank nearly gagged on the lilac fragrance floating in through the living room window. A loud booming noise, like a large metal ball slowly descending the staircase, hitting each step with a thunderous blow, came closer and closer. Then a megaphone blared in his ears, "Frank, I'm leaving."

Harriet stood in the doorway of the living room. She set down one of the two large suitcases she'd dragged down the stairs and picked up the photo Frank had taken fourteen years ago at the Socorro County Fair of their son William in his cowboy outfit. "And I am taking this with me."

Frank tried to speak, but his tongue stuck to the roof of his mouth. He got out a "Nnngh," but by this time the cab driver had loaded Harriet's suitcases in the trunk and opened the rear passenger door. Frank looked at the clock on the mantle—9:45. The train from Socorro to Albuquerque would be leaving at 10:30.

Should I try to stop her? Frank thought. He tried to sit up, but a large rubber band snapped around his head. Last night he had tried to explain to her again.

"Harriet, this was the last time I needed to go to White Oaks. Everything's set now." Frank lied; actually, he needed to go one more time.

"You said that the last time, Frank, and here you are, drunk again. I'm finished," Harriet said. "First Billy, now you. We have nothing left, Frank."

Frank lay back on the sofa. He'd rest a little longer before going to the train station to stop Harriet from leaving.

It was one in the afternoon, and, still shaky, Frank decided to drive, rather than walk, to school. A little hair of the dog would have helped, but he didn't want the smell of alcohol on his breath. Frank pulled his car into a faculty parking space next to Cramer Hall on the campus of the New Mexico School of Mines. Most of the parking spaces were empty. Spring classes were finished. Unlike Frank, most faculty members had already handed in their final grades.

Of course, the parking lot hadn't been full for more than three years now. Most of the students had been drafted, as had three of the younger faculty members. Admitting female students had helped keep enrollments up. Sarah Feinburg had joined the faculty as an adjunct to help teach the organic chemistry course after Sam Weatherton was killed in Italy.

This was all about to change. Germany had surrendered, and the Japanese were on their last legs, waiting for an American invasion. The department had already hired Richard Pugh as the unlucky thirteenth member of the faculty, and student applications were flooding in from newly discharged soldiers ready to go back to school under the GI Bill. There was a heightened interest in New Mexico uranium mining, and rumor had it that something earthshaking was about to happen over at White Sands.

Molly was sitting at her desk in front of the chairman's office. As soon as she spotted Frank, she called out, "Dr. Mitchell wants to see you right away."

Frank tried to slide past Molly's desk, but she was up, blocking his way.

"He'll see you now," she said.

Frank turned toward the chairman's door, but before he could knock, Molly had rushed over and opened it for him. Molly always smiled, but not today.

Hugh Mitchell looked up from his desk as Frank stepped into the office. Molly closed the door with what Frank thought was a deliberate slam, although Mitchell seemed not to notice.

"Sit down, Frank." It wasn't a friendly invitation.

"Sure, Hugh. How're things? Where are you and Peggy going this summer?" Frank said.

Mitchell ignored him. "Frank, are those grade sheets in your hand?"

"Yes."

"Give them to me." Mitchell ripped them from Frank's extended hand. "I don't know what happened to you. You used to be a good teacher. The kids loved you. You had some nice research publications, nothing great, but still respectable. What the hell happened?"

"What's going on? Why are you asking me this? It isn't time for my annual evaluation." Frank was thirsty.

"Frank, you're finished."

"What do you mean, 'finished'?"

"I mean, you're fired." Mitchell sat back in his chair and sighed. "For the last year you've screwed up every assignment. Your teaching stinks. All the students complain about you."

"Nobody ever complained to me," Frank said.

"Of course not, you're never in your office. As far as I can tell, you missed almost every scheduled office hour this semester. And when students were unlucky enough to catch you after class or, God forbid, in your office, you blew them off with some bull about how they were doing fine and not to worry about their grades."

"Well, sure, standards have slipped a bit with the war, but we'll all be back to normal next year," Frank said.

"Your normal isn't good enough anymore, Frank. We're going from fifteen students this year to over sixty next year. Johnson and Poundstone will be back from the service. Yarnell is being released from his assignment at Los Alamos. The new guy, Pugh, is replacing you in engineering drawing and math. I'm keeping Feinburg for the time being."

"You can't get rid of me, I have tenure. For Christ sakes, Hugh, I'm fifty-two years old. What am I supposed to do?" Frank was almost in tears.

"You're supposed to drink yourself to death, like every other drunk, Frank. I have confirmed reports that you came to Monday classes intoxicated at least five times last semester. I'm going to do you a favor for old times' sake. I'm going to let you resign. If you don't, I'll fire you for cause; it will go into your personnel file, and you will never get another teaching job."

"Shit, Hugh. You know I'm not a drunk. It's my research. I have to drink," Frank said.

"You have to drink to be a mining engineer? What kind of bullshit is that?"

"Okay, look, Hugh. I mean, I need to keep something under wraps for the time being, you understand?" Frank said. "Can I trust you to keep this under wraps?"

"You can trust me to fire you unless you have a goddamned good explanation for your behavior."

"I think I've discovered a grave," Frank said.

"Ah, great. A mining engineer finding a grave," Mitchell said, with a look of feigned astonishment on his face. "In the ground, I presume."

"Look," Frank said, "it's the grave of a famous missing person."

"Aha, so Amelia Earhart wasn't lost in the Pacific. She crashed in New Mexico," Mitchell said, widening his eyes in apparent surprise.

"Okay, make fun of me," Frank said.

Mitchell paused, having momentarily run out of ridicule.

Frank continued, "I've been stringing along an old greaser, buying him a lot of booze, drinking with him. You've known me for years, Hugh. I don't even like to drink."

"For somebody who doesn't like to drink, you've been doing an awful lot of it."

"But that's the thing. I can't let the greaser figure out what I'm after. He might buy the land before I do, or maybe rob the grave. Look, Hugh, this place is going to explode with all the military research they're doing over at White Sands. A tourist attraction like this will be a gold mine," Frank said.

"Frank, I don't care if you did find Amelia Earhart's grave. You're a mining engineer, not an historian or an archeologist. What the hell are you doing looking for graves, anyway?"

"But don't you see, it'll be a gold mine," Frank said.

"Frank, you're paid to teach people how to dig real gold mines, not to find artifacts that would be as good as a gold mine. What I see is a faculty member who's more interested in drinking and going on a wild goose chase than teaching students. Frank, if you'd told me you're having a rough time because of William, or that Harriet had left you for another man, I might have given you a second chance. But this crazy-ass story just convinces me I'm right to fire you."

"Please, Hugh. I can get myself straightened out by September. Everything is coming to a head this summer. I'll either find the burial site, or I will give it up forever," Frank said.

"I had Molly clean out your office and box up all your things. Move everything out today, or I'll have the janitors take it to the dump."

Mitchell got up and left Frank sitting alone. After a few minutes, Frank went to his own office. The door was locked, and his key didn't work. His books and papers were packed into boxes by the door. A moment later, Molly came by with a hand truck.

"Do you need any help moving the boxes to your car, Frank?" Molly said.

"I'll be okay, Molly," Frank said.

She gave him a smile that looked more like a wince and went back to her desk.

Ever since the chief mining engineer of the Old Abe Mine in White Oaks had invited Frank's senior engineering drafting class over for a field trip at the beginning of the fall semester, Frank had been making regular trips to White Oaks on the pretext of giving engineering advice. Frank went to White Oaks every third Friday of the month, when there was no faculty meeting, and spent Friday evening, most of Saturday—except for a quick trip to make an appearance at the chief engineer's office—and Sunday morning at Lupe's Cantina.

Last September on his first visit to the Old Abe Mine, Frank and his engineering drafting class were all guests of Old Abe's chief mining engineer. A goat had been slaughtered and roasted for the occasion, and local performers entertained Frank and the dozen prospective mining engineers with songs and stories of the old west. Frank had had a difficult time keeping up appearances during the reception, until he heard the local minstrel tell the story of how Billy the Kid had not gone east to Fort Sumner after escaping from jail in Lincoln following his murder conviction, but had, much more logically in Frank's opinion, gone west into the mountains through Capitán and into the lava fields known as the Valley of Fires, where even the Mescalero Apaches wouldn't be able to track him. According to the minstrel, Pat Garrett had killed the wrong man in Fort Sumner, maybe a look-a-like hired by Billy's gang. Having become famous for killing Billy the Kid, Garrett would have made a fool of himself admitting he killed the wrong man—and so the case of fatally mistaken identity became part of history.

Frank understood why Billy couldn't be tracked into the Valley of Fires. The fields were treacherous: broken terrain riddled with fissures, brittle overhangs, almost no flat surfaces and many sharp projections. Even in late April, when Billy escaped from the Lincoln jail, the lava fields became an oven during the day due to the black surface and lack of any shade. A single slip of the foot by man or horse would likely leave one or both disabled in a waterless wasteland, with no hope of help from passersby.

So every third weekend Frank traveled to White Oaks and, just to be friendly, bought drinks for any seemingly knowledgeable locals to get them to open up about local legends, history, and gossip. He didn't push anyone to talk about Billy the Kid, but when the opportunity arose he would ask the right question to steer the conversation in that direction. Gradually, Frank learned that Anglos, Mexicans, and Indians all believed different myths about Billy the Kid, depending on how badly he was thought to have treated their particular group while alive. Finally, during his April return visit to Lupe's Cantina, Frank met Miguel Herrera, an aging part-Mexican, part-Mescalero Apache miner.

"Muchacho, haven't I seen you working at the Old Abe?" Frank said.

"Si, I work there," Miguel said. "You work for el ingeniero?"

"No, I teach at the School of Mines in Socorro. I just come here to show the students how it's done in real life, not in books. How long've you been a miner there?"

"Long time," Miguel said. "My father also miner at Old Abe."

"Grandfather, too?"

"No, he full-blood Indian. Before there reservation at Fort Stanton. He got grandmother embarazada over on finca in Oscura. He have regular Indian wife back in mountains. Go back and forth," Miguel said.

"What kind of work did he do?"

"Hunting, stealing, like all Apaches back then. He wait for people go in lava field, fall and die, then he take things and sell," Miguel said.

"There were a lot of famous people around here back when your grandfather was alive. Did he ever meet any of them?"

"No, he mostly stay away white man, except they die in lava field," Miguel said.

"Nobody famous died in the lava fields, I guess?"

"Grandmother tell us one time grandfather find dead gunfighter in lava field. He take gun, knife, spyglass, boots, saddle. Horse already dead from fall," Miguel said.

"Really, was it a famous gunfighter?"

"No sure. Grandfather no speak Ingles. No read. No care about papers on body. Just things to sell. No know name of gunfighter, but had gun in holster a la isquierda," Miguel said.

"Isquierda?" Frank said.

"Si, over here." Miguel pointed to his left side.

Nearly two months after his resignation in May, Frank had saved enough gasoline ration coupons to make the trip from Socorro over to White Oaks. On his prior expeditions, he had used ration coupons from the school, since he was on official business. He waited for the sun to begin to set before making the trek across the Jornada del Muerto, where the daytime temperature could easily reach 110° in early July.

Frank left Socorro around 5 PM, going south on the Camino Real to San Antonio, and then turning his Willys east across the Jornada del Muerto to White Oaks, where Miguel would be on his way to Lupe's Cantina, as he was every Saturday night. Once he had passed through Farley and reached Carthage, Frank was stopped at a military roadblock. After assuring the soldiers that he was on official business from the School of Mines, he was allowed to pass, but they warned him to stay on the Roswell Road all the way to Carrizozo and not to make any detours south onto the military testing grounds.

Lying before him was the Jornada del Muerto, the ninety-mile shortcut off the Camino Real between Santa Fe and El Paso. The Jornada was an empty plain filled with lava that the winds had abraded into a sandy basin covered in low shrubs. There was no reliable source of surface water for a trip that had taken several days on horseback. The Muerto whose death inspired the name for "Dead Man's Route" was El Alemán, a German trader whose body was now submersed somewhere under the Jornada's sea of volcanic sand. *A dead Kraut thousands of miles from home*, thought Frank. *Dying in a distant land.*

The waning afternoon light hit the desert scrub at an oblique angle, making the surface appear dark, even though the sand underneath was a light creamy brown. The desert basin shimmered in the heat like an ocean of choppy, dark water lying between the islands of the Fray Cristóbal Mountains to the west and the Sierra Oscura Range to the east. The late afternoon wind had raised a sea spray of dust. Frank sailed across this sea of sand in his Willys much as America's sons had sailed across the English Channel toward Normandy on D-Day, now more than a year ago. *Sinking beneath the surface, lost forever in a distant sea*, Frank thought.

Passing through Bingham and another military roadblock, Frank was again warned not to stray off the road. The Willys ascended the bumpy road up the Chupadera Mesa, a bottle of Don Cuervo Especial Tequila bouncing on the back seat. Frank would use it to pry out the last bits of information about the burial site of the dead body Miguel's Apache grandfather had found out in the Valley of Fires some seventy years earlier. Crossing the top of the Mesa, Frank descended into the breach in the northern and southern ranges of the Sierra Oscura; darkness quickly surrounded him.

"I've got to find that grave," Frank said out loud to himself; since losing his job, he only had himself to talk to. Harriet had wanted to talk to him, but he had lost interest almost a year ago. He didn't actually miss talking with her that much. Since she'd left, Frank found he preferred cooking his own meals and eating alone. Ever since he had heard about Billy the Kid, talking things over with Harriet at dinner invariably led to a fight.

The next day was July 14, two months since Frank had lost his teaching job. If everything went well tomorrow, he'd soon be welcomed back at the School of Mines. His strange and erratic behavior would all be explained, or at least excused, by the significance of his find. *Okay, it wasn't a mineral in the ground, but it was a significant discovery; and it was underneath the earth, and it did have to be excavated, even if it wasn't exactly a job requiring the skills of a mining engineer,* Frank thought. *Uncovering a grave of this historical importance will show Mitchell a thing or two about the noteworthiness of my research. More important, it'll shut Harriet up about how I've lost my mind, about needing to pull myself back together.*

Frank wasn't sure he wanted Harriet to come crawling back to him from her mother's farm in Iowa, but he would feel vindicated if she tried.

The Don Cuervo Especial had done the trick. Miguel got good and drunk and told the whole story of his grandfather's grave robbing. *Okay, that was unfair; Miguel's grandfather had dug the grave for the gunfighter, buried him deep enough and covered him with enough rocks to keep the coyotes from devouring his remains,* Frank thought.

Of course, the old Indian had unburdened the unfortunate corpse of its unnecessary worldly possessions—possessions that, if left with the body, might well have tempted some unscrupulous person to defile the grave and disturb the spirit of the recently deceased. The gunfighter might have led a turbulent life and suffered a painful death, but that didn't mean he shouldn't rest in peace.

Frank left White Oaks the next morning as early as his hangover would allow and headed south through Carrizozo. Miguel's story about his grandfather and the dead gunfighter had given Frank the landmarks he needed to find the grave. Frank was stopped by yet another military roadblock on the road to Alamogordo and again warned not to leave the main road. Reaching the village of Oscura, Frank found the trail into the Valley of Fires closed by a barricade proclaiming the area on the other side to be a restricted military zone; a single sentry sat in a jeep next to the barricade.

It was 3:30 in the afternoon; the sentry would change at 4 o'clock. Frank parked the Willys a quarter of a mile down the road and waited. At 4 PM the sentry drove off toward Carrizozo to exchange the jeep with his replacement. Frank shifted the Willys into four-wheel drive and drove around the unguarded barriers, following the trail through the narrowest point of the Valley of Fires lava field.

On one of his periodic visits to his Mexican wife, Miguel's Apache grandfather had seen the gunfighter ride through Oscura on his way into the lava field. The Apache followed the gunfighter on the prospect that an untimely accident might provide some valuable prizes. Miguel said his grandfather had guessed that the gunfighter wanted to cross the lava field, and then ride up its western edge. With a spyglass, the gunfighter could keep an eye on anyone following him on the eastern side of the flow; he could be long gone into the mountains by the time any posse could cross the treacherous lava fields.

The gunfighter had a good plan, Miguel's grandfather had thought, until he wandered off the established path, probably to make tracking more difficult. The gunfighter had got himself onto a precarious ledge running alongside a ravine where the brittle lava failed; the gunfighter and his horse fell, both suffering a painful death.

Fortunately for Frank, the army had built a patrol road with an easily circumvented roadblock right where the path used to be. Frank had written down all the rock features he would need to find his way to where Miguel's grandfather had buried the gunfighter: *The Tortoise with the Broken Leg, The Coyote with One Foot Raised,* and *The Hawk Catching the Ground Squirrel.* Before dusk, Frank had found them all.

Frank set up his camp at the foot of a twisted juniper tree that grew out of a crevice in a black lava platform. Lightning had split the juniper tree's trunk decades ago; the separate halves of the trunk had continued to grow, agonizingly twisting themselves more than 360 degrees in opposite directions. The night air was cooling fast, but the black lava still radiated the sun's heat. Just behind the deformed juniper lay an oblong mound of rocks marking what Frank believed to be the grave of Billy the Kid.

It only took Frank an hour to restack the rocks covering the grave into a wall around the edge. After removing three flat slabs of volcanic lava, Frank saw in the ebbing light that the remaining dirt had subsided, collapsing into the empty cavity that had once been a human body. It was too dark to continue; the rest of the excavation would have to wait for the new dawn.

Frank started a fire and prepared his meal. In the deepening dusk, the split and twisted trunks of the juniper looked like the desperate arms of a drowning soldier reaching out of a dark sea, hoping to find someone to pull him to safety. Frank took a long pull from his flask and lay back on his bedroll for a rocky night of sleep.

Frank woke before dawn, needing to relieve himself. He restarted the fire and put on some coffee. The eastern sky was just starting to blush a soft pale blue. Another half hour until dawn, and Frank could finish excavating the grave.

Drinking his coffee and waiting for the light, Frank opened his wallet and took out a worn pocket snapshot of his son, William, dressed in his cowboy outfit at the Socorro County Fair. Tears ran down his cheeks.

"Oh god, son, I wish you could be here with me now. I couldn't save you from drowning off Normandy. If only they could have sent me your body to bury, to have a grave where I could visit with you, to know you weren't lost forever."

Frank sat on the wall he had built from the rocks covering the grave of the body he believed to be Billy the Kid, holding the picture of his dead soldier-son. In the west, the sky burst open with an enormous flash of light. The flash was so bright that Frank could read the note Harriet had written on the other side of the snapshot: *William 'Billy the Kid' Tombe, 1931.* A brief eternity later, and the snapshot burst into flames. Frank's eyes blistered and went black, but he could still hear. The earth quivered, and the sound of a thousand locomotives raced toward him. Time passed very slowly; then a tidal wave of wind hit Frank so hard his burning body was thrown backward into the open grave, collapsing onto and becoming part of the desiccated remains.

In a few seconds, the grave was filled with debris. The campsite was obliterated. Frank's Willys was incinerated and thrown into a nearby ravine.

Another Tombe had been buried in an unknown grave, in an unknown place no loved one would ever visit. The area was covered with radioactive fallout and declared off-limits for twenty-five years.

October Wildfire 2003

Bobbie Jean Bishop

When things I love go up in flames over and over,
    blackened landscapes mushroom in my heart.
Days before the wildfire flashed through
    drought-dead pine, skeletal chaparral—
a gopher snake slid like a quiet train across a path while
    I waited for it to disappear into the underbrush.
I recall its graceful body seamless as a stocking in
    the face of now televised images of
suffocating clouds, charred mountains—the steep
    grade of Milk Ranch Road where I could climb
out of an ordinary self into forests of filtered light,
    needles trembling in a fairy breeze.
As I picture havens like Azalea Glen going up in smoke,
    arbor of burnished manzanita west of Dyar Spring,
I wonder who can flee from such a blaze—
    wild turkeys in black-feathered coats, tawny deer?
Will Kumeyaay ghosts still roam their "place where it rains?"
    Bones of oak stand stark along the highway, once
canopied with leaves on the way to Stonewall Peak.
    I won't live to see new growth trees, only ash from
"Ahhakweahmac" drifting over my balcony, hood of my car,
    dark rain from a smoldering wilderness—Airplane
Ridge, Soapstone Grade, Granite Springs—places
    mapped in memory with lingering trails, their
burrs in my socks, light blessing of dust on my shoes.

Ring of Fire

Toni Timmons

Mt. St. Helens exploded one day. I am growing worried and afraid of living in the ring of fire.

The mountain blew violently after giving many warnings of impending doom. It shook, and news bulletins flashed information. Scientists were interviewed, telling people to leave the mountain. Harry Truman owned a lodge on the mountain. Despite many efforts to dislodge him, he decided to stay. After all, he had spent most of his life there. I watched him explain on TV one day, prior to the catastrophe, that he would not leave his wife who was buried there near his home.

Sunday, May 18, 1980 the mountain's pent-up anger swelled to the point where she blew, taking 57 people with her (including Harry Truman), decimating forests and rivers, erasing lakes, and covering part of southern Washington State five inches deep in ash (including Yakima and Spokane). The wind blew the 12-mile-high ash east, affecting air over countries worldwide. Day turned into night, cars wouldn't run, and people were trapped out in it.

The effect on me comprised annoyance and interest in the scientific aspects, but not fear. We lived across the Columbia River in Oregon, south of the mountain. Most of the ash blew east, and the sun kept on shining where we were in Milwaukie, near Portland.

The dangerous ash caused us to wear protection over our faces so that we would not inhale it. It cut our eyes, and we could not wear contact lenses. I hated going back to glasses. The worst part for the young people at school where I taught fifth grade was the ash that rose from the grass and blacktop when they ran out to play. Firemen came every day to hose down the area, but as soon as it dried the ash lifted in clouds around the children. On days when the mountain sent out more ash and steam plumes, we could not allow them outside. That was difficult for them, as school was almost over, and the warm weather said, "Come play!"

The ash ruined many cars. We had just bought a new Buick, and every night we ran out to cover it with a tarp so the glassy ash wouldn't scratch it. I drove to downtown Milwaukie one day and suddenly looked up into the sky, and there it was! A huge ash plume jutting into the sky! I hurried home in case the wind changed, and it would blow down on our little town, turning sunshine into dark night.

Mt. St. Helens stood, beautiful, in her glory days. Her top now burned and scattered, her side scarred, she lay there, beginning her time of renewing. I saw her scar from an airplane window. It hit me. This is something to be afraid of. It's much more than an annoyance. It is deadly.

During the years between 1980 and 1990, she had twenty periods of eruptive activity to rebuild her dome, and now a large glacier is forming. She gets active, and then quiets down. We ask, "Will she have another huge eruption like before, or will she just continue rebuilding back into her beautiful self again?"

An old Indian legend says that Mt. Hood and Mt. Adams both loved the calm, elegant Mt. St. Helens. They argued over her so long that they eventually blew their tops, and, through intermittent battles, devastated the Columbia Gorge area. Eventually, they stopped their battle and are now proudly showing their towering, white, snow-capped peaks. But the story hasn't ended. Mt. Hood rattles once in a while. Steam and a bit of ash waft out of the top. Is it ready for another battle? If it blew, would it land here in the middle of Milwaukie or Portland or Salem? We're only forty minutes away.

We're centered in the ring of fire. Mt. Rainier is heating up and, if it blew, it could bury Seattle in ash. In the Cascade Range lie Mt. Jefferson, Three Sisters, and many more volcanic peaks. In 2004 an up-swelling of land near Three Sisters and the rattling of earthquake swarms alarmed us. Geologists check the area often. Mt. Mazama blew many years ago, leaving a gigantic hole that filled with water, now called Crater Lake. We sit on earthquake faults that run right through our town. One is under a school. Another is under the west hills of Portland. More are in the ocean nearby.

Friends who live elsewhere ask, "How can you live there? Aren't you scared? Why don't you move?"

We know living near our active volcano is no joking matter. Our descendents will cope with it for many years to come as it grows back to its regal splendor. We live in the ring of fire, and we hope and pray that our mountains keep their furnaces cool. *Rattle if necessary but don't blow your tops*, we say to them every time we drive the rugged Columbia Gorge and pass by Hood and Adams. *Keep your tempers under control.*

I remember Mt. St. Helen's eruption, not with annoyance anymore, but with great fear, respect, and interest in observing the destruction and rebirth of a great mountain.

Remote

Tillie Webb

The rarefied air at 12,000 to 14,000 feet in elevation crept up on my bodily defenses quickly and without warning. Result: vertigo.

As I began to fade away, my condition was not helped by the near claustrophobic sensation of the narrow streets with tiny shops pushing in on me. Immense gray clouds descended on the town, while strains of music provided by flutes and plucked instruments began to seep into my consciousness. I hung onto the fact that evening had arrived through the smell of burning charcoal. This meant that the inns and homes had started preparations for the evening meal.

Unbeknownst to me as we threaded our way through the small lanes, Olivia was studying my face and my gait. Finally, she said with perfect Latin sensitivity, "Mathilde, I invite you to stop and have a cup of chocolate with me." Providentially, we were standing outside what served as a small bistro with hard wooden chairs. We were served thick, steaming South American chocolate. In minutes, I had revived.

Back at the hotel, a full course dinner was offered, complete with the customary tea made from coca leaves. The unprocessed leaves have many culinary and medical uses, we learned. And, indeed, a soup and tea from this plant was served next day before we took the arduous train ride on a narrow-gauge track that snaked its way between the Andes mountain peaks. Once again, my body betrayed me with the old familiar motion sickness as the cars rolled along the railroad right-of-way at the edge of the almost vertical precipices.

All of a sudden, a valley opened before us, and we were gazing down on the famed ruins of the Inca city of Machu Picchu. Inconveniences of travel forgotten, we stood in awe as our Peruvian guide pointed out the observatory, the ball court, the university, and the priests' hostel. The slopes were terraced with intricate irrigation systems. Experimental farming had counted successes with several unlikely crops, such as cotton.

Back in the pre-Columbian commercial center of Cuzco, I reflected that this experience would not be forgotten, not only because of the totally different sights and sounds it afforded, but also for the spiritual understanding of gigantic leaps in human progress evidenced in a truly remote age and place.

From Rhodes to the Belgian Congo
—Notes from my father, rewritten as a memoir

Albert Russo

I was born on the island of Rhodes—'Heliousa Rodos'—the capital of the Dodecanese, which lies opposite that part of the southwest shore of Asia Minor known in ancient times as the Doride. According to legend, Apollo fell in love with the nymph, Rhoda. One of the sons of the sun god was the father of Camiros, Ialyssos, and Lindos, who gave their names to the three largest cities of ancient Rhodes.

Like many parts of Greece, this island has a rich history. The son of Antigonus of Syria tried to conquer the city in 305 B.C., but had to capitulate when faced with the islanders' resistance. To express their gratitude to their goddess for this victory, the Rhodians erected the gigantic and celebrated Colossus, one of the original seven wonders of the world, which was destroyed by an earthquake. Then came the Romans; after their demise, Rhodes fell under the rule of the Eastern Empire of Byzantium. During the era of the Crusades, it became one of the main ports of call on the way to the Holy Land, and, in 1306, after having belonged to Venice and Genoa, it was sold to the Knights of Saint-John of Jerusalem. In 1522, Suliman the Magnificent conquered the island, and thus it remained part of the Ottoman Empire until 1912, when Italy occupied the island after their victory against the Turks. In 1923, the Treaty of Lausanne officially turned Rhodes and the other islands of the Dodecanese over to Italy.

This, then, is where I was born, around the time the Italians came, into a large and poor Sephardic family. The Sephardic Jews—Sephardic means 'Spanish' in Hebrew—were persecuted during the Spanish Inquisition, and they either had to convert to Catholicism or leave the country. The majority of them were expelled in 1492, under the reign of Ferdinand and Isabel.

At the age of eight, I accompanied my parents, two brothers, and four sisters to the Turkish city of Antalya, for Father had been offered a job there by the branch manager of his Rhodes' employer.

In 1918, war broke out between Greece and Turkey. I witnessed the most appalling massacres and the sad flight of the Greek inhabitants, who were either killed or expelled from Turkish soil. The situation became dangerous for everyone. We were lucky that, in the meantime, Father had obtained Italian naturalization, since it was not long before the Italian Navy disembarked in Antalya to protect its nationals.

The schools were closed for several months, and Father asked a Turkish merchant to employ me in his shop. In spite of my young age—I was only nine—I managed to satisfy my boss with odd jobs, working as a door-to-door salesman, as a warehouse assistant, or serving the ladies in 'our' store, as my boss specialized in ladies' materials.

Foreigners were not well considered by the Turks and were frequently harassed by the local population. Merely wearing a hat was disturbing. So, in order to be left in peace and to pass as a native, I exchanged my classic hat for a typical red fez.

Looting and banditry plagued the towns, and the ringleaders, known as Tchetas, were rough, ruddy, and discontented mountain folk. At first, they tried to adapt to urban life, but soon realized they faced a world fraught with unexpected hardships. To do away with this new scourge, the Turkish government had to take drastic measures. As soon as one of these Tchetas was caught, he would be hung in Antalya's Central Square. The sight of these public hangings was dreadful, especially for a child; if you had to cross town to go to work, you couldn't avoid seeing them. A sheet of paper was pinned on each criminal's shirt, listing his crimes.

Apart from these nightmarish images, I still cherish some pleasant memories of my stay in Turkey. Thanks to my father's good reputation, we made a circle of fine friends and were often invited to their homes or farms, enjoying their hospitality and taking part in their festivities, such as engagement parties and weddings.

As the schools still remained closed, my father decided to send me back to Rhodes in order to further my education. That was in 1922. A kind old couple, Mr. and Mrs. Abraham Hasson, took me in as a lodger. They had a son my age named Elyakim, with whom I shared a bedroom for several years. The Hassons were long-time friends of my parents and virtually considered me as their second son. Elyakim and I felt like brothers. We had our little quarrels, of course, but there was never any jealousy between the two of us.

A few months after my return to the island, I was sent to a teacher whose name was Jacob Capuya. He taught me how to read and write Ladino, a liturgical language derived from ancient Spanish and written in Hebrew characters, for that was the only way I could correspond with my father and get news of my family, who still resided in Turkey. Following that, I attended the Italian school up to the third technical grade and took night courses in accounting.

Living conditions grew more and more difficult in Turkey, due to economic and political instability. As a consequence, my whole family moved back to Rhodes. Unfortunately, they arrived just as the World Crash hit Europe. My father, who had worked for the same firm for more than twenty years, had to accept a much lower salary than previously. It was barely enough to feed his large family. We couldn't buy new clothes, so Father managed to acquire an unsold stock of the cheapest materials then available, which my mother and my elder sisters sewed into garments for us.

Seeing the conditions my father was toiling under, I took the initiative of interrupting my studies, in spite of his insistence that I get at least a technical degree, and found employment as a bank clerk, a job I kept for a few years. Still, the little money I could bring home did not alleviate our plight. In the meantime, Father had been appointed by his firm as a traveling salesman. For weeks on end, he would shuttle between the islands of the Dodecanese and leave us without news. It was very trying. He always came back in such a pitiful state that I decided something had to be done, so I wrote to an uncle of mine who had immigrated to Montgomery, Alabama, in the United States, asking him if he could get me a work permit.

Several months elapsed, and no answer came. In the meantime, I received news from my bosom friend, Elyakim Hasson, with whom I had shared a room for many years in his parent's home in Rhodes. He had left for another part of the world, the Belgian Congo, in the beginning of 1929. I wrote back, explaining to him how difficult things were for us. A couple of months later, I received in the mail a labor contract with a well established firm in the Congo for a job in Kamina, an outpost in the southern province of Katanga.

I talked the matter over with my parents. They were appalled that such a young boy might go to a place they had never heard of, to be lost somewhere in the middle of the African jungle! But I insisted and, after much recrimination—my mother couldn't stop crying, my father feared for my life there in the bush, and my brothers and sisters thought I had gone crazy—I convinced them that this was the only way I could help them.

In order to get an entry visa for the Belgian Congo, I wrote to the Belgian Consulate in Alexandria, Egypt, sending them my Italian passport. Once I received all the documents, duly signed and approved by the Belgian and local authorities, I was ready to leave. An acquaintance of mine, Isidore Malki, had made the same decision, and we were to travel together.

Heartbroken, my parents finally gave me their consent, along with their blessings. With part of his savings, Father bought me new clothes, but he had to pawn some of my grandmother's jewelry so he could give me the 42 pounds sterling and 12 shillings I needed for the boat fare.

My departure, set on the 8th of November 1929, was quite moving, for God only knew when and if I would see them again.

The sea was very rough that day, and the boat couldn't anchor in the harbor, so we had to embark on a trawler and, from there, to the S/S Rodi of the Italian Puglia Line. Our first stopover was Alexandria, where Isidore and I got off. An old Egyptian friend of my father's met us on the quay. He waved at us and shouted my name several times until I recognized him from an old photo my father had given me. He held a responsible post at the city's Court of Appeals, but apart from that I knew nothing about him.

The big, bearded man immediately felt drawn to us and spent the whole day showing us around the city, explaining the small and important facts that gave Alexandria its glory in ancient times; he mentioned Cleopatra and the great library that had attracted scholars and merchants from the entire Mediterranean.

That same evening, he put us on the train bound for Port Said. We arrived there late at night. He had recommended me to his relatives, who put us up.

After three days, we embarked on the S/S Aviateur Rolland Garros, a French liner of 6,000 tons. I only had 13 pounds sterling left in my pocket, and neither Isidore nor I could afford a cabin. The only alternative was to sleep on deck. Nights were chilly, especially when it rained and the wind blew in from the west. Thanks to the kindness of a French sailor, we had a blanket for the two of us.

This was our first big trip, and a fascinating one at that. It took us thirteen hours to cross the Suez Canal. We were filled with curiosity.

From Djibouti (the only memories I have of that place are blurred by those of the scorching heat) we sailed to Mombasa and, finally, after a journey of nine days, to Dar es Salaam. There was only one train a week from this ocean city to the inland town of Kigoma on the shores of Lake Tanganyika. Isidore and I had no more money left, so we worked for a Greek hotelier, doing all sorts of menial jobs for him in order to pay our board and lodging.

We arrived in Kigoma on December 2, 1929, and on the same day we boarded a small ship that brought us across Lake Tanganyika to the town of Albertville in the Belgian Congo. What a surprise to meet there one of my childhood friends! We were so happy to be together that he put the two of us up in his tiny, hut-like abode for several days. At last, we had something resembling a bed, with proper sheets and pillowcases, and we ate fresh vegetables, grilled chicken, and tropical fruits—mangoes, avocadoes, and papaya—that we had never tasted before and relished to the last morsel. What luxury! To us boys, coming from the impoverished island of Rhodes, it seemed as if we were living a fairy tale, full of new sounds and potent smells. Some of them were terrifying, especially at night. We even asked our host if a lion or some hungry crocodile might come and eat us while we slept. He laughed his head off, yet kept us wondering. And how delighted we were, the next morning at cock's crow, to see that we were still alive and in relatively good health, although both of us had lost weight for, during the boat trip, we had subsisted on canned food, dried dates, and stale bread.

From Albertville, we boarded a train with wooden planks for seats. Steam locomotives in those days were extremely slow and broke down often, but we did arrive the following day at Kabalo, where we embarked on the Prince Leopold, which sailed down the Lualaba River. This, too, was a unique experience, lasting almost a week. The boat made frequent stops to refuel—its boilers required wood coal—which allowed our captain and other amateur hunters to use their skills and bring us back some game; this is how I got my first taste of antelope, wild pheasant, and warthog meat.

The boat also served as a floating market for the villagers ashore. Hardware and clothes were sold in exchange for fresh fish, fowl, vegetables, and fruit. More than once, the boat became entangled in large banks of papyrus. Hours of work and dozens of African hands were needed to free us.

That river crossing remains one of the most spectacular adventures I experienced in the heartland of the Congo. Bukama was the terminal point.

My new boss, Mr. Ruben Amato, came to receive me on the quay. We barely had time to get acquainted; two hours later, I jumped on the train headed for Kamina in northern Katanga, my final destination.

Kamina was the connecting point between the Lower Congo and Katanga's copper mines. There I met my boss's other two partners and the fifty-odd workers and employees of the firm. Appointed shop assistant at the grocery store, I started working the very same afternoon of my arrival.

There were seven of us at that branch store. Late in the evening, around the dinner table, I got acquainted with my fellow employees and the different activities of our company. I thus learned that it owned two bakeries: one for Europeans and one for Africans, who passed through the area by the hundreds, hailing from as far away as Kasai province, to rejoin the famous copper mines of the Union Miniére du Haut-Katanga. There was also a bar, a general retail store, and a butchery, for the region had rich pastures for cattle breeding and stock farms.

Three days after my arrival I fell ill with a high temperature. I must have contracted malaria during the boat and train trips. I had to be confined to my room—if you can call a barrack made of mud wall held together by bamboo rods a room. The sheets on my iron bed were constantly wet from the rain that leaked through the roof. One of my fellow employees came to my rescue and, using four wooden pillars and a blanket, he installed a metal basin above my bed to absorb excess water. Of course, the basin had to be emptied several times during the day after the storms, which along the equator can be terrifying as well as ear-splitting. At night, I had to do it myself, so as not to disturb the other employees. Finally, after two days and two nights, a bush doctor was called in; he gave me quinine injections at regular intervals. That is how I was saved from certain death, for many people in those days succumbed to that very debilitating sickness. Within forty-eight hours after the doctor's last visit, I was able to resume work.

There wasn't such a thing then as fixed working hours. All depended on present circumstances and on the requirements of our clients. Most of them were transit passengers, and very often I had to attend to them at the bar until one or two o'clock in the morning…and the following day, I might be up as early as 5 AM, delivering loaves of warm-baked bread to the numerous natives who worked in the mines.

The train drove through Kamina twice a week, and one of our duties was to supply the dining coach with fresh food. Since there existed no restaurant or hotel as such in our tiny outpost, we were asked to provide accommodations and serve hot meals to any stranger, traveling salesman, or manager who passed by, whether they belonged to our company or not.

The store itself was built with corrugated iron, which made for quasi-untenable heat during the day, becoming drastically cold at night. Because our customers could appear at any odd time of the day or night—they might be stuck in the bush, if they happened to drive a car that broke down because of flooded roads—I decided to sleep in a corner of the store on a bare mattress that I found tucked away in the storage room. But after two weeks of that regimen, I became weak and sick. Happily, my plea was heeded, and I was offered a small mud-wall hut all to myself, making the changes in temperature more bearable.

I was only nineteen and already many responsibilities had been thrust upon me. Apart from the various jobs I held in Kamina itself, I was instructed to go and visit the firm's twenty subsidiary stores, which were scattered all over the bush and in the surrounding villages. These stores were managed by trained Congolese shop assistants. My tasks consisted of supplying them regularly from a Ford company truck, checking their accounts, and taking stock of the goods at the end of each month.

The World Crash reached the Congo in 1931. The railroad company, then called BCK (Bas-Congo-Katanga), whose headquarters were located in Kamina, had to dismiss three quarters of its personnel, both black and white, which naturally affected the whole business community and our company in particular. Many of our customers became insolvent; others had to sell their personal belongings, such as watches, old cars, and family jewels, and always at a heavy loss. Many of them, Belgian nationals, mainly, just left the country for good and returned, penniless, to the motherland. Other European expatriates had no alternative but to stay on and make do with the current situation.

Our firm was not spared, but instead of dismissing us it presented us with two alternatives: we could either accept half our previous salary, or receive a one-way ticket back to our home in Europe. I chose the former and stayed in Kamina. Very difficult days loomed before us. We had to resume eating canned food, for the train that usually supplied us with fresh meat, vegetables, and fruit passed through our town only once a week. Thanks to the kindness of villagers, we sometimes received fish, game meat, and bananas, which we had to consume immediately for, in those days, we had no refrigerators, and in that heat the food would very quickly rot or grow stale. When we were lucky enough to receive corned beef or ham, we had to wrap the morsels in mosquito nets and store them where there was a draft. They were the prey of flies and other bugs, and half of the meat had to be thrown away, lest we catch one of the many diseases brought by infected food.

The first galvanized refrigerators did not reach our district until 1934.

The only entertainment we had was the BCK Club, where I was in charge of the refreshment bar. We used to listen to 78 rpm records played on an old manual gramophone. Once or twice a month, amateur accordionists touring the Congo gave performances. We thought they were great and thoroughly enjoyed their limited repertoires.

In Kamina, our means of locomotion consisted of a second-hand 1929 Ford van, which we used to make the rounds of our customers, supplying them with canned food and other staples, and which often broke down in the middle of the bush. The firm also owned a dozen rikshas, each one of them pulled by seven Congolese men, two in front and five in the rear. These rikshas could carry loads of merchandise up to 300 kilos. They traveled far into the bush, sometimes a distance of 400 kilometers, to supply the foremen and the workers who were building the Dilolo railroad, or the Territorial Administrators of such far-flung places as Kindu, Safakumba, Kabongo, or Mato Sungo. The trip might last anywhere from eight to fifteen days. Along with another Belgian company, Interlina, we were the only suppliers for the whole Kamina area.

On the way back, the riksha boys used to bring us papayas, pineapples, bananas, mangoes, and vegetables, which they would pick along the paths. Three or four rikshas traveled at the same time. We could hear their chants as they approached Kamina, expressing their pain and their relief. They knew we would welcome them back home.

Things, of course, didn't always go smoothly, in spite of the fact that the economy had picked up. Hazards such as tire punctures, broken wheels, leaks in the carburetor, or breakages caused by overloading provoked delays of up to a fortnight, the riksha boys having to wait for us to send them repairmen and fresh supplies. I often had to meet them in the most ungodly places.

During those years of hardship, we could bear almost anything, for stability reigned all over the country, and we would always find a village or a cluster of huts where we could eat and sleep. African hospitality is no mere legend! And I shall be forever grateful to the innumerable Congolese who let me share their berths and their food, no matter how poor they were.

Once the World Crisis and its catastrophic effects had ended, we received a few brand new American trucks, which greatly facilitated the transport of goods and put an end to the era of the rikshas.

I had been working 16- to 18-hour days, 365 days a year. I didn't know what the words 'rest' or 'vacation' meant. And this went on for eight solid years, until I became so thin and emaciated, weighing less than fifty kilos, that in 1937 my boss insisted I recuperate for a couple of months at a seaside resort in what was then the Union of South Africa. A trip to Europe was more than I could afford, as I was sending the greater part of my allowance money to my family back in Rhodes. This didn't represent much, as I started out earning about fifteen hundred Congolese francs every month (the equivalent of thirty U.S. dollars). By the end of my eight years of employment, my salary had risen to twice that amount.

On my way to South Africa, I passed through Jadotville, and then stopped over in Elisabethville, where I stayed for a few days, visiting with some childhood acquaintances of mine who had the privilege of living in the relative comfort of the provincial capital. I marveled at the relative sophistication of that town and enjoyed its invigorating climate. There, for the first time in my life, I saw a talking movie. Otherwise, we spent our idle time playing cards and Ping-Pong, and, on the rare occasions where someone owned a car, we were driven through the few paved streets of what was then hailed as the Pearl of Katanga.

From there, I traveled by train through Northern Rhodesia (today's Zambia), then Southern Rhodesia (contemporary Zimbabwe), changing coaches and locomotives three times until, finally, after a journey lasting five days and five nights, I reached Capetown at the southern tip of the black continent, one of the world's most beautiful spots.

Thanks to the city's bracing climate and its air rich in iodine, I recuperated in a matter of weeks. I was overwhelmed by the beauty of the country: its variegated and colorful landscapes, its mile-long sand beaches, as immaculate as baby powder. Yet, at the same time, I felt the shock of institutionalized racial discrimination. Segregation existed, of course, in the Congo, but it wasn't as petty and clear-cut as in South Africa, and, although frowned upon, miscegenation in my adopted country was never a crime. I shall be the living proof of it, but it is too early yet to broach that subject.

Whenever I saw benches marked 'For Whites Only', whenever I saw that the entrances to the post office and other administrative buildings were separate, that some busses were reserved exclusively for Whites and others for the so-called Coloreds (this term included all the non-white population: Blacks, Asians, and people of mixed-blood), I felt that something was fundamentally wrong and immoral. Because of these unforeseen circumstances, I planned to cut short my vacation in South Africa—the first in my adult life—and instead rejoin my family in Rhodes, albeit for a much shorter stay, since I could not afford the length of time I would have spent in Capetown. But my wishes went unfulfilled, for I received a telegram from my firm requesting that I return to Kamina immediately. That could have been my last chance to see my family and convince them to accompany me to Africa. But destiny decided otherwise, and the worst tragedy humankind was to experience was going to take place a few years later. Nobody, at the end of the thirties, could ever have fathomed the magnitude and consequences of that disaster.

Back in Kamina, I continued to work as eagerly as before and to transfer money to my folks. I was thus gradually able to pay off the dowries of two of my four sisters, who married one after the other. Again, I insisted they join me in the Congo, at least the newlyweds, assuring them that I would find stable jobs for them there. They didn't want to hear about emigrating to Africa, but a few months later, their husbands managed to obtain visas for the United States, and the two couples finally went on to settle in Montgomery, Alabama, next to that cousin of ours who never responded to my letters—it was I who was supposed to go to the States, in the first place, remember? After having begged them to change their minds, I then sent three one-way boat tickets to my two younger brothers and one of my sisters. They very reluctantly conceded to my plea, saying at first they preferred to live in the poverty they knew rather than launch into what was still described as one of the most dangerous and savage regions of the world. If I hadn't known better, I would have suspected them of reading Conrad's *Heart of Darkness*, which describes a situation no longer true. As for my parents, they categorically refused to leave Rhodes and kept my baby sister with them.

I am amazed at the fact that half the world still believes the Congolese are ill-treated and, what's more, these rumors continue to be spread by reporters of so-called reputable newspapers. It is tantamount to claiming that slave trade has not disappeared in the south of the United States. From the minute I set foot on Congolese soil until now, I have never witnessed any violent attitudes, lashings, or acts of torture on the part of the Belgian Administration. I'm not denying that there was discrimination and that the Europeans acted in a paternalistic manner that nowadays would be unacceptable and humiliating. But they were far more humane than the other colonial powers, some of which were clever enough to form a political elite among their subjects, to the detriment of the populace—the Belgians did the exact opposite and ended up losing everything—and I could verify this later on after my visits to the Portuguese, French, and British colonies, not to mention South Africa. One easily forgets that, when the international scandal broke out at the beginning of the twentieth century, when King Leopold II still owned that huge chunk of land, exploiting it unashamedly for his own personal benefit, Belgium, which never wanted a colony in the first place, was forced to take over the country in 1908. Consequently, the lot of the Congolese began to improve, and forced labor gradually disappeared, giving way to decent living conditions. The motherland, of course, greatly profited from the country's immense riches, but so did the African population. By the year 1958, the Administration had built more than 3000 hospitals and free clinics throughout that land, which was eighty times the size of Belgium, and the international commission that visited the country under the aegis of the United Nations found the results to be quite remarkable and unparalleled. The communications network alone was second to none. All this, sadly, has gone to ruin after fifty years of independence, and I still hear some of my African friends whisper in my ear: "If only the Belgians could come back and restore order to the terrible mess our politicians have wreaked!" A most politically incorrect wish that even few Congolese journalists dare state.

Second Runner-up: Best Poetry Contest

The Scorpion

Ruth Moon Kempher

> *Scorpius is also the name of the eighth sign of the Zodiac…the sign Scorpius is now about 30 degrees west of the constellation Scorpius with which it once coincided, about 2000 years ago.*
> —excerpt from "Scorpius," The American Peoples Encyclopedia

This presents a confusion of terms and of order—
the curious sign precedes the stars
    while the crawling beast itself—
an ancient fossil type, still bearing primitive features
the united head and thorax…cousin to the spider
    creeps
unconcerned across the cutting board, the sink, retreats
under stacks of coffee cups, an antiquated shape
    lurching in segments
raising fears our ancestors bequeathed—
old myths, old dreads that rattle into modern bones
    hissing Kill it! Kill it!
shivering the kitchen air, 'til it's smashed with a pot
and the fear ebbs, relieved.
    Only then there's time
to stand at the window, and see how the stars have tilted;
how there's a new slant to the red heart star, Antares
and find in the sacrifice of that small life
a disconcerting grace.

Vanity

Jane Boruszewski

Vanity is nothing but a little creature with a swollen head that wags its tail as if to say, "Feast your eyes on me, World, and see how great I look."

At the end of World War II, thousands of others like myself, displaced by the war, were hoping to return to our beloved Poland, a free Poland, but, because my country was given away to Stalin, most of us never went back. Some of our people went to Canada, Australia, and England. I chose England.

Marysia, my older sister, introduced me to Walt, and we began to date while working in one of the textile factories in Batley. When I married Walt, I was still a foolish teenager, barely out of that Polish orphanage in Africa where I had waited out the end of the war. Because he knew that, in the past, I had no pretty clothes to wear, my new and loving spouse often bought me new outfits. The first one was a brown pleated skirt, a pink blouse, and a pair of brown high-heeled shoes. Trying to walk upstairs while wearing those shoes for the first time, wagging my vanity, I fell down.

Walt and I would parade in the park on weekends, where I managed to be a big showoff in a small body. I itched for my old roommates and schoolmates to see how much I'd changed, but none of them were in England. I was sure I looked as good as as Princess Elizabeth and acted like royalty, letting my tail wag faster than ever. I did collect some admiring glances from young people, but that was not enough for the likes of me.

While traveling to America on a Britannic ship, I received enough attention to tickle my ego, but then I slowly became obsessed with the thought that I could overwhelm our sponsor with my sophisticated appearance. He had been my teacher in Africa. After his return to the USA, he bought a farm so that he could bring Polish refugees over from Europe and Africa. I was one of them; he had hired Walt to be his manager, and I to be his housekeeper. Unfortunately, I was a housekeeper who couldn't cook and had no idea how to use a vacuum cleaner.

I knew my teacher remembered me as a shy, plain girl in pigtails, wearing dull school uniforms. Soon, he was to have his fill of my new female beauty, which now belonged to my beloved husband, Walt. But still...

We arrived in New York in July, the hottest day of the year. My vanity made me put on a blue, long-sleeved dress to bring out the blueness in my hazel eyes, along with high-heeled shoes and silky stockings to make me look like someone important.

"Our sponsor will see me soon," I whispered under my breath, careful not to let Walt hear me. I was so certain he would meet us the minute we stepped off the ship, but I was in for a surprise. I saw tall skyscrapers reaching up toward the merciless sky, horrendous traffic on the streets, and crowds of pedestrians on the sidewalks, all rushing to go somewhere—but not a sign of our future employer. I was even more disappointed to realize that no men even looked at me here, with me dressed to kill.

A stranger called a taxi for us and instructed us to get on the train to Syracuse at Grand Central Station. On the train I began to notice how much I was sweating, but that didn't worry me, for I still had my makeup on, especially mascara to make my lashes long and thick, and red, red lipstick on my lips, which I kept puckered up. But in the train's bathroom, I looked in the mirror and gasped. My face was streaked with running mascara, and my lips were smeared into a red blotch. Och, there was nothing for me to do but to wash in the sink, and I did just that. I also tied my lame hair into pigtails, for it hung in strings around my shoulders. When I looked again at my reflection, I saw the shy, plain teenager from my African orphanage days. I was so upset, I didn't even bother to reapply the makeup I carried in my purse.

Our dear sponsor was waiting for us when we arrived in Syracuse. I looked down humbly at my feet after our greeting, just like in the old days. He took a second to look at me, and then smiled the smile I'd known in school.

"Janka, you look sweet." *Sweet*, I thought, my heart sinking to my feet. "And just as pretty as you did in Africa. I'm so glad you haven't learned to use the awful makeup our women mask their faces with."

Pretty—that's better, my vanity whispered inside of me. And I grinned a shy grin.

So my first lesson in my new country was that one has to learn to dress properly for the climate, and that it's not appearances that make a person, but what is inside of one. From that day on, I was careful not to paint my face too heavily. More importantly, even that foolish creature called vanity agreed with me.

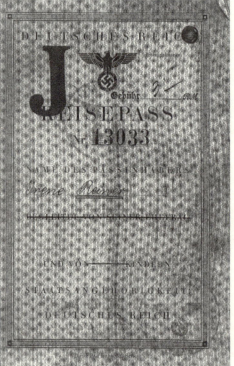

Enemy Alien

Irene Etlinger

These days we hear a lot about "illegal aliens." I often think of the times I have been designated an alien—not an illegal one, but an "enemy alien."

When I left Austria on December 9, 1938, I carried a German passport because, in March of that year, Germany had annexed my country—forcibly, but with the enthusiastic approval of many citizens. My passport had a black swastika stamped in it, as well as a large, red "J," designating Jewish blood, in my case 50%.

I was sixteen years old when I fled Vienna for London to wait for my U.S. visa. The political situation in Europe had become dangerously unstable, and it seemed wise to leave German territory before a war broke out. A kind British family—the Nathans, who were friends of some Viennese acquaintances of ours—agreed to host me for a few weeks until I could obtain my visa. They lived in Golders Green, a nice, middle-class part of London. I helped with the housework and the children, ten-year-old Elizabeth and six-year-old David. My visa was supposed to come through in three to four weeks, but due to the political situation and the American quota system I was still waiting in September of 1939, when the Nazis invaded Poland and Britain declared war.

Mr. Nathan was concerned about his family staying in London. It was expected that the Germans would start bombing England immediately, so he decided that his wife, the two children, and I should move to a farm in Somerset, near Taunton. He would stay in London to do his work and come to visit us on most weekends.

Wibble Farm was a three-mile walk from the town. The countryside was green and gentle, with fuchsia hedges instead of fences to mark the fields. We had two rooms in the big farmhouse, which had indoor plumbing, but no bathtub or shower. Each morning we made several trips to the kitchen to fetch hot water for our ablutions.

I remember eating rabbit in every possible form: stewed, fried, in pie, even curried. Mr. Wibble shot the rabbits in his fields before they could eat up all the vegetables he had planted.

This was the time of the "phony" war. Nothing was happening. There were no air raids over England. So, each day, we would walk into town. There was a little library tucked into a corner of the chemist's shop. I borrowed and read many old books, which had been donated by the community: *The Scarlet Pimpernel, Lorna Doone, Little Lord Fauntleroy, The Last Days of Pompeii*. We also bought a newspaper every day, most often the Daily Telegraph, which was considered less stodgy than the London Times.

One day in October, 1939, there was a large notice in the newspaper to the effect that all "Enemy Aliens" were required to register at the nearest police station. Any person carrying a German passport was considered an enemy alien, regardless of background. In all countries overrun by Germany, if you were lucky enough to have a passport at all, it was a German one.

On the morning after the notice appeared, I walked to town and dutifully presented myself at the little police station. Two middle-aged, uniformed policemen were on duty. "I am here to register as an enemy alien," I said.

In retrospect, it seems like a scene from one of those British comedies on PBS Television. The two men looked at me in surprise. They probably had not read the morning papers, and had not yet received instructions from headquarters about the new law. Here was a small, young girl, speaking English with a German accent, claiming that she was an enemy alien obliged to report to them.

The older man, a paunchy, fatherly type, offered me a chair. "Now, now, my dear, what can we do for you?"

"The notice in the Daily Telegraph says that I must register at the nearest police station. I have a German passport, even though I am an Austrian."

"Well, young lady, you don't look very dangerous to me, but we all have to obey the law, eh?" He turned to his colleague. "Ring up Headquarters and find out if they have any instructions for us."

It took quite a while to get an answer from Headquarters. Meanwhile, the policemen gave me tea and biscuits and asked questions. I felt that my problem was probably the most interesting one they had encountered in a long time. Surely, there was not much crime in that little town, and there certainly weren't many foreigners.

ENEMY ALIEN

After about two hours, a young policeman on a bicycle pedaled up to the station. He had come from Headquarters with forms and instructions for the registration of enemy aliens. All three officers helped me to fill out the forms and took my oath that I was not a subversive intent upon overthrowing the British government. They wished me good luck, and told me that I was free to return to Wibble Farm.

All this had taken most of the day. Since Wibble Farm had no telephone, I could not let Mrs. Nathan know I would be late. When I finally arrived, she was relieved that I had not been detained by the authorities and interned for the duration of the war. This had been the fate of Germans and Austrians in England during World War I.

I left England for America in December, 1939, before the Blitzkrieg. My encounter with the police in that small English town has remained an amusing memory.

By December 7, 1941, I had been in the United States for almost two years and had graduated from Lincoln High School in Portland, Oregon. I was attending Hastings Business College and living with my sponsoring family, the Pallays. They owned and operated several movie theaters and worked at night. I stayed with the children in the evenings and got them off to school in the mornings.

A few days after Pearl Harbor, there was a notice in The Oregonian to the effect that all enemy aliens had to register at the Federal Post Office on Broadway and Main Street. I had already been there the year before to file my Declaration of Intention to become a U.S. Citizen. After that filing, it took another four years to get citizenship, five years altogether.

Registering with the U.S. federal government was not nearly as much fun as it had been with the English small town police, but it was much more efficient. I filled out the forms, showed the clerk my passport with the red "J," and asserted that I was an Austrian whose country had been invaded, not a German enemy. The clerk did not acknowledge my statements, only warned me that I was subject to a 10 PM curfew and obliged to notify his office if I changed my address.

Soon after this registration, the Pallays' neighbor, Mrs. Bronner, came to see me. She very excitedly told me that someone from either the FBI or the INS had visited her to inquire about me. They had also gone to other neighboring homes to ask questions. She said, "I told them you were just a nice refugee kid and certainly no threat to our country." I never heard from any government agency about my status as an enemy alien.

That left the matter of the curfew. I did not get to go out in the evenings very often, since my job was to stay with the Pallay children. Occasionally, though, I was allowed to go to a USO dance or a party at a friend's house. I never paid any attention to the curfew. Since none of my friends owned a car, we often walked home after midnight. Secretly, I really hoped that one day the police would stop me. I imagined myself as a kind of Joan of Arc. "I am an Austrian," I would declaim. "My country was overrun by our common enemy, the Germans, and I had to flee because of racial and religious persecution. Now you, the representatives of the U.S. Government, are wronging me by treating me as an enemy."

As it happened, no policeman ever apprehended me for breaking the curfew. I still regret that I never had the chance to make my impassioned speech.

An Immigrant Life: Snapshots

Joan E. Zekas

"Come, Tafillie…lookit!"

Tafillie pushed herself away from the kitchen table. She wondered what was bothering her sister-in-law. She hiked up her cotton stockings, put on her eye glasses, and shuffled to the window.

"What's the matter, Rŏzé?"

"Poor chicky chick…no head…run crazy…all over yard," said Grammie Rose.

The Strishes next door were great neighbors in every way except one. When they axed one of their chickens, they just let it run headless in their yard until it stopped and fell over.

But not Grammie Rose. When she killed a chicken out on the back stump, she held onto it—between her knees, almost reverently—until it stopped shaking. It was a fine point, a little finesse in the hard life of a Lithuanian immigrant in Northeast Pennsylvania.

Tafillie, the compassionate sister-in-law, just shook her head and sat down. Grammie Rose lifted the silver-colored kettle from the coal stove and warmed their tea. Her hands shook, and a few drops of water spilled on the oilcloth. Tafillie pretended not to notice and quietly nudged them under her saucer.

Grammie Rose put her hand to the side of her face and pondered. "What you tink, Tafillie? Pranas—he gonna stay in America dis time? He *like* dis coal country?"

Tafillie's hand curled hard around her cup. "Mano vyras (my husband)!… he better, or I don't know vat I gonna do!"

"Oi!" said Grammie Rose. "Mario brolis (my brother)…so strong in head! Even in old country he make our motina vorry. Yes…no…dis vay…dat vay…"

"Yeh…all he say: 'Go to America, go to America, tings good in America.' So ve go to America," said Tafillie. "Den he say 'Go back to Litwania, tings no good in America, go back to Litwania.' But ve have two babies den. Not so easy to go back to old country. I tell him, like dat—too hard, too hard to go back. Den, my Pranas, his eyes so sad…so ve go back to Litwania."

Grammie Rose put her hand over Tafillie's and sighed. She just didn't understand her brother. But he was a sweet man with a kind heart, at least most of the time.

"You know, Rŏzé, ve be still in Ellis Island, if…" Tafillie's voice trailed away. Her shoulders shook.

"Tafillie, don't make cry. Is all right now." Grammie Rose knew this part of the story well. Her brother, Pranas (Frank), Tafillie, and their two babies were denied readmission to America because they had no birth papers for the two little ones, who had been born in the U.S. It took the effort of Anna, Grammie Rose's mother-in-law, to authenticate matters.

"I tank God every day for Anna," said Tafillie. "You tell your Jonas… his mother is good voman…is *Saint!* So far to Ellis Island she go…old, sick, English no good. She tell Big Shot man at desk how she be baby lady (midwife), how she pull my babies into America."

"God bless Anna," the two women said in unison.

"Rŏzé, *you* are good voman, too…like Anna. Ve make you *squash*…like sausage. No room to move…four more people in house. But ver vould ve go? I see Big Shot man ven I close my eyes, and I shake."

"So? Ve be sausage!" pronounced Grammie Rose.

Compassion ruled the hard times and kindliness was its fine point. There were now ten people—four adults and six children—in the small house.

The stove cast a rosy tint on their faces. Grammie Rose went over, shook down the ashes, and shoveled in more coal. The stove hissed, crackled, and roared, causing eerie screeches.

Grammie Rose quickly crossed herself. She and Tafillie held hands and said a prayer. The women believed those sounds from the stove were really the cries of souls suffering in Purgatory. The prayers of the living would give them release.

A staccato rap on the kitchen window caught the women's attention. This was on the Lavages' side of the house. Grammie Rose set aside the pot of petunias and pushed up the sash. A wooden spoon with steam rising was thrust through the opening.

"Rŏzé, what you tink?" Anelka Lavage used Grammie Rose as her official taster. "My piccalilli…more sugar?"

Grammie Rose ran the wooden spoon under her nose, sniffed, then tasted the piccalilli. "It's nice, Anelka. I tink is good."

"Rŏzé, I see mailman come. You get letter from Marta?"

Marta was Grammie Rose's sister, the only sibling who remained behind in Lithuania. Grammie Rose, her eyes bright with tears, shook her head no.

"Sorry, Rŏzé."

Slow, slow, slow, Grammie Rose closed the window, blinked back her tears, and sat down.

"Oi! Oi! Oi! Is time!" Grammie Rose shot up from the table. The men were coming to double-check the measurements of the house. And Grandpa John was due any minute from the mines.

There it was—the thump of footsteps on the porch. Men talking back and forth in broken English. Grandpa John and the workmen had arrived at the same time. But Grandpa John stayed on the porch. Blackened bits of coal dust slurried in the water bucket as he washed his hands and face.

The men surveyed the house and made long lists of notes. Grammie Rose could hardly believe it. It was really and truly going to happen: the house was going to be *raised!* Grandpa John had finally saved enough money to raise up their coal company house. Each week, he checked and double-checked his pay to be sure that the mine bosses had not cheated him, a not yet fully literate American.

Day by day, Grammie Rose readied the house, packing up the dishes and hanging old carpets over the windows to keep out the dust.

Now, at last…the big day! All the children were wide-eyed, watching the burly men troop into the yard. The kids had to be shooed away again and again, till Grammie Rose, in exasperation, sent them next door to the Lavages. She and Tafillie stationed themselves on the front sidewalk. Their husbands were, of course, at work—far beneath someone else's house, digging coal.

One by one the men rolled their jacks into the yard. The foreman called out the positions. When all the jacks were in place under the house, the foreman blew his whistle. The men stood at attention. Another whistle blast and, in unison, each man cranked up his jack just *one notch*. Again and again, the whistle; again and again, the crank of the jacks. And, one notch at a time, the house rose until 143 South Empire Street was sitting high and sassy.

Peering at the uprooted house through the Lavages' windows, the children made big "Oh's" with their mouths.

Next came the digging, the back-breaking work of unearthing the new floor. The workmen wiped slick beads of sweat from their brows as they dug, dug, dug. Mounds of dirt piled up in the yard, dirt destined for a vegetable plot in the rear.

Over time, the men got it all done: erecting the new joists, pouring concrete for the foundation, sawing and nailing the wood for steps, and putting in the window for the coal chute.

It was a proud day when Grandpa John could walk down, down, down his own cellar steps. Many of his coal miner buddies could only manage shallow cellars, but *he* could stand fully erect. He made sure of that! After twelve-hour days spent hunched over in a coal mine, he could stand tall in his own home.

It was a fine point.

Questions

Dorothy Boggs

Questions raced through Dorothy's brain. Mrs. Bond, her third grade teacher, had opened the door by asking, "Who were the Minute Men?"

A freckle-faced third grader with reddish-brown, curly hair, Dottie skipped and ran on her way home. She kicked a stone and jumped over a line in the cement sidewalk.

The year was 1926, and the economy was booming. Women wore shorter dresses. Men sported business suits. Money was flowing. Women showed up in neighborhood saloons with an escort. A thought was floating through the population. *The world was going to hell in a hand basket.*

It was Dottie's turn to help Mom with the evening meal, but she took the long way home. She was thinking about her questions. *Where did the Minute Men meet? Boston Gardens? Boston Commons? Did the British Soldiers notice them?* Mom and Dad would know the answer. Dottie opened the door and dropped her books on the kitchen table. She saw that her mother was annoyed because she hadn't come right home from school. Dottie got busy setting the dining room table, trying to placate her mother.

"Do you know who the Minute Men are?" Dottie asked her mom.

"We'll talk about it later. Your father and brother are hungry."

It's always later! Dottie glared at her mother, but she started to mash the potatoes.

Her father came into the kitchen to see if dinner was ready.

"Dad, do you know anything about the Minute Men? Did they fire any shots in Boston Commons?" asked Dottie.

"I'm not sure if a shot was fired at the Commons or Concord. Dorothy, we're having company, and they'll be here in an hour. I want you and your brother to help your mother clean up the kitchen. We'll talk about history tomorrow."

Dottie watched her dad leave the room, and made a silent decision. She wanted some answers to her questions.

It was a beautiful spring morning. You could hear the click of horse's hooves on the cobblestones. As Dottie started out the back door, she spied four empty milk bottles. Twenty cents! She grabbed a paper bag to put the milk bottles in and went to the neighborhood grocery store. Twenty cents went into her pocket. With her lunch clutched in one hand and a sweater in the other, Dottie left the store. Spring fever and adventure was tweaking the third grader's heart.

At the railroad station, she purchased a round trip ticket to Boston, thirty miles away. Walking quickly, trying to look tall and confident, she found a seat by the window. She avoided looking at the adults, in case they might see the excitement in her eyes. Her sweater went over her arms and shoulders; the lunch sat on her lap. She saw people pause, look, and wonder why she wasn't in school. Dottie stared out the window.

Thirty minutes later, the train rolled into South Boston. The passengers slowly exited, walking towards the ferry that would take them to the business area of South Boston. Dottie fumbled in her pocket for the transfer. She felt the ten cents at the bottom of her pocket. She pulled up her shoulders, tucked in her tummy, and walked briskly. Twenty minutes later, the ferry tied up to the pier across the harbor. Everybody disembarked.

Dottie stood at the crossing. Should she take the Rapid Transit or walk? On a post, she saw a board with the prices of rides to different parts of Boston. It would cost her ten cents to ride to the Commons. She decided to walk. She knew the way to downtown Boston, because her dad had taught her.

Nine-year-old Dottie crossed the road, singing a song to herself, a half smile on her lips. Pretty soon, she would have answers. The sun caught the red highlights in her hair. Dottie's shoes created a melody on the cobblestones. Now and then, she stopped to look in the shop windows and dream. *When I grow up that dish will sit on my table.* She forgot to count the blocks. *What did Dad say? Look for landmarks? Odd-looking buildings?* She sat on the curb. Watched the traffic flow by. The Commons were a few blocks away. Dottie walked past Filene's Department Store, stopped, looked at a beautiful dress. *I am going to look like that someday.*

Finally, the Commons! Now to find somebody who could answer her questions. A man was talking to a group of people. She watched them for a while. When she got hungry, she sat on a bench and ate her lunch, while tourists walked by.

QUESTIONS

Dottie joined the group. She tried to understand the leader, but he seemed to be talking in another language. Who could she ask?

A policeman walked by and smiled at Dottie. She smiled back.

"Did you go to school today?" the policeman asked.

"No, I didn't. There were some questions I wanted answered. Everybody was busy. So I came here. Do you know anything about the Minute Men?" Dottie asked.

"Sure," the policeman said. "What do you want to know?"

The policeman and the nine-year-old girl sat on a bench for quite a while talking about the Minute Men, Concord, the War. He was patient and answered all her questions.

"Thank you!" Dottie said. "I have to go home now. Can you tell me what street I should take to get back to the ferry?"

"What's your name?" Now the policeman had questions for Dottie to answer. "How old are you? Do your parents know where you are?"

"My name is Dorothy Kane, 121 Washington Street, Lynn, Massachusetts. My dad's name is Michael Kane."

"How would you like a ride in a squad car? We may be able to take you home. Okay?"

Dottie smiled and nodded. At the police station she was treated like royalty. Her parents were notified that she had been found at Boston Commons, and she would be brought home in a squad car.

Dorothy's parents were relieved that she was alive. By the same token, they were very angry for all the grief and fear she had put them through. She was severely punished, and would think a long time before embarking, unaccompanied, on another journey.

At an Age When

Annette Stovall

When I took as wrenched away from parents,
this youngen had nothing but my tears
in the matter. Of my tender lad year,
I kin just guess at 8th or seventh.

That age ripe for training me tasks fit for
I toil in light yard and house stints.
Sad and weepin as missin my parents,
I'd even cry 'side the games kids for.

As for learn me education, few cared.
Not even ole massa give a hoot.
Some them well meaning them folk what gives a hoot,
was run from the outdoor school all scared.

At age 10 or 12, I was fit for more tasks.
Such for gather corn and bale cotton
while I worn them shabby seams grown rotten
and run-down shoes fit for the trash.

Later when ah's physically at adult age,
my burden, yea, day long tasks.
I ploughed, planted seed, while feeling sun's hard rap
and massa whip my bruised back that age.

At last comes the age ah was jes happy.
I and many another like me,
we all given our long deserved freedoms.
Oh, how I praised God! What plans ah had!

Things I dreamed for years on doing, at last,
for truth when some folk blanked on where go.
I had it head far as north is from south, though.
There should other freedoms come to pass.

And many like me give response applauds
"head for said northern prosperity."

Where the ache none worse than southern agony,
there we's hoping it for less discord.

Oh, the celebration we shouts in the glee
with country food, dance, and toe-tapping.
'Twas enough to remember through all infinity.
For I and all slaves, we's, now, set free.

May Day

Eleanor Whitney Nelson

The buckskin stallion glared at us. He pinned his ears back, shook his head and stamped the ground. Behind him, his herd of mares and foals galloped off toward a low sagebrush-covered hill.

Our horses planted their feet and stood like statues with drumming hearts, but under my saddle I could feel my Paint gelding bunching, ready to spin and bolt. My husband's mare snorted and swung her haunches sideways into my leg. Frank tightened his reins and drove her forward with his heels, forcing her to face the wild horses.

When the last of the herd disappeared over the crest, the stallion wheeled away, bugled a shrill whinny and thundered off to join his family. Powdery dust churned beneath his hooves, spreading low across the ground. Like a thin morning fog, it hung in the air long after he was out of sight.

In the late 1980's, drought browned the countryside in northern Nevada, leaving the oily sagebrush and junipers explosively dry. Wildfires were never more than a careless cigarette, dry thunderstorm, or random spark away. Water holes dried up, and the bands of wild horses moved progressively closer to populated areas in search of food and water. Stressed by the harsh conditions, many of the mares dropped their foals and moved off with the herd, leaving their babies behind. A handful of foals were rescued and brought to veterinary clinics to be raised in adoptive homes; most died abandoned and alone or fell prey to coyotes and mountain lions.

During the years we lived in Reno, Frank and I spent much of our leisure time exploring the mountainous rangeland in that part of the state and nearby California, occasionally on foot, more commonly on horseback. Weekends became a blur of small events: sightings of wildlife—a herd of deer, an eagle—wildflowers in the early spring, sunburned noses, a lost horseshoe, a sudden windstorm or snow squall in July. Those small events blended into what has become a generally pleasurable memory with no single happening standing out dramatically above the others—except for one. May 1, 1988 would become a landmark date in our lives.

On that particular day, Frank and I loaded up our horses in the trailer, tied our dogs in the back of the pickup, and headed toward one of our favorite riding areas on the northern outskirts of Reno. Even though it was close to town, this rangeland provided almost unlimited open space in which to ride, with only the wild critters that called it home for company. Once covered by low scrub junipers, it had been scorched by fire three years earlier and, except for isolated clusters of trees, it now sported only young clumps of sagebrush that were beginning to reclaim the hillsides. The steeply rolling, granitic foothills of the eastern Sierra Nevada provided beautiful, coarse sandy footing for our horses.

This first day of May was unusually brisk for the season, but it was a vast improvement over the screaming winds and spitting snow of the previous day. Fortified with a warming stirrup cup of Chilean brandy, Frank and I set off for a leisurely Sunday picnic ride on our four-year-old horses. Frank's mare, Lily, trotted across the sandy ground, slapping her dinner-plate feet securely one in front of the other. A Clydesdale-quarter horse cross, she always made us think of the children's rhyme: "Fatty, fatty, two by four..." My Paint gelding, Cajun, pranced stiffly along behind, threatening to buck before settling into a smooth ground-covering jog.

Ratso, our Chilean rabbit-hunting dog, loped freely across the countryside on greyhound legs, a perpetual smile on his face from the pure joy of running. Covering five miles to our one, he kept us guessing as to his whereabouts. We would spot him on the hills to our right, and then he would appear streaking out of a low draw on our left. At times, when we began to wonder if we had lost him, he would bound up with a grin on his face that said, "I knew where you were all the time."

At first, Rocky, our ten-month-old butterball yellow lab-mix puppy, tried to keep up with Ratso, but as he galumphed along he quickly fell behind, his chunky legs no match for his fleet companion's. With a resigned expression, he trailed along after the horses, his tongue hanging to the ground.

Not wanting to stress either the dogs or the horses, we moved slowly across the wildflower-dotted hills, pushing toward a water hole where we planned to stop for lunch. Even on cool days, the dogs depended on their water breaks. Whether they wallowed in a muddy cattle tank or soaked in a watercress-clogged spring, they always lapped noisily at the refreshing water until the thirsty horses pushed them aside.

As we neared our destination, Ratso joined us, but we noticed that we no longer had our caboose; Rocky had vanished. Shading my eyes, I searched the hillside and, finally, there above us at the base of a prominent rocky outcrop, I spotted his yellow coat. He was motionless, fixated on something among the boulders. We called, but he refused to budge. The clear, pale sky beyond the top of the hill was dazzling, and I squinted, trying to make out what was hidden in the shadows. It took a moment before I realized what I was seeing; Rocky was nose to nose with a tiny brown foal.

Expecting to see Mama charge out from behind the rocks and trample him, we feverishly called Rocky off. Reluctantly, he returned to us. While Frank kept the dogs with him, I rode up the hill and cautiously circled the foal at a distance, looking for any sign of the mother—dead or alive—or the herd, but I saw no other horses. As I neared the tiny foal, Cajun's head shot up. He pranced and pawed at the ground. He became so agitated that I had to dismount and lead him back down the hill for Frank to hold.

When I approached the colt a second time, he took a few steps, stopped and pressed up against the smooth outcrop behind him, trying to nurse the warm rocks. I reached out to him, and he stood quietly while I stroked his neck. He was emaciated, his body appearing to be nothing more than ribs pressed against his hindquarters. No stomach was visible. A long string of partly dried umbilical cord hung down from his belly.

I had no way of knowing if he was abandoned, or if we had scared the mother away. I knew that, when the wild mares were ready to drop their foals, they wandered off from the herd to find a private place, but as soon as the foal was on its feet and strong enough to follow her, the pair rejoined the group.

Realizing that Frank had his hands full with all the animals, I slid back down the hill on the heels of my boots. As I left, the colt turned and took a couple of wobbly steps toward me before returning to the security of his warm rock wall.

"What do we do now?" I asked.

"We leave him here," Frank said. "We have to give his mother a chance to come back for him."

"If she doesn't, he'll starve or freeze to death…if coyotes or mountain lions don't get him."

Frank shrugged. "That's the chance we'll—he'll—have to take."

Little else occupied our thoughts for the rest of the day and that toss-and-turn night. At some hour in the early morning, we agreed that I should try to find a way to drive our truck to where we had found the foal. If he was alive and alone, we would return in the afternoon when Frank was off work and bring him home in the back of the pickup.

Soon after dawn, I hopped into the truck with Ratso for companionship and my .38 revolver snugly on my hip for security, and set off on the forty-five minute drive to where we had parked our horse trailer the day before. Once on the other side of the fence, there were no more paved roads, but I found the area crisscrossed with rutted dirt tracks. Most were passable with a four-wheel-drive pickup. Which one would bring me closest to the foal was the puzzle.

Following what seemed the most probable route, I eased the pickup across the bumpy surface. The road dropped down into a hidden valley, where I passed a lion hunter's camp. The staked-out hounds set up a baying that should have woken the dead; Ratso tore at the windows answering their calls with angry barking. Not wishing to encounter strange men, I was relieved when no hunters appeared from their tents. Two miles farther on, I came across an abandoned mining camp. Ghosts hovered between the shambled buildings, and my skin crawled from their touch. I hurried on.

Before long the road veered off in the wrong direction. I tried several intersecting tracks, but none brought me closer to my destination. Finally, I decided to start all over and backtracked to where we had parked the day before. Retracing yesterday's route by driving cross country seemed the only answer.

An hour later, I found myself at the bottom of the hill where we had seen the foal. With Ratso tugging me up the slope on the end of his leash, I slogged through the stickery brush. Scanning the base of the resistant rock rib, I saw no sign of life, but no sign of death, either. I was on the point of breathing a sigh of relief that the colt was gone—that the mother had come back for him, that he had not been eaten, that he had not died of exposure—when a little head popped up and stared at me. The startled figure lurched to his feet, staggered to his security wall and tried to climb it, wedging himself into a slot in the rocks. I went to him and gently extricated his tangled legs. He was noticeably weaker, and it was obvious now that he was on his own. There was nothing I could do for him by myself, so once again I left him. And, once again, he turned and took a couple of steps toward me.

Hustling back to town, I began a round robin of telephone calls—to Frank, who said he would be off work at four o'clock, and to my veterinarian, who said he would get some goats' milk and prepare a stall for the foal. In the midst of making all the arrangements, my college-age nephew, Mac, called from the bus station. We had known he would be arriving for a visit, but had not known the exact time. An extra pair of hands would come in handy.

Hardly had I collected Mac when Frank appeared home early, so we all piled into the pickup, stopped at the veterinary clinic for the goats' milk, and headed off to rescue the colt. Mac, who lived in Los Angeles, commented that this was straight out of Disney—Disney, perhaps, but a very real life and death situation for that tiny creature.

The chestnut foal with two white stockings on his hind legs, flaxen mane and tail, and a bold star on his forehead was standing about twenty feet from where I had last seen him. This time he whinnied at me. With Frank and Mac flanking him, I corralled the colt for the third time in twenty-four hours. The little foal halter I had bought dwarfed him as though it had been made for an adult horse, so, latching it around his chest, I turned it into a harness. By holding onto it, we could support him on his unsteady feet.

We offered him the calf-nursing bottle, which the veterinarian had filled with goats' milk, but he seemed unsure what to do with it and displayed no instinct to nurse. In our eagerness to get food into him, we forced milk on him too fast. Soon he was sputtering and coughing, white froth bubbling from his nose.

After he had drunk a few swallows, we tried to coax him down the hill, but his legs were dragging, and it was obvious he would not be able to make it unless Frank carried him. Even though he was way below normal size, possibly fifty pounds instead of the seventy or eighty he should have been, he was a heavy load to negotiate down the slope.

Once at the pickup, we placed him half-sitting, half-lying on a foam mat in the back. While on the bumpy road with Mac on one side supporting him and me on the other, he seemed all right, but when we reached the smoother paved surface he relaxed and sank down onto the foam. Thinking he had succumbed to exhaustion and was trying to adjust to a totally new situation, I let him go. It took me a few moments to realize he had stopped breathing.

Desperation and anger overtook me. "No! Not after all this. You won't give out on me now!" I snatched him up, but he just lolled in my arms. I laid him down and pounded on his chest. I yelled at him. His eyelids flickered, and he looked up.

For the rest of the drive back to town, I made him stand while I cupped my arms under his chest and belly to steady him. When his head started to droop and his knees buckled, I released him, making him struggle to stay upright; when he had his feet under him again, I would renew my support. A very long forty minutes later we arrived at the veterinary clinic.

As soon as we placed him on the ground, he became aware of the other horses in the corrals nearby. His whole posture changed. He whinnied, and we were able to guide him into the barn on what seemed like much sturdier legs. Once inside the thickly-bedded stall, he nursed eagerly on the goats' milk. The veterinarian said his lungs were harsh, and she was worried about pneumonia, but she would keep a close watch on him. There was nothing more we could do that day, so Frank, Mac, and I left, knowing that if he was going to make it he was in good hands.

May Day, as we named him, did develop pneumonia. During the week that he was in the hospital, he was treated using an IV to administer medication because his stomach was not sufficiently developed to handle oral drugs. We stopped by to help out during the day, and someone on the staff stayed with him each night to bottle feed him every few hours and administer medication. When we took him home, our veterinarian asked us to pay only for out-of-pocket costs for medicine and supplies: $160. Everyone at the clinic—two veterinarians and the staff—donated their time.

During the time that May Day was in the hospital, we prepared a secure stall for him in our barn with deep straw bedding for warmth. The afternoon we brought him home was bitterly cold with fine snow flurries swirling in gusts of strong wind. Even though we had wrapped him in a horse blanket and the drive was less than ten minutes, he was shivering when we got there. Concerned about his recent pneumonia, we dressed him in Ratso's dog jacket. Although Ratso was only a mid-sized dog—no more than fifty pounds—the jacket was many sizes too big, but it did the job.

We spent three touch-and-go weeks with numerous visits from both veterinarians before we could say that May Day was out of danger. Soon, his belly was no longer tucked tightly against his haunches, and he was cantering around the corral on growing legs.

Our three horses greeted him with different attitudes. Little Man, our Appaloosa gelding, saw him as a challenge, and we knew we could not allow him near the colt. Cajun seemed to have no memory of his encounter on the hillside and hardly registered that May Day was there. Lily was entranced and stood for hours on end with her head hanging over her stall door across the aisle, her eyes locked on him while she uttered soft nickers. Although it seemed she might make a good substitute mother, we didn't dare stall her with May Day for fear she might crush him. She did, however, provide much needed companionship.

May Day had two strikes against him: he was both a wild horse and an orphan. Most wild horses are difficult to train. They seem to possess more imagination than the long-domesticated bloodlines, but handled with patience many can become exceptional mounts. In general, those wild horses that are gathered young submit more willingly than their older relatives. This should have meant that May Day would be agreeable to what we asked of him. But he was also an orphan, and orphan horses are notoriously difficult to raise, because most grow up with no respect for their handlers. May Day was one of these. Perhaps the relationship is too close. We spent hundreds of hours bottle feeding him, nursing and caring for him when he was a baby. While we disciplined him, perhaps we were not firm enough, or perhaps our methods were not understandable to his equine way of thinking. Perhaps there was something within his nature that did not lend itself to being domesticated.

May Day turned into a good-looking horse, but he had small mean eyes. When he was old enough to be turned loose with the other horses, he became aggressive, refusing to accept the normal authority of the older members of his herd. Even though he had been gelded at a very young age (five months), he retained many of the dominant characteristics of a successful wild stallion. He would rear up, grab the other horses on the neck behind the ears, and shake them until they squealed in pain.

We gentled him to ride and found he had comfortable gaits, but he submitted reluctantly. Each day was like starting anew with his training. When grooming him or trimming his feet, he would cow kick, a dangerous jab to the side with his hind foot. Eventually, when I was approaching him with a net full of hay, he struck out and hit me just above the knee, dislocating it and tearing the tendons. Even after surgery and many years of healing and therapy, few days go by when I am not reminded in some small way of May Day.

When he was four years old, we made the decision that he was not meant to be a family pleasure horse, and through a friend's recommendation we found a ranch willing to take him. In his new setting he would no longer be a pampered back yard horse, but would have to spend long hours moving cattle to earn his keep. Knowing May Day as I did, I was sure he would thrive on hard work. Even so, and despite the problems we had had with him, I was apprehensive about turning him over to a rancher, afraid he would be handled roughly by cowhands abusing his mouth with severe curb bits and spurring him into submission.

It was late in the day when my friend and I pulled into the ranch and drew up next to a large corral filled with horses nose-deep in feeders heaped with hay. The sun had already set, and a pale orange glow stained the horizon.

As I opened the back door of the horse trailer to unload May Day, I saw a lanky man standing by a hitching rail, saddling a bay quarter horse. He looked up, adjusted his hat and ambled toward us. Before I could unfasten the safety chain behind May Day's rump, allowing him to step out, May Day twisted his head around and peered out the side of the trailer. In a sudden panic, he flung himself against the restraint. Again and again he hit it. Unable to push free, he ducked his head, crouched down on his knees and shot out under the chain. Scrambling to his feet, he planted his hoofs and stared at the unfamiliar surroundings with wild eyes.

The lanky man, whom I took to be the rancher, stopped beside me and regarded May Day, spat a squirt of juice from a wad of chaw into the dust, and drawled, "Well, that's one way to do it." Calmly, he strolled over to the trembling horse, reached out, took hold of the lead rope and stroked his sweaty neck.

"Raul." He turned toward a group of cowhands who were pitching hay to horses in a second corral. "Throw a saddle up on him. Let's see what he can do."

While Raul cinched up the girth of a well-used roping saddle, the rancher grabbed a gentle, loose-ring snaffle bridle off the hitching rail and slipped the headstall over May Day's ears. He rubbed him between the eyes, speaking softly to him.

Handing the reins to Raul, the rancher turned toward me and fished in his shirt pocket. He drew out a few bills and handed them to me. "That's what we agreed on," he said.

Before I could flick through the money and stuff it in my pocket, he was halfway to the saddled quarter horse; Raul was already swinging on board

May Day. Once settled in the saddle, he sat quietly for a moment, allowing May Day to adjust to his weight. Without picking up the reins, the cowboy nudged him forward with his legs. May Day resisted, ducking left, then right. He stopped and stared—uncertain, afraid.

Lettng his hand rest calmly on the saddle horn and the reins hang loosely alongside May Day's neck, Raul pushed him forward again, more firmly this time, touching him with his heels, and this time May Day responded, taking small, hesitant steps toward the bay horse that was already moving toward the far side of the corrals. Each step brought new confidence and, by the time he drew even with the cowpony's flanks, he was walking freely, keeping pace with the old-timer.

The hint of color in the western sky faded to gray as they strode into the desert; May Day pricked his ears forward and never looked back. Little puffs of dust kicked up behind his hooves as he disappeared into the evening shadows.

We closed up the horse trailer, and I turned the pickup back toward the long dirt road that led to the highway. A thick trail of dust churned up behind us, overtaking and surrounding us each time I slowed for a ditch or pothole. When the air cleared, I continued on; I never looked back.

Aging Horse

Sheryl Holland

> *In tribute to Deborah Butterfield's sculpture, "Untitled,"
> Cantor Arts Center, Stanford University, Palo Alto, California*

I've never loved horses
and they've never loved me.
But this one in the museum
draws me like an ancient mystery.
The aging creature turns its head
as if listening to distant voices.
Its body angles left, resting secure
on all fours. Worn pieces of driftwood,
its bones and muscle. Scraps
of dilapidated barn, some splintered
and jagged, some smooth from years
of wind and rain, fire and gravel.
These pieces of wreckage cling
to each other, as if life depended on it.
Colors, brown with gray, sand on slate,
grit turning to dust. I look down
dark hollows of eyes, glimpse meadows
and mates under apple trees,
deserted skies over parched deserts,
springs raining wildflowers, storms
and tornadoes. The sign says, *Do Not Touch*,
but I reach out, smooth its elegant haunches
still graceful and strong, touch time
in its weathered hide. It lifts its proud head,
perks its ears, turns to me, eyes like mirrors.

Life's Harvest

Sally Carper

When Ruby was twelve years old, she was riding with her family to their new home in Oregon, but shortly before reaching their destination she saw a big wooden sign hanging on a fence proclaiming the entrance to the "Ruby Horse Stables." From the back seat of the car, she announced to her parents that from now on her name was Rubye. Ruby with an *e*. No way was she going to have the same name as "those damn horses."

Rubye moved with her parents and three siblings to Bandon, Oregon in the early 1900's, where they homesteaded. The house they built was just one big room that served as the kitchen, dining room, and bedrooms. From the outside it looked like a barn, except for the shape of the roof.

Having moved west from Chicago, Rubye and her siblings loved living on the homestead. They may not have had any privacy in the house, but once outdoors they could roam alone over wide-open spaces, or communicate privately with the horses and cows.

Her mama was a tall buxom woman with her hair in a bun who wore long, simply-styled dresses. She had a pleasant face that smiled almost all the time, and she was the best cook in the world, spending most of her time over the big wood stove. Gazing at her open shelves lined with sparkling canning jars filled with colorful fruits and vegetables was like looking at a piece of art.

Pa, on the other hand, was small and wiry, and he was never seen in anything other than bib overalls. He did not spend much energy on conversation, but worked the homestead from dawn to dusk. His work of art was the woodpile, where the wood was stacked so precisely you could not slide a piece of paper between the chinks.

Rubye's favorite chore was to take Pa his lunch every day. Mama would pack a basket, and Rubye would head for the fields to spend precious time with her father while he ate his lunch. She did all of the talking, and he listened attentively, only occasionally offering some bit of advice or encouragement. This alone time with her Pa was the best part of Rubye's day.

One day, Mama told Rubye that she was taking Pa his lunch, and Rubye was to stay home with the baby. Rubye became very upset, and then angry that she was being punished for no apparent reason. After stewing awhile, she told her younger sister to watch the baby, and she headed out to complain to her father.

She went straight to the cornfield, where she knew Pa would be working. Quietly, she wound through the long perfect rows, straining to listen for voices above the soft rustling sound of wind blowing through the tall green stalks.

Then she heard them. Her mother and father were on the ground between the rows. Being a farmer's daughter, she was well aware of the "facts of life" and realized she had caught her parents in a rare and private moment of intimacy. Very slowly and carefully, she backed out of the rows, trying not to make a sound until, with a sigh of relief, she reached the edge of the field.

After four years and four more children, Rubye knew that, whenever Mama took Pa his lunch on a warm summer day, they would be reaping more than corn that year.

Mother Earth

Helen Benson

Every Spring my mother
Made a pact with the sun:
It would warm the earth
And her magic fingers
Would pat in the seeds.
Soon we had spinach
And lettuce and peas
And early blossoms
And harmony.
She traded plants and secrets
With like-minded folks
And we had potatoes
And string beans and lilies
And nasturtiums
And contentment.
In the fall crickets sang
And grasses died;
We had tomatoes and cabbage
And pumpkins and asters
And chrysanthemums
And love.

Fruity Freebies

Marian Wilson

On the citronic scale of cooking ability, I am not up to lemon level.
People try to give me lemons from their prolific trees,
but I cannot accept the fruity freebies.

A gourmet cook/lemon tree owner friend of mine
tried to foist a pair of the small yellow orbs on me once.
When I declined, she said she had never heard
of anyone who didn't use lemons.

Not wanting to send her into a xanthic funk,
I accepted a couple of the ubiquitous citruses.
The two sleeping canaries nested in my refrigerator drawer
and caused a tawny torpor to permeate the box.

In only a few short weeks the pair of cowards underwent
a melanomic metamorphosis in preparation
for entering the witness protection program.
Finally both soldiers had reached a rank worthy of departure.

Recently another dear friend offered the pungent little fruits.
I told her tartly, "I just couldn't." I don't mean to be a sourpuss,
but there's no sense in getting myself all in a meringue about it.

"Lemon Juice, That's Yellow Alert"

Janet Thompson

In the Air Force, "Yellow Alert" was a warning, just one step below "Red Alert." Red Alert came when the enemy planes appeared on the radarscopes, and they were right on top of us. The drill worked like this: the Officer in Charge of the radar site called to tell the Base Commander, the Base Commander called other important people, such as the State Governor, who called the National Guard and the President. Down the line, someone notified Civil Defense and many others, all obviously very quickly. Yellow Alert occurred when the planes were further away, and there was more warning. Everything about a Yellow Alert warning was handled the same as Red Alert, except that no one called the President.

To set the stage: in early spring of 1951, I was recovering from polio. Our house backed up to the vacant agronomy farm at Colorado A & M College, now Colorado State University. I was learning to walk again, and our house had a big picture window overlooking the vacant space. I used my reflection in the window to check on how I was walking, if I was listing too far to one side or the other. I usually was.

On both sides of our house, a local builder was building new houses. His son, Duane, was working for him, and he saw me walking in the yard; he was wondering why I would just walk back and forth, over and over, like that. Finally, his curiosity got the best of him, and he came over to check it all out. Introducing himself, he explained that it was his dad building next door, and he was working for him so he could finish school at A & M.

He was majoring in music and was in school on a wrestling scholarship. He played the violin and often sprained his fingers wrestling. Thinking about this picture, I thought this combination was quite funny, and I found later that he thought the picture of me walking back and forth, over and over, was funny, too.

All of my regular boyfriends had given up on me. It wasn't cool for a guy to have to carry his date upstairs or into the ballroom for dances, and then have to leave her sitting them out while he danced with someone else. Once

I was able to stand up, if I hung on tightly to my partner and just scooted my feet around without picking them up, I could fake it and look as if I were dancing again. Still, it wasn't the best arrangement.

Duane and I started dating, and he was kind, considerate, and didn't mind my disabilities. He wanted us to get married for his last year in school.

For the previous eight months, my mother had had a full-time job caring for me. There were the treatments taught to her by nurses from the National Foundation for Infantile Paralysis. She had worked feverishly during my illness, hot-packing my poor body every few hours, day and night. This duty entailed soaking wool blankets in the hottest water she could use, then wringing them out in an old wringer washer. She would wring out the blankets and, while they were still hot, lay them all over my backside. A plastic shower curtain was wrapped around the wet blankets, and more dry blankets placed atop the shower curtain to hold in the heat. To get my legs moving again and for exercise, she would lift my legs, bend them, and apply resistance. This went on until I was able to stand up to try to start walking again. I will never forget the first time I stood up again, and it felt like my knees were going to bend backwards instead of forwards!

After all her care and concerns, Mother was outraged that I would even consider marriage in my condition. I was always headstrong, so, blithely and against her wishes, in August I married anyhow. I got pregnant probably on our wedding night. Duane graduated the following May, and our son, Mike, was born in June of 1952.

Duane had received an ROTC commission as a Second Lieutenant and now had his military responsibilities to fulfill. In August, Lieutenant Thompson, disabled wife and infant son set off to California for his basic training. The Korean War was raging.

First, a little inside scoop about how *not* to be a proper Air Force Officer. Officers were not even supposed to carry groceries. Their right hand and arm had to remain free to salute other officers and return the salutes of enlisted men. Here was Lt. Thompson with his disabled wife, who could barely walk. He also had a three-month-old son, whose mother could not even carry him. Obviously, officers were especially not supposed to carry wiggling children! What a sight we made: I, walking, clutching onto one of Duane's arms, with Mike being carried in the other.

After only about two weeks of basic training, the military decided that Duane would make a perfect Radar Officer. His next posting was to Geiger

Field in Spokane to receive radar training. If I remember correctly, his radar training probably only lasted about three more weeks before he was in charge of a crew of enlisted men at the radar site. It was these men who looked for the blips (for bogeys) signaling planes showing up on the radar screens. If the blips were not for known or identified aircraft, it could mean enemy aircraft were approaching. With his skimpy three weeks of training, the brand new Radar Officer only "supervised." Being the new guy, he naturally had the night shift. It wasn't long before, at one or two o'clock one morning when Duane was on duty and in charge, one of the radar operators at the screens excitedly shouted, "Lemon Juice, that's Yellow Alert!"

"Lemon Juice" is a simulated Yellow Alert. For Lemon Juice, no one outside the base is notified. You can imagine the Base Commander's embarrassment, when it becomes obvious that some young, green Second Lieutenant makes a goof like this, and the Commander has just called the Governor, the National Guard, and Civil Defense!

Quickly, Duane received a three-week leave, and we were given enough time to go home to Colorado for a two-week vacation, while the Air Force figured out what to do with its green officer. I will never forget coming around the Grand Tetons and seeing the whole sky and atmosphere change. After the dreary, autumn gray skies of Spokane, seeing the clear, bright blue skies made me cry for joy. Experiencing the energy of sunshine again was like a religious experience. Spokane was a lovely town with beautiful people, but a couple of fall months of cloudy days with no blue skies and no sunshine had been mighty depressing. Probably, this mood hung on me even more because, in those days before the birth control pill, I was pregnant again, and Mike was only about four months old.

Next, the wisdom of the Air Force assigned Duane to Mather Air Force Base near Sacramento. Any other guy by this time would have found himself in Korea, but because of my condition this assignment luckily didn't happen for us. At Mather, reviewing Duane's radar history, the powers that be decided that, since he had been in the building business, he would make a good Base Installations Officer. This job put him in charge of the care and maintenance of all the base property and buildings.

It was at Mather, in March, that our daughter, Sharon, was born, two and a half months premature. Fortunately, we had been given Officers' Quarters just above Colonel and Mrs. Larson's unit. Dear Colonel Larson was the doctor in charge of the Base Hospital. After about a day and a half in the hospital, trying to hold off delivery, I had to drop Colonel Larson's name to get serious attention. I was trying to convince a "Nurse Cratchit" that Sharon was coming, and, indeed, she was coming, NOW. At that point, I didn't care whether that inconvenienced or embarrassed Cratchit or not. Sharon was born, unassisted, on the gurney, racing down the halls to the operating/birthing room, where she arrived weighing only two pounds and thirteen ounces.

In those years, wives were mostly a burden and a care to the Air Force. The doctors told us she "probably would not live, so don't even bother to name her." They immediately put the wrinkled, grayish-looking, tiny child into an incubator. They moved me into a room with about four other mothers, who already had had their babies and were nursing and cuddling them. It was more than a little weird! Oddly, Sharon was born with all her parts, with tiny fingers and toenails, eyelashes a mile long, but not a lick of hair on her tiny, teacup-sized head.

After I got home from the hospital, Mrs. Larson invited me and a couple other officers' wives for coffee. It was wonderful to be invited out, and I was overjoyed to have the female company. I drank many cups of coffee without realizing that my milk was coming in (what I knew about childbirth was zilch!), and there would be no baby to suckle. I quickly learned how miserable it was, how much it hurt, and why wet-nurses are so treasured. Mrs. Larson showed me how, using torn sheets, to wrap my breasts tight against my chest to discourage this natural lactating business.

Little Sharon thrived in the hospital and came home after six weeks, weighing almost five pounds. However, for the last several weeks, the nurses had taken her out of the incubator at night, held her, sung to her and played with her. At home, her days and nights were reversed, and the other three of us got no rest at all. It was *not* pretty!

Mike, now nine months old, was not yet walking. Now, this Officer-father must always make two trips, first carrying babies in both arms and next with his arms loaded with groceries.

Duane, always an entrepreneurial fellow, decided that maintaining the base buildings and grounds wasn't keeping him busy enough. He learned about selling Easterling sterling silver and fine china. It was sold like Tupperware to groups or individuals. He also saw all these young women WAFs, who would make perfect customers by starting their hope chests with sterling silver and china. The beautiful silver was manufactured by Gorham.

The snowy white porcelain china was designed by the famous industrial designer, Raymond Loewy. Duane signed up to sell the products. Given my need for help with two babies, baby-sitting was a neat way for the young women to pay for their down payments. Duane started making money hand over fist, because he has always been an excellent salesman, and he had an almost captive customer pool.

Some of the streets on the base had no curbing, so Duane received orders to get some curbs built. A problem arose when he discovered there were no workers available to do the construction. Wouldn't any entrepreneur quickly figure out there were some guys in the brig who weren't doing anything but sitting around? It wasn't long before the higher-ups saw prisoners outside the brig having a field day, joyful in the sunshine, building curbs. Well, while effective, this solution was not "regulation" in the hierarchical Air Force. Again, Duane was given leave to go home for a couple weeks while the Air Force could, once more, figure out what to do with him.

Next, we were off to Hamilton Air Force Base near San Rafael, California. This was the crème de la crème of Air Force bases. Higher-ups, returning from overseas, relished landing there on their first return stateside from the Far East. Hamilton is a beautiful base on top of Mount Tamalpais, overlooking San Francisco, the bay, and the ocean.

Duane's conservative religion allowed no drinking, so he had never taken a sip of booze. On learning this, the mucky-mucks decided he would make a safe and perfect Club Officer, who wouldn't drink up the bar profits. In charge of the Officers' Club, here was a young guy with a heady duty. He was at the Officers' Club all day. I relaxed and hung out at the Club pool most of the day. The indebted WAFs cared for our children, and Duane peddled silver and china at night. Now, with plenty of money and household help, we were living high on the hog! You can imagine how all the other officers and their wives soon envied us. After all, young, fresh out of ROTC, second lieutenants are supposed to be compliant and put up with being the lowest of the low in the Air Force pecking order.

Luckily, before they put a hit out and murdered us, the Air Force declared a "reduction in force." Newer, younger (and misfit) officers were allowed to end their tours after completing just a year. So the saga of our Air Force days was over in August, 1953, and once again we were allowed to return home.

For us, it had been a good year—a *mighty* good year!

Audience

Judy Ray

Company mail carriers, cold as the sleet
sliding down the office windows, each day
thump down the heavy-duty grey bag
with its drawstring and metal clip, pick up
the MAIL <u>OUT</u> BOX with its heap of SASEs,
and bang out the door without a word.
We in the office do not know why there is
this surliness, this excommunication.

One day a new mailman steps in
out of the cold wearing a woolly hat.
He asks if we write the stuff in this magazine
we publish. He must be the first
in his department even to turn a page.
He has the old complaint—he likes rhyme
and meter, doesn't understand the rest.
He quotes some lines of Frost—"…in fire
…in ice"—then says he'd like to say for us
a poem he wrote when he was courting his wife,
lines about a man and a woman at daybreak,
at midday, and at sunset thankful for love
lighting the clouds with orange and peach.

He gets breathless as he recites. Bowing his head,
he says to one of us, "I'll remember you
by your smile." And to me, "I'll remember
the voice." And to all, "I'll remember your listening."
He goes out the door like a cheery robin whistling
an old owl's tune, lifting our excommunication.

Those Letters from Sally

Jean Ritter Smith

Well, these letters kept zinging in. Actually, I'm no more curious than the average female, but I'll bet they'd have had you gasping, too. Can you make sense of this one? I couldn't.

Dear Hattie,

'Scuse the long silence, sweetie, but the summer riot has started, and it's hard to find a chair since the last sturdy one shattered under Rick's dad. The kids, at least, can sit anywhere—except that the porcupines leave quills on the lawn. That's important, since the Medlars are visiting this week, and they have six. Kids, not porcupines. Luckily, we live informally (what a great word for it!), but the Kimberley's patio cocktail party was a welcome change. Blue jeans do get tiresome.

The weather is gorgeous—city gal, you can't imagine!—and we think the altitude has cleared Steven's asthma. At last, he has quit kicking, and I wear shorts again. He did get a little choked when he found Sassie stuck 60 feet up in a pine tree, but it was a slim tree, and Rick cut it down to rescue her. Rick said, "NO MORE Siamese!" after the power line came down with the tree, but the repairmen came out only a day later and were really awfully nice about it. Was a little difficult with all of us getting ready for the square dance, but with candles, and the creek so...

Country life has finally gotten to the poor girl, I thought, and just skipped that one after the ringing in my ears died down. I went my merry way, which consists of combining a satisfyingly successful business with a decently happy social life in the Big City. No rings, and I like it that way. Incidentally, Mother approves of the life I lead.

Several more of these puzzling letters came slamming in. I made a studied effort to ignore them; never Sally, of course. My attention was diverted by the new men in the next office (UCLA, Navy, and Yale), and I splurged my raise on a not-too-simple black cocktail mini. Then this next letter arrived:

Hatti, honey—

Do plan to drive up this coming weekend. Swimming and water-skiing are in full swing—so good for your city pallor. The community masked ball was great fun (except for the fireplace chimney fire, and even that lent a certain excitement with little damage). The Cables and the Greers enjoyed it all, too. I did tell you they were coming that weekend?

Jerry, Ina, and their kids drove over for three days; that must have been the week the antenna fell into the sunporch windows. No casualties, thank goodness! Wish I could say the same for the family picnic last weekend, but I guess a sprained ankle, burned elbow, and assorted hurt feelings isn't a bad score considering that "only 34" came—not my quote, as I don't know where we'd have stacked more bodies.

We'll look for you Saturday noon-ish; map enclosed. Rick is hopefully planning a cookout at Shadow Lake in your honor. Perhaps it will also help Katie forget her broken arm for a bit. The fall didn't slow her horse craziness an ounce, but we just haven't room to keep one. Although if I thought quartering one (or is that what they do to beef?) in the back yard would keep the deer out of my petunias, I'd be tempted.

I surely told you about the helicopter that landed in the side meadow? Mike is still entranced that someone would accept literally my casual invitation to "drop in sometime." Actually, the pilot is on some ranch crop spraying contract, and when we met him we didn't know about the helicopter bit. He'll be at the cookout; such a nifty guy. We'll expect you Saturday!

Now, while I must admit I don't know too much about the activities of the busy, youngish, married set, I do know that our bustling city paper's "social column" never carries items like this. I read this one over three times. It affected me like itching powder in an air conditioner. Then I sent off a hasty acceptance note. I had to.

Since you still don't understand, I'm sure, let me tell you a little bit about Sally. We were roomies at school and, believe me, you know a person inside and out after that. She was a plumpish little blonde; yakky, but didn't say much, if you know what I mean. She always managed a presentable date for a really big event, but I swear her library stack card meant more to her than a frat dance bid. Somehow, we hit it off fine. I had her future all mapped out in my mind: dull-but-nice husband, couple of average kids, PTA, garden and book clubs, with the church social as the big event in her outings. Fine for Sally, but not for me!

I hit it pretty close, except for her personality-plus husband (will wonders never cease?). And their three kids are much more enjoyable than I ever thought kids would be. We still write often, and before they moved to the country I dropped over to their little town several times. It was a pleasant drive, and Sally does love to pamper an occasional guest and show off her placid domestic life.

Then Rick was transferred again, this time to somewhere out in the hills. A little curve in the creek, I gathered, called Pine Valley. After a few months, these crazy letters started stuttering in. Knowing Sally so well, it was easy to figure that her deadly quiet country life was starting to get her down, but she couldn't bear to have me know that. I mean, even a good novel doesn't pack in *that* much action.

I decided a weekend in the country wouldn't kill me if I could cheer the gal up a bit. So Saturday morning I rose bright and early, showered and gulped black coffee. Beige linen slacks and low pumps seemed ideal for my "Day in the Country." Rick knows very well that campouts, etc., are not my cuppa martini, though Sally, in her own obtuse way, does love to tease me. I tucked in my bikini and cap, remembered the books I'd chosen for my honorary—and literate—young niece and nephews, checked out my little imported rag-top, and was off. Well, how was I to know I should have girded my loins and climbed into the nearest Sherman tank?

Once out of freeway traffic and headed into the hills, the scenery was heavenly. That high mountain air had me all set for one of those nice, peaceful weekends at Sally's, with her waiting on me hand and foot—no, no, she really *likes* to. Mulling over those crazy letters, I was more sure than ever that Sally, while trying to prove to me she hadn't curled up and gone soggy in the country, had just overdone the gag a bit. As I drove, I noticed masses of people swarming in, on, and around the several inviting lakes I passed, so probably a few old friends did manage to drop in occasionally. Since Sally is sort of unorganized, that surely would have her going in circles.

Turning at last off the highway, the Triumph and I twisted around various dusty red roads, carefully following Sally's map. I spotted their mailbox at last and turned off into their lane. It was so still that the noise of the car seemed to intrude on the swaying pine trees and the cinder road winding ahead of me. The unnerving quiet, with only a squirrel or two for company, might be, as Granny used to say, "Nice for them as likes it." I'll take the corner of Grand and Emerson anytime.

I rounded the last pine tree and pulled up short. Would you believe seven cars, a pickup, a motorhome, a Hog, and assorted bikes, all crammed among the surrounding pines on what appeared to be a futile attempt at a side lawn? I squeezed between a weathered stump and a Jeep, but even before I turned off the motor a blast of shrieks and whoops of laughter from the house and far lawn assaulted me. Valiantly, I stepped out—beige linen and patent shoes, remember?—and picked my way to the back door. I always use Sally's back door.

Everybody else does, too! The door slammed open in my face, and what I think is known as a "horde of kids" charged around and past me. No damage, when I got enough breath to check, and every last one of them had yelled some variation of "'Scuse me!" as they disappeared into the woods. Maybe the end of a Boy-and-Girl Scout something or other? Rick is great with kids.

Before I could reach again to knock, Sally came racing out, shrieked, hugged me and passed me on to Rick. He gave me that nice, cheeky grin, handed me a glass of wine to "brace me through the introductions" and was drawling something that sure sounded like, "Forgot to tell you this is Kiddie Camp-Out Weekend," when Sally came flying back. Between Sally pulling me at a mad gallop through an adult mob while I stumbled gracelessly over that darned Sassie, I caught a few of the names she flung over her shoulder, and only bit of something about "…and the same size…to my jeans and…." Well, it's no use, you wouldn't begin to believe the rest of that weekend.

That was about ten days ago, and I think I'm past the recovery stage, almost. My sunburn only killed me for three days, and Don thought the new freckles were "adorable." Can't beat that. (He's the helicopter pilot; it *was* in the side meadow.) I can bend my scraped knee without moaning now, and I only had to take one day off at the office to recover from the horseback riding. Loved that grey mare! My boss is a nice guy, even if he is a city slicker.

Another of Sally's grand letters arrived today:

Hi, Toughie!
Wasn't that weekend the greatest? Jake and Don (don't you love his beard?) thought you were the best sport ever—as well as a pretty sexy-

looking broad. I nearly had a heart attack when your raft smacked that rock in the rapids. Hope we really fixed you up okay. Handy that Rick used to drive ambulances. All fourteen kids said it was the best camp-out ever—and "will Hatti cook the special hotcakes again next year?" You really learned to flip them, and with so little practice!

Only the Browns and the Frazers are coming next weekend. Since it will be so quiet, we're planning a steak fry, and of course there's the square dance. That "fawncy" English guest you were so enchanted with will be calling again, not to mention Don and the Forestry guys.

Now, my question to you is, don't you think this letter is saying that Sally really expects me to come up this weekend? I have always had an open invitation to her house, and I really should return her jeans and sweatshirt promptly. Also, this past week I just happened to run across the swingingest square dance skirts ever and bought her one for a hostess gift. I only bought the other one because…well…Sally must get tired of loaning me clothes, and Don did say he thought I had a real knack for square dancing, and it seems a shame not to be prepared. I'm beginning to wonder if I shouldn't check that sleeping bag sale again…

My Uncle Jack

Esther Brudo

Gosh, I wish I was there to see it! I know it's a terrible thing to say because Uncle Jack could've gotten killed, or Grandma, or anyone else in the store. But it's so thrilling that my very own uncle was in a shootout with a crook!

My uncle is sort of the king of the American Delicatessen. Our whole family helps out, though, and we all live in the apartments upstairs.

You never know what my uncle is going to say. He makes jokes with the customers and gives them all crazy nicknames, but they don't get mad. I think they like it. Some of them come in every day and hang around the soda fountain and maybe buy a coke or play the pinball machine.

Everybody in the family thinks Uncle Jack works too hard, especially Grandma. She wants him to get married, and he really gets mad when she says it. He doesn't like anybody to tell him what to do, even if it's a good idea.

When he's in a bad mood, I stay out of the store. But I usually like to hang around and watch him and all the stuff going on. The kids in the neighborhood think I'm lucky because I can dip myself an ice cream cone and read comic books free.

But nobody knew that Uncle Jack keeps a real gun hidden behind the counter. If you asked me if my uncle knew how to shoot off a gun, I would have said you were crazy.

Grandma told me a man came into the store and asked for a pack of cigarettes, and when my uncle turned around to get them, he pulled out a gun. When Uncle Jack saw that, he reached down to a shelf behind the counter and pulled out his gun. So there they were, pointing guns at each other.

The crook pulled the trigger, but his gun didn't go off.

My uncle pulled his trigger, and his gun didn't go off, either.

Gosh, don't you wish you were there to see it? Well, then Uncle Jack tried one more time, and his gun went off. The crook turned to run out of the store, and my uncle shot at him again. There are holes in the wall to prove it. If you don't believe me, I'll show you where.

Grandma and Louise were behind the refrigerator case in the back of the store because my uncle yelled at them to go back. I'm glad Mom wasn't there. She's got a nervous stomach.

The police came, but they couldn't find the crook. The next day they called to say there was a man at Casualty Hospital with a bullet in his leg, and they needed someone to come and see if he was the one. Louise went. She works in our store. She said if it wasn't him, it was his twin brother. But the next day her family told her not to get mixed up in it, and she decided not to talk to the police anymore. We were all disappointed, but nobody blamed Louise.

Then the police said that, when the doctor took the bullet out of the guy's leg, they could check and see if it was from Uncle Jack's gun. And then my uncle found out the guy wouldn't let the doctor take the bullet out, and he didn't have to. After that everybody in the family was disgusted and didn't want to talk about it anymore.

I'm really proud of my Uncle Jack, though. The customers tease him and joke about it, but I can see they're proud of him, too. Uncle Jack jokes right back. When he laughs, one of his eyebrows goes up high, and I'm glad he's happy.

Day

Janet Kreitz

Oh feet swing from blissful slumber
alight to meet the weathered floor.
Oh the festival of light is near
the golden globe will debut.
Oh the territory awaits to witness
the tirade of light.
Oh the cabinet of hours
will document the supreme gift of day.

Just Another Day at Golden Acres

JoAnn Sunderland

"It is *not* an emergency," I said. "Fire is an emergency. Broken pipes are an emergency."

Francine was hysterical, sobbing.

I did my best to keep my voice hushed. Alan rolled away and put his good ear down on the pillow.

"A plugged toilet is not something to get us out of bed for in the middle of the night." I listened to more gibberish while I looked at the large numbers on the clock. "Okay, it's not the middle of the night, but four in the morning is not office hours."

Alan groaned and rubbed his tousled white hair. He squinted bleary eyes at me and mumbled, "It's okay, I might as well go. Likely she'll call every five minutes until I get there."

"Calm down," I told Francine. "Alan's coming. Just don't flush."

Alan muttered as he pulled on his sweats and shoes. "Typical way to start the day at this funny farm. I've done this so often I could probably clean out a drain in my sleep."

I dragged myself into the bathroom. I wouldn't go back to sleep anyway. It's harder getting going these days since my surgery, but it's not as bad as when I was having radiation and chemo. I still get a surprise when I look in the mirror and see my curly gray hair. Better'n bald, for sure, but never would have guessed it would come back in curly. I touched the scar where my left breast used to be. Wondered if I'd ever get used to that.

Alan's been real good to me through this; he did all the work managing the apartments while I was sick. Took care of me, too. He thinks it's time for us to retire. I think we need to hang on a couple more years till we get the pickup paid off.

I dawdled over getting dressed, wrote some letters and spruced up around the apartment. I was at the sink filling the coffeepot when Alan came in, walked up behind me and kissed me on the neck.

"Only coffee, don't cook anything for me, Dee. That job took my appetite. What a mess! Do you think they'll ever learn?"

I left Alan in the shower and headed out to the office. Maybe I could get some paperwork done before the phone started ringing.

The smell of fall was in the air as I walked the two blocks beneath the red and gold of old maple and birch trees. Patches of bronze and yellow mums brightened the borders along the sidewalk. It is sure pretty here. Two hundred units on fifteen acres, you can tell it was built back when a developer could afford to spread out. Not like those warehouses for old folks they're building now.

The phone jangled as I entered the office. I couldn't understand the words, but I recognized the slurred, lisping voice.

"Put in your teeth, Alice." I waited and heard the clicking as she installed her dentures.

"Darlene, have you seen that man in 58 sitting outside in his underwear feeding the squirrels?"

"No, Alice, haven't been by that way this morning."

"Well, his table scraps are all over the yard attracting bugs and vermin. It's downright indecent, him sitting there with his big belly hanging over; it looks like he's naked. I just can't—"

"Thanks for the call, Alice. I'll see what I can do."

I had to cut her off; she was warming up for a long harangue. I called Bill Spears's caseworker and left a message. By then it was after eight, so I took a deep breath and dialed Bill's brother. The phone rang for a long time before a sleepy voice answered. Oops, not good to wake him up. Well, anyway, I'm in it now.

"Mr. Spears, this is Darlene Olson at Golden Acres. We've been having some difficulty with your brother. He's outside in his underwear, and it's offending his women neighbors."

"Well, Mrs. O., why don't you tell those dried-up old biddies to just stuff it up their droopy butts. What business do they have complaining about what a man does at his own place, anyway? Don't you get paid to take care of these squabbles? I don't expect to have to come over there and handle your problems."

I barely managed to keep a lid on my temper. "I just thought you would want to know that he's getting worse." Then I hung up quick, before the idiot could start in again.

Annie, our cleaning whirlwind, stopped by the office to get her housekeeping schedule for the day. She flopped like a six-foot rag doll into the chair next to my desk, flashed her famous smile and gave her usual greeting. "Good morning, sweetie, how's it goin'?"

I shrugged and said, "I hope you're ready for a messy day's work. Get right over to George Moore's place. He heated a can of baked beans for his dinner last night. Put the can right in the oven. Problem is, he forgot to open it. Blew the oven door off and pretty much beaned the whole kitchen. After you get through scrubbing up, let me know if we have to paint."

A frown furrowed Annie's usually cheery face. "Talk about your helpless tenants," she said. "I found Judy Elmer wandering yesterday; she got lost on her way home from Bingo. I took her into her apartment and got her to lie down. Went into the kitchen to make her a cup of tea and found a burner on. She's going to start a fire one of these days."

"I know," I answered. "But every time I bring up assisted living to her son, he vows she's fine here, says she would be upset if he moved her. It's probably about money."

After Annie left, I spent some time stewing over Judy. Judy is a small, vague person, getting more shriveled and distant every day. It's like she's just fading away. She comes in with her rent check dated ten years ago. She leaves her laundry in the dryer, and when I bring it to her she thinks I'm giving her clothes.

The sound of the door roused me. It was Alan. After forty-six years, I still thanked my lucky stars every day for that man. He looked fine, but I could tell he was tuckered out—been up on the roof cleaning gutters. Climbing up and down those ladders is hard on Alan's old heart. Larry, our landscape guy, should have been doing it, but he didn't show up this morning.

"Sit a while and catch the phones for me, Hon," I said. "Annie's having a busy day, so I need to clean up after the morning coffee."

I was glad to get away from the phone and take a little walk down to the recreation building. There were still a few people finishing their coffee, so I sat down a minute to chat.

"How're you doin', Claire?"

"Honey, when you're ninety-two, just being able to get out of bed makes it a great day. How about yourself? You're looking good this morning, Darlene. You been feeling better?"

"Not so bad. Better than yesterday, not as good as tomorrow. Cancer is no fun, but right now I'm just glad to be alive and kicking."

Fruit and rolls were left on the serving plates. Some residents get embarrassed about taking stuff home. So I said, "Drink up, folks, kitchen's closing in five minutes," and took a load of cups to the kitchen.

When I got back everyone was gone. Annie came in to make sure someone was there to clean things up. She was tsk-tsking about the empty serving plates. "Looks like a herd of locusts has been through here."

"It's all right. I only put out what we can afford. You know that this and their 'Meals on Wheels' lunch is all some of them will have to eat today. Get along, girl, I've got this handled."

I hummed to myself as I loaded cups in the dishwasher. I sure hope that the owner finds managers who care about these people when we leave.

On my way back to the office Merle wheeled up on his three-wheel bike. "Better watch out, Darlene, these old geezers see you walking around in that snazzy yellow outfit, they'll get over-excited. You're a real medical hazard."

I smiled and waved him off.

Merle has been depressed since his wife died, but you'd never know it. When he starts getting gloomy, he gets on his bike. He can hardly stand without a walker anymore, but rides three or four rounds of the complex every day. On the way, he stops to chat with most everyone he sees.

My good mood disappeared when I got back to the office and saw the frown on Alan's red face.

"Well," he said, "I found out where our wayward handyman is. Larry just called from jail. He was kind of sketchy on the details, so I talked to the officer in charge. He and his buddy got drunk, drove his truck through a fence, and took out shrubbery and a lamppost. Caused a big commotion and both landed in jail to sober up. I'll give him a talking to when he shows up."

I gave Alan "the look," and he laughed.

"I know, it's not worth getting my blood pressure up over what happens at this funny farm. Want to run away with me, Beautiful?" He hugged me, then let go at the sound of the door and headed for the back room.

A feisty little fighting cock of a woman flew into the office. "Henrietta's been stealing my critters again."

Grace's wiry gray and red hair stood up like a coxcomb. Her big sweater ballooned around her skinny arms and neck like ruffled feathers when she flapped her hands in frustration. It took me a while to figure out that she was clucking about the lawn ornaments that decorated her patio. Grace Carson and Henrietta Simmons have an ongoing feud when they're not being best buddies.

Our Annie calls Henrietta "a few bricks short of a load." When Henrietta's neighbors complain about missing things, she says she found them in the dumpster. It's true, we can't seem to stop her from rummaging around in the trash, but we know she picks up things in other places, too.

I told Grace that we'd look into the problem of the 'missing critters' and shooed her out the door.

After lunch, Alan and I looked at the rental applications stacked in my basket. I've learned to be tough, but tears came to my eyes when I told him about the woman that came in yesterday with blue and yellow blotches on her face where the bruises were healing.

"I got a job cleaning at the motel out on the highway," she said. "That and my Social Security total up to more than eight hundred a month, so I can make the monthly rent. I'm going to have trouble coming up with the deposit, though."

"We can work out a payment schedule for the deposit," I said. "You can take as long as six months to pay it off. Can you get any help from your family?"

"My kids live out of state, and they don't need to know what that drunken bum did to me. I can manage this on my own, just don't want to still be living in my car when winter comes. I went over to Housing and filled out an application for the low rent. I can get it, but the waiting list is two years long. I'll have to hold out until my name comes up."

Alan agreed that she should get the next opening. I reached for a tissue and blew my nose. I stamped her application "Approved."

I picked up the next application and handed it to Alan. "I may have to turn this fellow down. He has lots of medical problems. I don't think he can manage living alone."

"Yeah, Dee, we've already got more old, sick folks than we can take care of."

"But someone's gotta do it, Alan. I swear, sometimes it feels like we have several hundred children."

The sound of a fire truck engine interrupted us. We hear that familiar noise at least once a week around here. My heart darn near stops every time.

At least, they turn off the siren when they come here so they won't start a panic. Alan came in to report.

"What now," I said. "Fall, stroke, or heart attack?"

"Fall," he said. "Good thing Henry was wearing his Lifeline Alarm. I told the guys you would call his family."

"I'll do that right now, then I'm heading home. You coming soon?"

We had finished supper and were watching Wheel of Fortune when the phone rang. The outdoor lights on the other side of the complex weren't working. It's that darn thirty-year-old wiring acting up again. Alan was out until after ten. When he got back, his tail was dragging, so we turned in.

Pounding on our door woke us. A disheveled Martin Smallet fidgeted on our doorstep in his pajamas.

"There's flickering in the kitchen window at Judy's place. It sure looks like fire to me. I knocked on her door, but she didn't answer."

Alan dashed out with Martin, while I dialed 911. By the time I got on a robe and slippers and ran the block to Judy's place, I could smell the smoke. Alan broke her bedroom window, and he and Martin lifted her out. Just then, a fire engine pulled in our drive, and the professionals took over.

Alan was a sooty mess, and his eyes were still red from the smoke. "Sure enough," he said. "Judy left a burner turned on under the teakettle. A towel and some paper bags lying on the counter caught fire. We're going to have to explain to the Fire Marshall why the smoke alarm didn't go off."

"I bet Judy had her son disconnect it," I said. "The sound made her frantic when she couldn't turn it off. We just got lucky that Martin is a night owl, and the fire was still small."

Heading for home in the darkness, I started to cry. Alan put his arm around me and said, "This is enough for today. I'm going to unplug the phone till morning."

Ah, Those Lovely Golden Years

Gloria G. Ammerman

    Where could those spectacles be?
Now I can't even see.
    "I just had them on," he said.
Oh, thanks, on top of my head.

    Hey lady, watch where you're going!
Where am I going? I don't know.
    My grocery cart just moves me so,
Oops, out of my way as with the wind I sway.

    What! I'm having a bad hair day.
That's why I'm wearing my cap this way
    To cover the bald spots and that awful gray.
I'd rather have my hair pure white.
    That would be a much prettier sight.

    What was that? It wasn't very clear!
I said, "I'll meet you in the car, dear."
    Of course, I wax out each ear,
but I still can't seem to hear.
    Well, I'll just look for your cute red hat,
and I'll know where you're at.
    The way you walk, you won't be too far.
I'll pick you up in my new car.

    Good! A restroom, but it's "out of order"—
wouldn't you know.
    Oh, I have to go, I have to go!
Hang strong, stay dry; don't get wet,
    you'll soon have time to "have a sit."
Let's hurry and go to the car.
    The gas station's bathroom is not too far.
Whew! I just made it!

    Yes, there are those wonderful days,
when I get hugged and even praised
    for just remembering to shave my face
and sit at the table at the right place.

At the Y

Shirley Oppenheimer

Drinking coffee after working out
we talk about
Viagra
having five husbands
having two boyfriends commit suicide
the pope on his pope mobile running over a dog
dirty old men
selling paintings
Yoga
Hinduism
being fat
Nazis
terrorism
our mothers
New York
babies
drought
coloring hair
Thailand and Vietnam
long distance telephone plans
a skinny man with boobs showing through his sheer T-shirt
Jane Fonda
the Vietnam war
knee replacement
Barack Obama
weight lifting
Ed's girlfriends
Dana's $250 purse
China
Mao suits
T-shirts honoring the Lohse Y's 15th birthday
chemical imbalance in the pool
an Elvis wannabe with a shiny black pompadour
mules falling into the Grand Canyon
Mike's knee support and yellow crocs
lunch on Wednesday for Jack's 78th
how much we love being here together

Kids and Cars

Frank Frost

In the late 1930's and early 1940's, when I was a teenager, the availability of an automobile was every bit as important to a kid as it is today, and probably far more important in the case of country kids like me. My nearest friends lived about two miles away. My regular circle of friends lived within about a six- or seven-mile radius from my home. There was no public transportation of any sort. Consequently, access to an automobile was essential to any sort of social life.

As we plunged into war following the Japanese attack on Pearl Harbor on December 7, 1941, the country immediately mobilized for war. Production of automobiles for civilian use simply stopped as car manufacturers shifted to the production of war materials. Practically overnight, any used cars that ran or could be made to run were at a premium. Naturally, most of the cars that we high school kids could afford were those that few adults were interested in. But they ran—or were persuaded to run, more or less.

Another problem was that tires were also practically unavailable. In those days, there was no such thing as a tubeless tire. Every tire required an inner tube, which was also unavailable. Since tubes suffered aging problems like anything else, they tended to deteriorate and require patching. Some, it seemed, eventually became almost more patch than tube. Standard "don't leave home without it" equipment included a jack, lug wrench, tire irons, cold patch kit, and a hand pump.

Gasoline was tightly rationed. For drivers who needed their cars for work, restrictions were fairly liberal. Few of us in high school could qualify for anything but an "A" ration card (we had good school bus service). An "A" card gave us the opportunity to buy three gallons of gasoline per week. Also, there was a wartime speed limit of 35 miles per hour (presumably the most fuel-efficient speed for the average car). These were not exactly invitations to unlimited joy riding. Although we did play by the rules pretty much (well, maybe not quite so much in the case of the speed limit), we also had a tendency to be creative. For example, gasoline for farm equipment and commercial fishing boats was not rationed, nor was white (unleaded) gas or kerosene. Since most of us were closely related to either farmers or commercial fishermen, in emergency situations, like the Senior Prom or an out-of-town football game, we could sometimes wheedle a gallon or two from a disapproving yet understanding donor. This diversion of a scarce commodity was illegal and seemed unpatriotic, so it wasn't often pursued.

My close friend, Gene, somehow managed to acquire an ancient Chevrolet a good year or more before he could legally drive. It was no thing of beauty. Some of the windows were missing. The floorboards were rotted or rusted out and had been replaced with cardboard and lumber scraps. The remnants of upholstery were held together with old blankets. But he convinced it to run, and with it he taught himself to drive, and in turn he taught me. His car was so old it didn't even have a starter; it had to be hand cranked. I learned how to hold the crank so that if it kicked back it wouldn't (presumably) break my wrist. I learned how to rock the car free when stuck in the mud (we did a lot of driving on an open hillside next to his home). I learned where to set the choke and spark levers when the engine was cold, and how to set them when it was warm. I learned how to double clutch when down-shifting to avoid raking the gears. I also leaned to "speed shift" (up- or down-shift without using the clutch at all). Of course, some of this was just teenage show off stuff and meaningless to someone who has only driven a modern automobile, but it was an invaluable primer in developing an understanding about how things worked in an increasingly complex world.

I never had an operating car of my own in those years, but Gene managed to progress through a series of successively newer, although not necessarily much better cars. He developed into a competent mechanic and tinkerer. For example, when he read somewhere that unrationed kerosene would burn satisfactorily in a car engine if it was pre-heated before reaching the carburetor, he figured out a way to rig an auxiliary tank to be filled with gasoline with which to start the engine, then switch to the main tank full of kerosene once the engine was fully warmed up. The trick was to wrap a couple of turns of the main fuel line around the exhaust manifold so the kerosene would be hot by the time it reached the carburetor. It worked. Not as well as gasoline but, what the heck, it sidestepped the rationing problem.

Neither one of us was old enough to get a driver's license so, whenever practicable, driving was largely confined to back roads away from the watchful eyes of the local constabulary. In fact, since I had no car of my own,

KIDS AND CARS

I didn't bother with a driver's license until I was twenty and about to be married. I needed one then so I could borrow my Dad's car for our honeymoon!

As noted, Gene's car was no thing of beauty. Nobody cared. Thanks to Gene's genius we now had access to all the weekend adventures that three gallons of gas (plus kerosene) would permit. These adventures, at times, got a bit hairy. The combination of a broken-down car packed with teenagers, the conviction that we were, if not immortal, at least undamageable, and the ready availability of plenty of beer was a potentially dangerous mixture. There were accidents, of course. I was a passenger in several. A couple of times, I was in a car that, laid on its side, went sliding down the road amid a fascinating trail of sparks. Once, there was a complete rollover with the car ending up on its wheels at the bottom of an embankment; the neophyte driver had simply driven off the road (at about 20 miles per hour). A couple of times we hit deer, once we hit a tree, and any number of times we just ran off the road to get stuck in a roadside ditch.

Most of the cars with which I was familiar were really in pretty bad shape. Hydraulic brakes were not yet a reality. Tires were apt to blow out at any moment. Headlights and taillights were apt to black out at the most inconvenient moment. Safety glass for windows and windshields was a development of the future. But there were never any injuries in any accident in which I was a passenger.

Obsolete junker cars, daredevil or inexperienced teenage drivers, lots of crashes, but no injuries? What saved us, I think, was the very obsolescence of the cars. They were simply unable to attain speeds of more than 45 miles per hour or so.

A few of the incidents were a little on the scary side. I remember riding with Gene's older brother one night when his lights failed. Suddenly, there were no headlights, no taillights, no dashboard lights, nothing. It was the middle of the night, but there was a pretty good moon, so we kept barreling down the deserted country road, "pedal to the metal," as fast as his 1932 Chevrolet would go. Suddenly, there were two horses crossing the road directly in front of us. Oh boy! Somehow, we managed to roar between them with scant inches to spare on either side.

On another occasion (same car, same driver), we were barreling down a dike road in the Svensen area. It was at night, naturally. On one side of us was farm land. On the other side was deep water. With little or no warning, we hit a massive pothole that spun the car out of control and sent us careening down the bank toward the water. We were hell bent toward an unplanned immersion when providence stepped in. We hit something—a stump or a boulder. Whatever it was, it was solid enough to spin the car around again and send us back onto the road. The pair of impacts was brutal enough to break the windshield and send it flying in a storm of shards. Other than that, the car seemed to be undamaged. I can't say the same for our composure.

Of course, every incident was not a product of inexperience, a desire to show off, or the availability of beer. Nor did they all involve crashes. Probably the most unfortunate incident I can recall was due to lost car keys.

Deena had borrowed the family sedan to go to an important football game at another country school some thirty miles away. Five of us—Deena and I, my friend Gene, Deena's younger sister, Betty, and another kid whose name I don't remember—all piled in.

When the game was over, we all scrambled back into the car. That's when Deena discovered that she had lost her car keys somewhere, somehow. There wasn't much we could do but begin a search. We searched the car. We searched the sidelines. We searched the girls' restroom. We searched everywhere Deena had walked or stood or thought she might have walked or stood. We searched for what must have been two hours or so. We searched until the five of us were the only ones left at the school or field. When we finally gave up, poor Deena was in tears. She and her sister were farm kids and had their chores. Their particular responsibility was the evening milking of their small herd of cows. It was already well past milking time, and we were still thirty miles from home with no way to get there. This was no laughing matter; she was in trouble, and none of us knew what to do about it.

One might wonder if we couldn't have simply "hotwired" the car and driven it home that way. Not possible. The car was a Ford. With Fords from that period, the key didn't turn on the ignition. A simple toggle switch did that. What the key did was lock the steering column. The engine could be started, but the car couldn't be steered.

Gene went to work trying to jimmy the locking lug out of its notch in the steering column, but after a half hour or so he had to give up. We didn't know what to do.

Finally, Gene suggested that maybe he could break off the entire casting that held the locking mechanism. Nobody had a better idea, so Deena finally told him to go ahead.

After what seemed an eternity of heavy pounding and swearing, there was a crash, and the entire lock casting fell off in several pieces. It was an awful mess, but the car could now be driven. Without the support of the lock casting, the steering column wobbled, but it held together, and the car was steerable. It was already dark when Deena let us off at the Svensen crossroads and drove the last mile to home. She was a pretty sick-looking girl. I never learned what sort of reception she received upon her arrival. It just seemed one of those "don't ask, don't tell" situations.

Duct Tape Saves a Life

Diana Griggs

In my hummingbird garden of bottlebrush trees, shrubs and flowers
Xlasma leaves darken the family room and scratch at the window.
I take the shears to the offending branches
gather them to the trash can and stare in horror,
a baby hummingbird lying on its back in a nest attached to the cut branch,
mouth trustingly open to receive anything I might offer.

Aware of angry wings beating above my head
I rush for the most used *fix it* item in our house,
choose a place in the tree shaded by overhead branches,
bind the orphaned branch firmly to another
wait inside the house and hope to observe a reunion.

Two hummingbirds dart in and out of the tree
hovering, searching for their lost chick
to finally fill the hungry beak with nectar.

One morning the offspring stands on the edge of his nest,
feels the speed of his wings as his home tilts steeply.
I rush to institute further duct tape repairs
anxious again that my presence will disturb,
but I'm greeted with trust and an open beak
as though he knows my hovering concern.

Daily the newcomer balances more and more precariously,
I missed his maiden voyage, but I think it was successful
because this year a new nest with two eggs
rests on the branch among the remnants of year old tape.

Fragile Wings

Diane L. Rau

My oncologist's physician's assistant, a tall, blonde young woman with a model's litheness and features, rolled her chair within inches of mine. Our knees almost touching, she looked into my eyes as she spoke. I will appreciate her warm directness and soft voice forever.

Gently, she explained, "As you know, the CT scan showed extensive cancer in your endometrium. But squamous cells found in the D and C biopsy revealed that your cancer originated in the cervix. It is extensive in the cervix and vagina.

"However," she emphasized, "the great news is it hasn't invaded the bladder or rectum. But because the MRI indicated suspicious nodules in the lungs, abdomen, and liver, we'll order a PET scan 'eyes to thighs' to determine the full extent of metastasis."

I was extremely grateful it hadn't invaded the bladder or rectum, and her sympathetic tone was supportive. Nevertheless, I reacted stoically. Since I'd neglected to have a PAP smear in almost three years, I felt unentitled to cry. Regardless of my reasons—I was recovering from a nearly fatal automobile accident, negotiating an insurance settlement, and organizing my new business—I had been irresponsible.

Even worse, I had ignored bleeding and discharge, two fail-safe symptoms that would have reduced the metastasis; I attributed intermittent spotting to a flare-up of my Bartholin cyst and treated discharge with vaginal cream. The prevalence of breast cancer had ensured my compliance with mammograms, but cervical cancer was the furthest thing from my mind.

Despite self-recrimination, I asked a hopeful question: "Can it be treated?"

"You'll never be cancer free," she intimated, "but it can be greatly reduced. We will send tissue samples to a laboratory in California for analysis. Applying various chemotherapies, they try to find one that reduces the cancer."

I felt hopeful and thankful for that scientific possibility.

Meanwhile, the prayers and support of my son and sister—my only family—were immediate and essential. My sister flew cross-country from Florida, bringing, in addition to her lovely self, her Delta-certified poodle as personalized pet therapy. Shortly after his arrival, I felt blessed when he anointed me with licks.

My sister also brought back a special ring. Adorning the band was a butterfly, intricately wrought, its fragile open wings set with semiprecious stones. Because she is a master gardener who nurtures butterflies from caterpillar through chrysalis stages, I had sent the meaningful gift to her on her last birthday.

Throughout adulthood we had cherished "The Gift of the Magi," by O. Henry, because his story recounts the sacrifices of love. Our gifts to each other were often a sacrifice in some way. When I purchased it, this particular ring was the only one in the shop, and I had really wanted one, too. Now, by sharing it with me, the ring symbolized our bond as sisters. Because butterflies represent hope, she wanted me to have it as comfort during treatment. I accepted it as a temporary return, and valued it as a talisman for my healing.

On another level, the exchange of the ring unified us. Because butterflies undergo metamorphosis, they represented changes in my sister's life as a recent widow. Although the loss of a husband and facing cancer were different, both of our lives were in major upheaval.

To face the reality of metastatic cancer, I needed more than good luck from the ring. Following my meeting with the physician's assistant, I had thought of many unanswered questions, which I wanted to ask the oncologist directly. I called his office. The message from his nursing assistant after consulting with the doctor was that all my questions had been answered.

Because I wanted him to understand the person he was treating, I wrote him a letter. In it I stated my belief in a doctor-patient *partnership* and integrative medicine. I described myself as a person who finds creative solutions to problems.

I explained my plan for self-healing: to lift my spirits, I would paint, dance, garden, and swim. Furthermore, I would investigate herbal immune-enhancing therapies, concentrate on nutrition, and embrace mind-body-spirit healing techniques.

Perhaps naively—considering my condition—I mentioned my desire to avoid caustic chemicals, which can damage the heart and vascular system. I questioned whether avant-garde immune-enhancing therapies could replace chemotherapy and radiation. Looking back, I was definitely assertive. Since then, I have read that patients who are proactive heal more quickly.

Intertwined with medical issues, during this crucial time I sought a pastoral dimension in the physician's role. In my letter I confided being at a crossroads, which he was undoubtedly familiar with in his patients' lives: celebrating every remaining moment without the ordeal of chemotherapy and radiation, or contending with their side effects in the hope of increasing my longevity.

Quality of life issues were the intended focus on my next office visit, but I was disappointed—perhaps they are beyond a physician's responsibility. Instead, the oncologist informed me dispassionately: "The PET scan confirmed Stage IVb. We consider treatment to be palliative." He didn't explain the term, but from my background as a home health aide, I understood: keeping a terminal patient "comfortable," but administering minimal treatment.

I asked if the lab results were in yet from California. He looked puzzled. I reiterated what the physician's assistant had explained, and the oncologist brushed it off with a wave of his hand.

Next I asked about immune-enhancing drugs or clinical studies. He said there were none, and that, before clinical trials, he wanted to try an aggressive regimen often used with ovarian cancer patients.

There *was* hope! I was grateful when he presented my treatment plan: eight rounds of low-dose Cisplatin to tweak the effects of 25 radiation applications; and depending on resultant cancer reduction, HDR (High Dosage Radiation) cervical implants.

I asked for survival statistics.

After a long pause the oncologist replied, "We have no statistics on length of survival, but there's a 40% chance that treatment will reduce the cancer." Obviously trying to communicate hope, he added: "You're lucky this isn't a recurrence, because they're more difficult to treat." Despite his seeming aloofness, discussing this diagnosis was difficult for him, too.

Having a "blonde moment," I then asked, "Why aren't there any statistics?" Again, he stared at me, deliberating over how to phrase his answer.

Then I realized why. Embarrassed to have put him on the spot, I expressed—almost answering myself—"Oh. That's because they all died." With the reaction of inappropriate humor that sometimes accompanies grave events, my inflection had been comedic. We both laughed, and at that moment our rapport began. We bonded like co-conspirators fighting an arch enemy.

Eventually, during cancer recovery my faith regenerated, but just after hearing the dismal prognosis, I didn't have much confidence that I would live beyond the expected time frame. I can best describe my feelings by discussing a "Photography as Meditation" cancer workshop in which I participated a few months ago. After we took photographs throughout the day, our teacher, Connie Reider,[1] asked us to select one that conveyed the negative emotion we felt just after diagnosis, and a positive image that related to the way we felt at present.

I selected a shot I had taken of an immaculate toilet bowl. Looking down into it, the static water was in dismal shadow. A major comparison to my first feelings, it conveyed: "My life is in the toilet." Throughout treatment, I had spent a lot of time using it, too.

For the positive image I selected a photograph I had taken of a waterfall plunging over boulders. The surging water was the power of my immune system, ultimately eroding the cancer cells—the boulders.

An important task was creating healing imagery to accompany my radiation therapy. An hilarious, meaningful (and, I believe, effective) visualization developed from a story my sister told about using a fly swatter to keep wasps away from her butterfly chrysalises. During radiation treatments, as radiation equipment arced over me, I envisioned hundreds of fly swatters rising up to smack the wasps—the cancer cells—and turn them into butterflies. Not only were butterflies symbolic in my healing because of the ring, imagining them replacing the cancer cells was powerfully curative.

Before my sister flew home, our little family of three indulged in favorite pastimes together: a day trip to the mountains; lounging by her hotel pool; eating forbidden foods, like breaded, deep-fried steak fingers and curly fries, and, as decadent dessert, enormous chocolate chip cookies. Then it was time to discuss treatment and quality of life issues. We relaxed in overstuffed chairs in my son's spacious living room.

---

[1] Please see Glossary.

Ultimately, they left the decision to me. I was undecided until an optimistic comment my son made inspired me to undergo treatment: "Well, Mom, when they say there's a 40% chance of rain in Tucson, I prepare for rain."

During 110° desert heat that summer, I had many opportunities for affirmation during the monsoons. Regardless of what chance of rain was predicted, in every downpour I ecstatically stood outside, drinking in the drops in celebration. As rain splashed over me, I felt cleansed of guilt and renewed with hope, feeling especially blessed when the forecast had been a 40% chance or less.

I have quiet faith and do not attend church, but the precept, "Faith can move mountains," has always been a touchstone. Just a few months before diagnosis, I had intuitively written on a refrigerator memo pad: "I am grateful for life and love." At my first chemotherapy session, I remember telling a volunteer (who was also a cancer support group leader) how my son's statement had become like a mantra for me and contributed to a life-affirming perspective.

Although I celebrated every moment and welcomed healing therapies, feeling unworthy of total remission gnawed at my hopefulness. While my sister prayed for a miracle, I prepared for the grim prognosis—deciding that, even if a miracle was possible, I was undeserving of it because I had neglected my PAP smears.

Healing became as much about resolving guilt for that oversight as combating the disease. Undoubtedly, my healing would have been easier if I hadn't blamed myself. Yet, looking back, self-forgiveness must have been one of the lessons I needed to learn, and which I am still learning.

Guilt was compounded by criticism of my negligence and trite jokes about assumed promiscuity, even from devoutly religious friends and co-workers on whom I had hoped to rely. I stopped disclosing that I had cervical cancer. I empathized with the stigma that AIDS and lung cancer patients face, because people fault them for causing their own illness. Where is compassion?

Important in my belief system was that I should be equally prepared to face either healing or death. Supported by wise philosophies, that attitude was fairly healthy: "Mind-body-spirit" practices emphasize "healing" rather than "curing." The Serenity Prayer asks for "serenity to accept the things I cannot change, the courage to change the things I can, and the wisdom to know the difference." I said that prayer often.

Feeling that my negligence had caused my family unnecessary stress already, I researched medical web sites for statistics. I wanted to prepare for eventualities: selling my household goods, getting on a hospice list, and making arrangements for my animals.

Limited studies of Stage IVb cervical cancer indicated that patients following the same regimen the oncologist prescribed generally lived from four to ten months. Usually, those who lived longer suffered irreversible complications from treatment, but *a few had gone into remission.*

Together with my own prayers, the solace of support and prayers from my son and sister, their church congregations, and my cancer group softened the harshness of facing my probable decline in health. Meanwhile, emetics lessened nausea after chemotherapy, and I cannot describe my days of recovery as bleak. Except for hemolytic anemia and critical platelet depletion from chemotherapy, and profuse diarrhea and urinary urgency from abdominal radiation, my recovery went smoothly. I do not make that statement tongue in cheek.

Regardless of my side effects or my doubts about being cured, every moment became a treasure. I took time for stillness, meeting a loved one's eyes, stroking a beloved pet. Self-directed therapy at home consisted of art and yard work. Initially, during treatment, I was consumed with raw energy and craved large muscle exercise—even pulling weeds was gratifying. Whereas painting "wearable" art had been a hobby, I now adorned larger canvases: painting the patio wall French blue like the house trim and embellishing garden benches and the carport floor with geckoes to match the wrought ironwork.

Work was the key word. I was determined to feel useful while I still had energy and endeavored to enhance my world with color and beauty.

Eagerly, throughout my recovery, I involved myself in yoga, NIA, meditation, and Chakra work, because these spiritual practices balance the mind-body-spirit connection and thereby enhance the immune system. My most joyful exercise was a NIA dance class, which combined modern dance with yoga and Chakra work.

For quietude I gazed on tranquil desert landscapes and meditated or walked with my trusty dog. Sometimes spending hours at home when I had little energy, pet therapy was at my fingertips—my dog and four cats intuitively comforted me, cuddling and nuzzling. Stroking them reduced my stress. The dog always responded by placing his paw on my arm, his eyes alight with affection. The cats arched their backs and squinted their eyes with pleasure as I caressed them, then rolled onto their backs for "tummy rubs."

Intuitively, I realized "laughter is the best medicine." (Or was it from years of reading that feature in *Reader's Digest*?) A humorous outlook not only relieved my stress, but counteracted any inclination to self-pity.

Consistently, my son enlivened my outlook with humor, for example, his quip: "Mom, you *have* to live, because I can't take care of all your animals!"

The antics of my cat clan provided at least one laugh a day. Watching the felines shadowbox, swing upside-down from the platforms of their cat trees, and surreptitiously snuffle the dog's fur provided amusement.

However, beneath my healthy outlook were precepts I had absorbed as a child in Sunday school. Paraphrased: We are subservient to God's will. Suffer in silence. Moreover, I took being positive to the extreme—denying myself an outlet for expressing my pain, in fact, I verged on being "in denial."

I certainly needed to discuss my conflicted feelings in a support group! Although I *thought* I felt comfortable facing death, joining a support group to discuss my feelings was an intelligent decision. But at first I had reservations about attending. My experience had shown that not all support group environments are helpful. Several I attended when I was a caregiver for my mother were "downers"—people spent their time complaining about the person they were caring for or mired in their own self-pity. Furthermore, anticipating what type of group I might find, I couldn't tolerate pollyannaish people. I've always thought that incessantly exuding happiness is fake. In a few words, I was pre-judging, so I decided to keep an open mind.

Fortunately, I found the right group because it was led by the right person, who guided members to uncover authentic emotions. Through weekly sessions I resolved my issues by listening to others' views, without faulting them or me.

I established an internal dialogue, allowing myself to express pain or fear if I didn't honestly feel happy. As a realist, I was also struggling against having "false hope." From the many definitions of "hope" set forth by group participants, I found a comfortable one: having hope means being optimistic, but also considering the reality of the situation. It does not *necessarily* mean you're planning the outcome or expecting a miracle.

At my first chemotherapy treatment, a witty and wise support group leader (the aforementioned volunteer), a sixteen-year breast cancer survivor, introduced herself. Not only didn't she blink an eye when I disclosed that I had cervical cancer, but she also shared stories of numerous breast cancer patients who had survived decades after being given dire prognoses. Thereafter, in the group I met so many courageous patients, I thought of our cozy meeting nook as "a roomful of courage."

Our "fearless leader," as I jokingly dubbed her, engendered an atmosphere that combined empathetic sharing of our pain with frivolity. Weekly attendance provided necessary levity, and I looked forward to her repartee.

However, in group, my refuge for acceptance, I began feeling uncomfortable sharing my cancer history. Although the leader and regular members were forgiving of me when I mentioned the omission of my PAP smears, sometimes new members would avert their eyes or shrug their shoulders. Therefore, I refrained from revealing my story until I knew someone well.

But, more important than any conflict, I was graced by a miracle: the continuous decrease of the cancer after treatment began in September, 2005. The CT scan one month later already showed extensive reduction; therefore, the radiation oncologist proceeded with implants to minimize it further.

In my office visit, awaiting the results of the October scan, I was prepared to cry with delight or sorrow. When the oncologist told me the good news, my tears of joy welled up; and, despite his low-key attitude, the doctor beamed. I also thought I detected tears glistening in his eyes. He seemed to be as surprised as I was at the results!

I thought about sending the butterfly ring back to my sister—her birthday was in November and, after all, it was only a loan—but she encouraged me to keep it.

After the CT of February, 2006, which miraculously showed eradication of all cancer, I joyfully relayed the news to my family and cancer group. However, my emotions were too blocked to celebrate my remarkable remission or cry with relief, because I hadn't yet forgiven myself. I needed the process of my Chakra workshop, just after treatment ended, to release pent-up feelings.

As we circled the room in soul-freeing dance to energize the "hara"—the energy center where the "Chi," or life force, resides—the teacher asked us to identify with an object that "spoke to" us. I identified with a flourishing corn plant that reached the studio's cathedral ceiling. To me, its height symbolized unlimited aspiration, and its lush verdancy represented health and renewal. Like the corn plant, in my cancer journey I had aspired beyond expectations and flourished.

Since diagnosis, I had only briefly achieved the healthy release of tears twice: within moments after the gynecologist revealed cancer in a telephone conversation; and again in the oncologist's office after receiving the news of reduction shown on my October, 2005 CT scan. The visualization and Chakra work released my imprisoned emotions. Like cleansing rain, unlimited tears of celebration flowed for the first time.

Bringing me to the present, it seems like another lifetime when I faced treatment and side effects, and I am blessed because the miracle of remission allows me to enjoy more time with my family. This morning, as I savor a chocolate-chip scone with coffee, I think about all of the gifts that remission has brought me. I appreciate a simple joy: the taste of chocolate, which was bitter during chemotherapy. I am grateful for the ability to swallow, which many patients are not able to enjoy.

Remission also gave me the opportunity to fulfill a dream. For more than a decade I had aspired to view Georgia O'Keeffe's paintings up close by visiting Sante Fe, the city where she lived and painted. I celebrated the first anniversary of the end of chemotherapy by driving—alone—to Sante Fe over the Christmas holidays to visit the museum that displays many of her paintings. Not only did I want to disprove the label of "chemo-brain," it was a pilgrimage: to pay homage to my good health.

I rented a car and drove the 2,500-mile roundtrip. Through isolated, yet serene, stretches of desert, I chatted with my sister by cell phone. "I only got lost twice, both times at night," I proudly reported later to her and my friends.

After unpacking in a small inn that the group leader had recommended, I hastened to the Georgia O'Keeffe museum. Elated, I stood within inches of Georgia's paintings, admiring her brush strokes, but marveling over the unique shadings of color she used to create the highlights and shadows that lend a velvety texture to her subjects. My favorites were not the renowned sensual flowers, nor the Pedernal butte, or the ghostly deer's skull. They were the bright blue and stark black lines of the church bell tower and the warm, velvety red highlights of her self-portrait nudes. Afterward, I watched the sun go down from the top of Canyon Road, the famous art district.

The beauty of nature and art that had inspired my cancer journey was encompassed in having this luxurious experience. I weep recounting it.

But I am touched even more, remembering yet another miracle granted me, which emphasized a lesson I had forgotten while congratulating myself on my cancer survival: *a higher power is in control.*

On my return home from Sante Fe, there was a blizzard outside of Wilcox, about an hour's drive outside Tucson. My son and sister recommended I stay there overnight, but I had surmounted bigger obstacles, had I not? Full of self-confidence and eager to get home, I drove onward, enjoying watching the landscape turn white.

Arriving in Tucson at nightfall, the city was shrouded in clouds; rain and fog reduced visibility, and I lost my sense of direction. Within just a few miles of my home, I took the wrong road and came to a sharp curve. Unfamiliar with the car and driving on ice, I hit the brakes too hard. As the car spun in a 360-degree revolution, I prayed: "God help me!" When the car came safely to rest, my gratitude was boundless. I could have careened into someone walking on the sidewalk or injured people in a car coming around the bend.

I had been smacked with a vivid reminder: no matter how powerful I think I am, a higher power is in charge. And, as the saying goes, "Somebody up there likes me!"

Epilogue

To what do I attribute my recovery, and what have I learned?

My recovery is a blessing that I did not earn, bestowed by a higher power, and which I will repay by growing in character. Different from being cured, my healing has been a combination of love, prayers, and spiritual belief with medical treatment, and plain good luck. For the moment I am cured, but I must work on being healed every day, through gratitude, prayer, and forgiveness—of myself and others.

The most important lesson in my cancer journey was family solidarity; and though there are only three of us, our love for each other packs a wallop in overcoming adversity. I wasn't surprised. We three courageously cared for my mother after she lost her speech from a stroke.

An essential lesson from my cancer journey is self-forgiveness. Judging myself and, likewise, other people was heavy baggage. Although I still cringe when disclosing that I had metastatic cervical cancer, I feel forgiven by whatever higher power governs the universe. As my sister says, "It will get easier every time you admit the story." Or, as Alcoholics Anonymous teaches, "You're only as sick as your secrets."

Over the three years I have participated in group, we have lost several members, whom we will always remember for their vitality, courage, and humor; but *this* time around, I was given an extension to savor life a little longer.

At plateaus of remission, I have considered the idea of giving the butterfly ring back to my sister, but haven't been confident to be without it. Guess I do believe in good luck charms. I need to keep the ring a little longer—as insurance. My sister laughed when I told her that. She had been aware of how I felt all along.

Glossary

1. PET scan – positron emission tomography "measures important body functions, such as blood flow, oxygen use, and sugar (glucose) metabolism, to help doctors evaluate how well organs and tissue are functioning."
2. "Eyes to thighs" – the examination area of the body that the scan includes.
3. Integrative medicine – medicine that combines traditional and alternative medical treatment.
4. Mind-body-spirit connection and work – theory that integration and wellness of mind, body, and spirit promote healing. Enabling exercises are, for example, yoga, tai chi, qigong, NIA, and Chakra work.
5. Alternative medicine – untraditional treatments, for example: acupuncture, healing touch, reike, and shiatsu massage.
6. Chakras – according to Eastern spiritual practices, there are seven Chakras—energy centers in the body, each connected to healing in that area. All combine to balance the whole of one's being; therefore blockage in one or more prevents healing.
7. Hara – "*Hara* is the Japanese word for a point in your body about two finger-widths below your navel. It is a major center of ki *(chi*, life energy)."
8. NIA – Neuromuscular Integrative Action is "a program of using physical activity to integrate one's neurology with one's body or musculature."
9. Connie Reider – a breast cancer survivor and photographer, who co-founded the F. Holland Day Center for Healing and Creativity in Maine.

The Ultimate Song

Megan Webster

Determined to die at home, my mother
waived tests, surgery, a stomach tube—

sought only the warmth of her bed,
her lilac and apple tree through the window,

the robin blossoming on a high branch.
As her breathing grew wispy, her fingers

tapped the sheet anxiously as if she had
an appointment. One night in the grip

of coma, she rose in her bed, stretched
out her arms, welcomed what only

her eyes could see, and in her Welsh
mother tongue, greeted her mother—

gone fifty years—and flew into her arms.
My heart leapt at this extraordinary

leaving, and I remember thinking
as I drew down her eyelids, brushed

my lips against her brow and held her,
how even on her last journey,

her mind already past the turnstile
of transition, she was leading the way,

teaching her daughter the mysterious
notes of the ultimate song.

The Perfect Gift

Leila Peters

October 17, 10:00 am

"The room is filled with light. The sounds of Autumn drift through the windows with the breeze. A small kitten lies curled on the bed at the fingertips of her sleeping owner. Except for the rattle of labored breathing and the rented hospital equipment in the room, you would never suspect this to be a dying place. It is, in fact, a beautiful, quiet sanctuary where there is a nurturing towards death, a place where death is recognized as part of the circle of life. The time is drawing near. The sparkling blue eyes which smiled at friends days ago are hooded now and looking inward."

Before the time that Sue's struggle was over, there were three operations to remove cancerous tumors, strong medicines, and countless visits to doctors. She became paralyzed in June. She smiled for friends, for the sun on the patio, for cool drinks, and for me. Suction tubes were inserted, catheters invaded, and still she held on to her own sense of self. Her beautiful, muscular body wilted and shrank. Breathing became more difficult. She turned yellow. The blue eyes still sparkled with light. There was a striving, in spite of the odds, for a rich, full life, praying for it, trying to stave off death through sheer force of will.

Fueled by the aching need to keep loved ones with us, we embark on a frantic, desperate time, filled with anguish because we don't know what to do. The caregivers of a dying loved one need help in re-orienting their thinking. It is essential to have a doctor who understands that the natural death of a suffering patient is not a defeat for them, but a release. Through their cool reason we can begin to understand that there comes a time when clinging to life must end and a new direction taken, a direction in which the main focus is providing care and comfort. It is not necessary to let go of our loved ones when realization comes that they soon will die, when we realize that none of our frantic efforts can save them. We are not powerless against the inexorable advancement of death. We can become even more involved and more an intimate part of their being as we prepare a smooth transition, keeping in harmony with the natural outcome of life even when that life is cut short by disease.

It is a monumental undertaking to care for a dying person in one's home. Procedures so common to the medical profession—irrigating catheters, changing soiled clothing, suctioning congested airways—are foreign, and shatter any illusions that "everything is all right." We are faced every day with the prospect that our loved ones are dying, and the finality of death looms undeniably in the future.

It is not something everyone can do, but with the help of a hospice program or home nursing care, it is possible. Even so, it will push the caregivers to their emotional, physical, and spiritual limits. If we can endure it, the comfort and fulfillment to our own souls will always be a part of our lives. We will have had something positive to do.

There is a profound correlation between the growth of a fetus toward birth, and the dying patient's progress toward death. There is, first, the knowledge of new life, and then tests for tiny shapes, the distorting of mother's body with new growth, anticipation, concerns for a normal birth, fear of pain and, at last, the journey down the birth canal from the safety of a protected, watery environment into a new and alien world.

The process toward death has a similar metamorphosis. The idea of death is presented to us. We see the signs of a body wearing down, atrophy, jaundice, lungs that fill with fluid. There is a growing fear for our loved ones' leaving this familiar world for the unknown. Death, like birth, has a natural progression, a positive movement toward an entry into a new place. We must make a truce with the fear of death, and generate a new resolve to make the journey a loving one.

We are not powerless. We can provide a beautiful nurturing place away from a hospital with its interruptions of probing strangers, its blaring intrusive noise, the sterile pungent smells, hard floors, hard lights, lack of privacy. We can make sure our loved ones are not removed from familiar surroundings that give comfort and peace to the soul. We can give the gift

THE PERFECT GIFT

of loving hands, soft lights, familiar music, and a quiet gathering of friends. Most of all, through the intimacy of our care, we can give the security of love, security even in the face of death.

October 17, 3:00 PM

> "Sue's body is beginning to shut down. She dozes most of the time, breathing heavily. Her hands and feet take on a bluish cast. She is semiconscious, unresponsive except for her precious music."

October 17, 4:30 PM

> "In the sunlit room our beloved friend turns inward and finds perfection. The struggle is over, stillness settles in the space, tangible, awesome, peace. Her mouth and eyes, half open, are relaxed, no movement, no torment, silent, beautiful face, sweet spirit released."

In the moments after Sue's death, I realized there is another gift, one to those left behind. The very thing we feared most bestows an unimagined serenity of spirit. Seeing the perfect peace on the face of a loved one who has just died is an indescribable gift, calm beyond understanding, a truth of the universe glimpsed for a moment, then gone, and we can only give thanks for having been a part of this transcendence.

Another Spring

Kathleen A. O'Brien

Someone had put him out to air
    the way women hang out musty curtains or
    open windows wide to let winter staleness loose.

Silently, he sat in his wheelchair
    across from our office
    near a bush laced in bridal white,
    watching four o'clock traffic
    stream lemming-like down Hoosick Street.
An orange blanket draped his lap
    like a sleeping cat;
    a Yankees cap tethered him to present time.

Someone had wheeled the old man to the walkway
    where he sat by himself in sunshine
    like a traffic cone,
    hands folded peacefully in his lap,
    savoring the gift of another Spring,
    wondering if it would be his last.

Winner: Best Non-fiction Contest

One Minute You're a Wife, The Next, a Widow

Vera Martignetti

My husband of forty-seven years died on June 9, 2007. No euphemisms—he didn't "pass on," "pass away," or "join the angels," and no one would have been more surprised than Phil if he "met his loved ones in heaven." He didn't believe in anything after death, but he did feel regret about missing the future. What was heartbreaking to him was not being in a world where his family would continue to unfold.

We shared a strong aversion to sentimentalizing death. Despite being an on-again, off-again practicing Catholic for most of his life, in the last twenty years he had grown to believe that after death there was only darkness—no awareness. Unlike agnostics, who start praying when the doctor says "terminal," Phil never wavered. He believed, as I do, that our children are our immortality. He specified very strongly that he wanted no mass or church service, no viewing, embalming, or coffin. Despite the fact that all four of our children are fervent believers, they and I worked hard to make that happen. He spelled out exactly where his cremated remains should be placed. "Having lived most of my life in close proximity to vodka," he thought an appropriate urn would he an Absolut bottle. It was typical of his black humor. To me—"I should start smoking again. What's the downside?" To a friend—"Danny, stop praying for me. I'm getting worse." Cracking wise at the Cancer Center, as if he had to keep his doctors amused while they gave him bad news. Asking, "What's the point of flossing?"

With our children's inherited irreverence and lack of propriety, they all understood and smiled along with him. Five days before he died, he sat at the kitchen table with the yellow pages, calling specialty liquor stores to find a place that carried not only 750 milligram bottles (one for me), but also airline-size Absolut bottles for our children, if they wanted one. They did. He stared at those bottles when he got them home and said, "I've got a man's work ahead of me."

We didn't realize it at the time, but Thursday, June 7th, became our last appointment at the University of Arizona Cancer Center. We knew he was failing, and that the third different chemotherapy had not been effective. We just didn't know exactly how much deterioration there had been.

Phil's doctor got right to the point—something we both liked about him. He said we would not be coming back for treatment. What could be done had been done. It would be "a matter of months," maybe less. He gave us a referral to hospice and a prescription for morphine in pill form, which he was sure Phil would need in the very near future. A liquid morphine inhaler could be delivered also, if necessary. Lord, I hoped it wouldn't come to that. An oxygen therapy machine to be used every four hours would be provided by our medical supplier. He gave us the radiology report, which clearly noted the growth of the largest lesion, and he brought the film up on his computer screen. Pointing to the lung mass, he explained what the term *atelectatic* meant—a partial breakdown of the lung due to an obstruction caused by the significant increase in size of the largest mass. Huh? It took us both a minute to understand that the cancer was causing Phil's right lung to collapse. The lesions were everywhere. Everywhere.

The doctor had given us so much of his time that Phil's portable oxygen tank was running out by the time the valet service brought us our car. Wide-eyed, he panicked when he saw the arrow pointing past the red, so I ran back in and "borrowed" an oxygen tank. It was one of the old, large, scarred, green tanks that look like a World War II bomb. I carried it out in my arms, put it between his legs, and connected him. Once he was breathing easily again, we laughed at how it practically reached his chin from the floorboards, and how no one had followed me out yelling, "Hey, lady!"

Three of our children live in Texas, Washington, and North Carolina. At home that evening, I asked when he wanted to call them to talk about our afternoon. "Not now. Not this evening." Nancy, who lives in Tucson, was with us that evening. Stone-faced, she heard the news from both of us.

The next morning, I went to pick up the morphine prescription. When he was making coffee just a few days before, he had asked for the more expensive, thicker, specially formed basket coffee filters. "Not the cheap ones that flop over, OK?" So, when I picked up the morphine, I brought the filters home, too. I showed them to him, and he looked at me blankly. Coffee filters?

We had received bad news in the last two years: when surgery failed to stop the growth of the lesions; when PET scans showed further involvement in other organs; when the latest round of chemotherapy had not been effective in shrinking the tumors. But we had always been offered an alternative—something new or different. Some hope for a remission or delay of the inevitable.

Fighting cancer had filled our days. Who knew that having a disease could be so much work? This time we had nothing. I think he was running a continuous loop in his mind about how the next few weeks or months were going to go. He didn't spend any time on the computer, which had been his lifeline to the outside world during the previous months. The last message he sent to friends, early on the morning of Friday the 8th, was a Peggy Noonan column entitled "The Greatness of 'The Sopranos.'" He was looking forward to the last episode, which was scheduled for Sunday. At almost the same time in the other office, I sent a message to our family with the subject line, "OK, here it is," detailing the bad news and telling them to expect a call from him.

As the day wore on, my gallows humor fell flat. The laughing had finally stopped. I asked again about calling the children to talk about the prognosis, or did he want me to do it? No, no, he would talk to them. I can imagine he was too emotional to talk about it just then. How do you tell your children that it's over? Should he ask Ed to come home from Iraq? One last family reunion? He spent much of the day staring into space. He called Tucson Medical Center Hospice, where he had volunteered for ten years, and asked a favorite nurse to visit us to talk about what the next steps would be for in-home care. They set up an appointment for Saturday morning at ten. Nancy stopped in briefly. "I'm happy you're here," he said, but little else. Susan and Lisa both called after work, as they had at least five days a week for months, but he waved the phone away. "I'm too tired. I'll speak to them tomorrow." Too tired even to eat, he had only gelato on Friday evening and went to bed very early.

For the last six weeks and for the first time in our lives, we had slept in separate beds. I got in the habit of checking on him when I went to bed between 10 and 10:30 PM, and again at 2 AM. At 10:30 that night, I helped him out of bed to go to the bathroom. He needed a walker to get around and was spitting blood more often than he had been. I collected the bloody tissues and walked him back to bed, bringing him two Tylenol and a glass of water when he said he had a headache.

At about 2 AM, I looked in on him, and it seemed as if he were sleeping—the oxygen concentrator humming, the cannula in his nose, the covers down around his legs. When I pulled the covers up, I saw he wasn't breathing. I called to him, shook him by the shoulders, held him in my arms, raised my voice and actually yelled at him. He was gone. I must have come in just shortly after he died. His face was warm and pink; his arms and body were flexible. Stupidly, I thought, This can't be. He can't die. I just brought home new prescriptions. Two days ago, he was opening jars for me, making coffee, watching the news and arguing with the newscaster. One minute you're a wife…and the next, a widow.

I dialed 911, and the EMTs confirmed his death within minutes. Or at least it seemed like no time at all. I don't remember hearing a siren. They stayed with me until two policemen arrived. I was feeling kind of fuzzy—disoriented. I called our daughters and daughter-in-law. I couldn't speak to our son because Ed, a Lt. Colonel in the Air Force, was in Iraq. They tell me I said, "Daddy died." It had been at least twenty years since I referred to Phil as Daddy. Confused and ignoring four decades of phone technology, I asked my daughter Lisa how I could get in touch with Susan, since I didn't know her hotel in Chicago. Kindly, she reminded me that Susan hadn't changed her cell phone number.

Susan asked to speak to one of the policemen, assured herself that I was doing OK, and said that she would leave the Chicago Trade Show and fly to Tucson that afternoon. I asked Lisa to wait in Houston for a few days so that she could come to stay with me through and after the memorial. The policemen called grief counselors. A man and woman arrived with a booklet entitled *Experiencing Grief: Coping With Loss*. I never realized that the Pima County Attorney's Office sends volunteer victim counselors out any time of the day or night. There I was, in the kitchen, looking at a list of mortuaries with them at 3:30 AM, explaining Phil's wishes. There were now five people standing and sitting in my kitchen. I felt as though I should make coffee or…something. The grief counselors asked me if I needed help to call a mortuary. "You don't want your husband's body to go to the City Morgue. You need to have him cared for by choosing a funeral home now." We should have chosen a mortuary well in advance. This was something we would have done that day when the hospice nurse was scheduled to visit. Had he died a few days later, all these choices would have been in place and I would have had to make only one phone call to the hospice emergency number, to say nothing of the fact that we could have talked about that last unsatisfying episode of "The Sopranos."

Karen, the volunteer, showed me a list of mortuaries in the back of the booklet. After I made a few calls, two people from a funeral home were on their way. Foolishly, I thought to call the funeral home closest to my house first; they made it *very* clear that the low-cost, no-frills service I was requesting was "best taken care of by another mortuary." "OK. I understand." I might have expected a bit more than those few, spare words, but it was 3 AM I settled on a mortuary that provided inexpensive cremation services. Thinking it must be the Costco of funeral homes, I liked it that Phil, who loved a bargain, would have been pleased.

I called Father Bob, a close friend for over thirty years who has been more than tolerant about our long-standing crisis of faith. Bob arrived before the mortuary employees removed Phil's body. Dressing quickly must be in every seminary graduate's job description. I was asked if there was something I wished to have before the body was removed. A ring? A watch? No, but I wanted his tee shirt. At least once a year, and sometimes more often, I had a *Poppy's Girls* tee shirt made for him with pictures of his grandchildren, front and back. He died wearing the latest one. I was promised that it would be returned to me when I picked up the remains. I was numb as I watched the gurney go through the door, although not so numb that I didn't notice he was in a large Hefty bag. "Phil's leaving our home for the last time." I was still amazed, convinced that there must be something I had forgotten to tell him.

We had been expecting this since the second chemotherapy failed in late winter. Certainly, we knew that the third type of chemotherapy was a long shot. But expecting his death in no way lessened my disbelief when it happened. It was so abruptly final. Despite the fact that he was more than five years older than I and had been experiencing various medical problems for the last six years, I thought we'd be together forever. No, not forever. Just a while longer. And I thought of myself as realistic? How little we know ourselves. Actually, he died under the best possible circumstances. He appeared so strong that I was afraid his body would linger with an awful, painful cancer death—wasting away, loss of bodily functions, morphine haze, the inability to recognize family, and still hanging on. But he died peacefully at home in his sleep with no signs of thrashing, pain, or suffocation. It sounds trite, a cliché when someone holds your hand and says, "It was a blessing," but in this situation it was absolutely true.

A few days later, the doctor said, "He probably threw a clot," presumably from his lung to his heart, causing the heart to stop instantaneously. Is that a massive infarction? Or did he mean a brain aneurism? I didn't have the presence of mind to ask for more details. The death certificate lists metastatic melanoma as the primary cause of death, with pulmonary amyloidosis and chronic obstructive pulmonary disease as secondary causes. Both secondary illnesses would have been terminal in time. His heart was also laboring with untreated aortic stenosis. Surgery couldn't be done to correct the stenosis because of his other illnesses. Every body has its limits. It is beyond hackneyed to say it, but "it was just a matter of time." Later, during that long day, which had started at 2 AM, I called two close friends, and then sent an e-mail to the same grouplist of friends to whom I had been sending medical status updates—part of the cathartic journaling process that brought me relief during his illness and made it real to me.

In reading this e-mail now, I'm struck by how dispassionate it is. It reads as if a close family friend had written it. Clearly, I was emotionally underwater, and it would be weeks before his death and its impact on me would fully register.

On autopilot, I showered, dressed, ate, and stared at the newspaper headlines. Nancy drove over, and we talked again and again about "last night and this morning." I think I even made my bed, all the time avoiding Phil's room. I picked Susan up at the airport and breathed in relief. We talked about everything we'd have to do as she drove home: a place for the memorial, a reception after the memorial, what food? A DVD of pictures of Phil's life? What music? A visit to the mortuary. I wanted to write the obituary.

She was surprised at all the medical equipment in the house. Through her eyes I saw the walker in his bedroom, the oxygen concentrator (as tall as a night table) by his bed, the spare portable oxygen tanks in his bedroom and the dining room, the "stolen" green tank in the living room, and the oxygen therapy machine in the kitchen. "Pillow cases in the night table?" "Yes, he was coughing up a lot of blood." Pill bottles and miles of medical tubing coiled everywhere. This had become the *new-normal*.

I don't remember that first evening after coming home from the airport at all. I think I may have been in denial. "There must be some mistake." "What just happened?" The next morning, Susan and I started cleaning out the pill bottles. The clinic told us they couldn't use pills that have been prescribed for someone else, even if the containers haven't been opened. What a horrible waste! So many expensive pills went down the disposal. I have since read that I was probably poisoning the aquifer. Who knew? It was cathartic for both of us. We started clowning around, flinging the bottles into wastebaskets, making two-pointers. There is a fine line between laughter and tears.

Susan had to return to her family and job in Seattle and wanted to bring pictures with her to start the DVD of Phil's life. She would create a compilation of pictures with captions and music. Forty-eight years of pictures—at least two hundred a year after all four children were born. Rolls of thirty-six pictures taken at every birthday, first day of school, first date, prom, school concert, swim meet, vacation, and graduation. Witch's costumes, Christmas trees, Easter bonnets. Thousands of them taken in and around two apartments and five different homes, some in tattered albums, some in our forty-eight-year old wedding album, some in recently bought, acid-free Hallmark albums, and some loose in boxes. My whole life lay scattered on tables, chairs, and floor. I don't know how we got it down to seventy-seven pictures. And then we had to choose four for the memorial program. Bob volunteered to have the memorial program done at his church and to find a memorial venue for about 100 people. What would I have done without my family and Bob?

My daughter-in-law, Tessa, called to say that Ed's commanding officer in Iraq told him his dad had died and made immediate plans for Ed to return to the States. He was expected to arrive home soon, and Tessa was already making plans for their family of six to leave for Tucson. There were reasons why our two oldest grandchildren in Seattle couldn't fly immediately. We decided to delay the memorial for at least a week. It would give everyone—family and out-of-town friends—time to get here and time for me to get the obituary published. It was also good to give myself time, some breathing room to focus and make decisions.

Writing the obituary was no chore. It flowed easily. I even managed to mention his two favorite dogs. But I ended up paying (literally) for my wordy, effusive article. When I emailed the obit and his picture to the *Arizona Daily*

Star, asking for it to be published Saturday, Sunday, and Monday before the Tuesday memorial in both the morning and afternoon papers, I was called by the editor and told that it would cost about $1,100. "How much?" I asked her to repeat it. Good Lord, that was hundreds more than the mortuary's complete services! Removing it from the afternoon paper and Saturday brought it down to $620. Phil had thought of everything and told me to put every cost (even the chemotherapy) on my personal VISA to build up my mileage plan for a vacation when it was all over. Prescription drugs after he exceeded his insurance coverage (the dreaded medical insurance donut hole), first-class airline tickets to accommodate the oxygen concentrator when he and I traveled, the photo shop for the DVD, the mortuary, the catered Italian food for after the memorial, the contribution to St. Augustine's High School for the use of their chapel, the flowers—all were included in his last gift to me: thousands of extra miles.

Susan and I went to the mortuary to sign paperwork and ask about the Absolut bottles. "Is that the strangest request you ever had?" "Not at all," the lovely lady said. "You'd be surprised." I had been asked to bring a recent photograph of Phil to be given to the cremation center for identification purposes. Thinking I had brought everything I needed, I found myself calling home to ask Nancy to find some paperwork giving me Phil's social security number. You never have it all with you. How many death certificates would I need? I hadn't thought about it. I guessed at six—more than one costs extra. Now, a year later, I still have six. We left with a thick folder and booklet. "Cremation is irreversible," the booklet explained. OK. You have to wonder which of their clients made it necessary to include that. The phrase became a refrain. When it all got too overwhelming, I could make myself smile by muttering, "Cremation is irreversible."

Susan left for Seattle, and Lisa arrived the next day. "What can I do for you?"—her first words. "Help me change the room where Phil died. The children will have to sleep there when they come." I had already stripped the bed and run out to buy a new coverlet and shams for it. So bizarre to be standing by the register of Bed, Bath & Beyond. They ask for your zip code. I wanted to say, "85712. My husband just died. My life will never be the same. Put it on my VISA."

The outpouring after Phil's death was overwhelming. Throughout the days, friends and neighbors arrived with food, plants, flowers, and kind words. We had offers of guest rooms and neighborhood casitas for our family and friends who were flying in from out of state. I love my friends.

Susan stayed in constant touch, giving us updates from Seattle on the design of the DVD. As we moved forward with the memorial plans, I couldn't stop thinking that Phil should have been there. It was his party, after all. We knew he was going to die, but we had closed our eyes to the inevitable arrangements. "We'll make plans later in the month, after the next doctor's visit, when we have a clearer idea of the progress of the cancer." It sounds delusional now in the retelling. Had I been more open about my emotions, we would have spent an entire afternoon talking about it, making choices. He loved to plan a party. I should have insisted.

When Susan returned, she, Lisa, and Nancy helped me go though the closets. A few things for our son and son-in-law, a few things for me to keep, most everything else for Goodwill. Phil never threw anything away. There were thirty-year-old cowboy boots, hiking boots, golf shirts from long-forgotten tournaments (some too small, some too large), ties from the 70's, suits that hadn't been worn in fifteen years, dress belts to go with them. There was a pair of black wingtip tie-string shoes bought in Jersey City in the 50's. Lisa found a Web site that explained how to figure fair market value for charitable donations and printed out my list.

Bob arranged for the memorial to be at St. Augustine's High School chapel—pushing the envelope on Phil's request for a non-religious service. But the room is beautiful, seats more than one hundred, has a lovely piano and sound system, and is spare in spiritual decorations. When we drove over to take a look, Lisa got into the spirit by pointing out that we could call that large symbol above the altar a "big plus sign," and the altar, of course, was just a high table. Bob and I argued. He wanted to wear his vestments; I thought it was just too religious. He showed his love for Phil and me by wearing black pants and a long-sleeved guayabera. Phil would have approved. I remember some of those days very clearly, and some of them not at all. Mostly, it was a blur punctuated by an occasional clear moment.

I surprised some friends by speaking at the memorial. I started with a joke about "counting the house," and how pleased Phil would have been with the turnout. I added a few words describing Phil as a man of excesses, including how excessively he loved us all. Susan stood up with Nancy and Lisa, speaking beautifully about the father he had been to them. Anecdotes were told about Phil's parenting—his daily phone calls to them during their first year of college.

I had requested e-mail remembrances from our friends to be read at the service. So many people wanted to express their thoughts that Lisa had to edit the sheer volume into ten heartfelt stories that she told on behalf of his friends. Our oldest granddaughter, Toni, stood up with the five other granddaughters and spoke lovely words about their Poppy. Ed spoke warmly about Phil as a mentor, father, and grandfather. He wore his Air Force uniform, which would have made his father so proud. Phil got a lot of mileage out of "my son, the Academy grad," "my son, the jet pilot," "my son, the Lt. Colonel." He racked up countless bonus points on the golf course by casually dropping his son into the conversation.

We sang his favorite hymns: "Just a Closer Walk With Thee," "Day by Day," and the Lord's Prayer. Phil always insisted that you didn't have to believe in God to love a song about Him. We directed everyone to the church recreation center where food, wine, and soft drinks were served and the DVD shown for the second time. The guests from out of town and dear friends ended up at our home for drinks and more laughing and crying. I must have been exhausted, because I can't remember when the party broke up, how the house got cleaned up, where everyone slept. All I know is I slept alone—feeling cold in Tucson in June—and I cried. Grief is immediate—ferocious and in your face. It's there every night, no matter how much your busy days keep it away.

So many thank-you cards had to be written for flowers, plants, food, casitas, mass cards, donations to Tucson Medical Center Hospice in Phil's name. I quoted St. Paul: "He fought a good fight. He finished the race. He kept the faith with us." I cried every time I wrote it. I was wrung out by the time I had written twenty and started again the next day.

Guests left town. Family left town. Lisa was the last to leave, and I was alone for the first time in weeks. I had been in the care of others—people who loved me. Now it was time for me to take care of myself.

Loss is "the extraordinary rent you have to pay" for living in this world, author Annie Dillard once observed. I coped, laughed, cried, and took care of widow business throughout the next twelve months of paying my extraordinary rent.

Things I've learned this year: Anger is fine. A good attitude is highly overrated. My life will never be the same; this is what is meant by a life-changing event. You can't get to recovery without laughing, most especially at yourself. It's OK to sit and stare at the wall sometimes. Some, but not all, friends will remain steadfast. The beneficial powers of crying should not be overlooked. I still cry, but not as often and not as fully. Tears are brief and unpredictable—rivulets running just long enough to ruin the Clinique. I could use a bumper sticker that says *I brake for tears.*

Across

Constance Richardson

You are free—released into the waters of Lake Champlain,
a great waterway that flows from the St. Lawrence Seaway
inland and to the oceans and beyond.

Take my hand and come with me on our last trip across the country.
From the hazy gray Atlantic, through Providence, Mystic, Bridgeport,
then towns named Hershey, Hagerstown, Cumberland,

along the crest of the Blue Ridge Mountains, through Morganstown,
Clarksburg, by congregations of bluebonnets and clover,
through cathedrals of alder, spruce, and oak.

You, my first-born, gave me my fearless protective maternal instinct.
I could have wrestled tigers to keep you safe, and did spend hours
watching your mouth form its first words.

God blessed you with many gifts: beauty, talent, and an intelligent heart.
You gave me the most beautiful name in any language: mother, mom.
It's not fair that you left us, sweetheart.

Down from Appalachia to the rolling Blue Grass hills of Kentucky,
a 16-wheeler with "Rush Trucking" signage passes,
reminding me how you rushed fearlessly into womanhood.

It's pouring rain through Nashville, Jackson, Memphis. We pass miles
of contorted roadside performers wearing green kudzu costumes,
some bowing, others saluting in silent homage.

By Oklahoma the country flattens out into plains, its bleeding red earth
like raw emotions laid bare, slowly warming
and stretching out in the noonday sun.

From Texas into New Mexico, there is more sky than earth,
more space to imagine the "what ifs?"
I wind back time daily because you left us too soon.

On the home stretch from Albuquerque to Tucson, our trip is almost done.
There, I will make a new life into old age. I'll let desert winds dry my tears,
and soft cool evenings cradle me to sleep. I'll build a community of friends.

We're here at last! Mountains frame Tucson to the north, east, west, and south.
You would love this place, but it's time to part.
Let go of my hand. Soar with the eagle to that ridge.

Mingle in the cool waters of Sabino Creek. Lie down by the arroyo.
Blake and Isabel belong to the future where neither you nor I can dwell.
Good-bye sweetheart. Good-bye.

Return to Provence

David Ray

Sam still lives for me in snapshots and memories. He still stands on the deck of the Rhyndam, a toddler in his orange life preserver when, in 1966, I traveled with my wife and two children to England—my entry into the expatriate life and our years of moving from place to place, country to country, living on a shoestring.

The Dutch couple we became so fond of on the ship took the pictures but never sent the prints as promised, yet the snapshots live in my mind, perhaps more vividly than what the camera might have captured—Samuel with that orange arch of a lifesaver over him, his sister, Wesley, sticking out her tongue and holding her ears, then the two of them in a pose I had ordered, no horsing around. It's good that I enjoyed those brief years of parenting and such unforgettable scenes, for I would one day be unable to summon much pleasure even from the best of those days.

Eighteen years after that voyage across the Atlantic, Sam's death following a drinking binge with his sophomore classmates at Carleton College seemed an indictment of my unworthiness. It seemed better that I exist in shards and fragments, my chaotic manuscripts suitable for nothing but my habit of pulling out a sheaf here, a handful there and dropping them into the flames. At least that ritual, indulged with quondam regularity over a period of years, stopped short of suicide, for which it was a substitute.

I have always envied the writers who were in control, who knew where they ended and their work began, whose neatly-tailored work never dissolved into fragments that left them weeping. If they were fathers, they knew clearly they were not their sons, but Sam's death was virtually my death, and such a devastation made me wonder anew if my father might have felt more for me than I had realized. Perhaps, after all, he had loved and cared, though I had looked for every clue and found no evidence.

In the fall of 1984, my wife, Judy, and I were staying in Southern France at the Karolyi Foundation in Vence, thanks to a writing fellowship. It was there that we got the news of Sam's death. Eleven years later, I was given an opportunity to return to France on a similar fellowship at the more elegant Camargo Foundation in Cassis.

Though I wondered if that setting might be too close to Vence, stirring up the grief, I hoped the Camargo fellowship could offer a chance to recover. But once back in France I fell into a blacker depression than ever, lost in the past, sick with remorse for my failure as a father to those two inseparable children, Samuel and Wesley, who had counted the suitcases as we moved around Europe, children who found new friends on an island in Spain only to have to leave them behind and find new ones on an island in Greece. And since they had stayed with their mother after we divorced, distance, loss, and alienation had long been woven into all our relationships.

I pondered whether the geographic cure would work, heal some of the grief. Wasn't it about time to leave Sam behind? And surely it was time to leave behind that little boy I had once been. Clearly, as I came to understand later, the trip was a counter-phobic effort: if I could live without Sam, accept his death, so near to where I had been when the news struck, then I could bear the grief anywhere. But within hours of landing at Nice and making my way by bus through Aix-en-Provence to Marseilles and on to the resort town of Cassis, it was clear that I was not up to the challenge. Even the view of Cezanne's bluish-green Mt. St. Victoire did not help me crawl out of the pit. As the bus hummed along the Promenade des Anglais, bordered on both sides by plane trees swathed in blue Citroën haze, the worst day of my life had already gone off like a bomb recycled and detonated anew.

Steeling myself for the return to France had muted the shock not at all. It is the subliminal glare, the air and light itself, the sudden glimpse down a shadowed corridor that could suddenly collapse the years between a catastrophic instant and its reverberation years later. And it was not the first time I had encountered the paradox that depression is more likely to strike in the most beautiful surroundings, not the gloomiest.

As I sat in my assigned seat on the bus, it was as if I stumbled again— strangely not bleeding and strangely not screaming—through Nice on that sunny day of September 6, 1984. And just as now, when I am flooded with a flareup of grief for my son, lost on that day of cataclysm, the world is in absurd, unbearable contrast with the blue sea and unshaken mountains in the distance. Such a glimmering world was sunny and indifferent then, and years later, unchanged, it seems to mock the tortured soul with its obstinate, uncaring insistence on survival. Suicide was ruled out for me only because Sam's death had taught me how much a lost loved one can inflict pain on survivors. I had made an ethical decision, but from the day of the phone call from the embassy I had lost my ability to trust sunny weather, unshaken seas, and even the brief happiness offered by an idyllic scene.

In Cassis, on the Mediterranean, the weather is perfect and the sea rarely rages. The beach is a three-minute walk below the Foundation, and the cliffs of the Cap Canaille and Couronne de Charlemagne are such impressive sights beyond the port and bays that many of the great painters of France have painted them. Yet in these almost too perfect surroundings, marred only by traffic and the *parfum de Citroën*, I learned anew that "the geographical cure doesn't work." Milton: *The mind doth of itself make a hell of heaven... and I myself am hell.*

I cast mordant eyes on the yachts, glanced enviously at the enthralled lovers and topless sunbathers, their languid breasts of glimmering bronze. I strolled gloomily past waterfront restaurants where the rich sat with their plates piled high with spiky sea urchins. The meaning of Ellison's phrase, "invisible man," rang with new poignancy. I was noticed only when, like an unwelcome child provoking responses of irritability and surliness, I employed enough French to make a few purchases, barely enough for survival. Alone for the first month there, while Judy was at home awaiting the birth of a grandson, I lived on cereal and canned tuna, cheese and baguettes, oranges and apples. I was a child playing house in my little furnished apartment at the Foundation.

My return to France, then, triggered new waves of regret and nostalgia—all perhaps covered clinically by that catchall phrase, "survivor's guilt." Why should I live and another, so much more deserving, be lost?

Eleven years before that sojourn in Cassis, I had spent the month of August, 1984, alone in Vence, and Judy had arrived on the first of September to share my little cottage at the Karolyi Foundation. I had greeted her with an armful of yellow roses, and the day before word of the disaster we had taken our one and only trip together in that region—a drive around the mountains in the second-hand Ford Cortina I had purchased for six hundred dollars. We stopped at Grasse, had coffee, admired the views, and walked around

RETURN TO PROVENCE

among the shops fragrant with lavender. The next day we returned to the little cottage at the Foundation from an afternoon swim in the Municipal Picine, the shining blue pool. We were glowing from our reunion.

Our hair still wet from our swim, we were as happy on that terrace looking out across a green gorge as we had been for years. There were deep sighs of satisfaction and rare contentment, just as I noticed a handwritten note, weighted with a pebble, next to my Olivetti portable atop my upturned wooden crate, which had once held salted shark. I assumed it had been left by the English girl who helped the ninety-two-year-old Countess Karolyi run the Foundation.

The note saying that we should call a phone number in the States did not strike me as urgent. Though the number was the Minnesota area code, where my remarried former wife lived, I heard no alarm bells, saw no red lights flashing. I had, in fact, been thinking how wonderful it might be if Sam and Wes—or maybe one of them—could come visit, and every time I passed the roadside phone booth near the Foundation, I had considered calling and making the invitation.

Somehow, the fantasy danced through my mind that Rita and her husband had come up with the same idea. Or it could be something related to school, or perhaps a request for me to pay for something special. Not long before, Sam had wanted a very special Japanese bicycle costing several hundred dollars. And on his sixteenth birthday he had purchased a Toyota, for which we had split costs, his mother and I. Sam had come to Kansas City, where we scouted a good buy, one that met his fussiness about color, model, number of gears, and no doubt its suitability for lovemaking, as I realized when he and his girlfriend set to work right away on the interior, turning it into a comfy den, a love nest. They even put up curtains and installed a little battery-powered fan to cool the back seat.

But that afternoon in Vence we had not been back ten minutes from the pool and still sat in our bathing suits when the English girl herself appeared. A glance at her face told me that something heavy was in the air. Such an ominous expression reminded me of a scene from my childhood. On hot summer days in Tulsa my mother would send me across vacant lots with an empty milk bottle to get refilled with root beer at the pharmacy soda fountain. On a fateful afternoon in July, the pharmacist, after handing me down the refilled bottle, hesitated, but then dutifully delivered a note. "Give this to your mother," he said, and within the hour the floodgates of her weeping changed our world forever. My father had abandoned us.

The note the English girl delivered took on the same presumed finality. She spoke to me with a concentration that ruled out her looking at both of us. "I think you perhaps do not understand," she said. "I think you should come now. The message came through the embassy. They had to find you here."

Then it would not be trivial. It could not be trivial. I looked more closely at the note. It said simply to call that number.

As we were about to follow the girl up the path, I said, "Wait. We have to take a minute and collect ourselves, prepare ourselves."

"You're afraid it's the children," Judy said.

"It could be any one of them," I said. "Let's just hope..."

We trudged up the path through grape terraces and trellises. The Countess was upstairs in bed, and the girl told us to go on up, that's where the telephone was.

No, that was not the case. Memory plays with us. The telephone was downstairs, and the girl helped me dial the number in Minnesota. I saw the Countess only a few minutes later, because she heard my outcry of grief and wanted to offer comfort. A second telephone was by her bed, but it was not the one in my hand.

The pain struck as if a sword had cut me down the middle with the precision of a samurai's chop. My outcry was an involuntary spasm of shock.

"What happened?" I managed.

"We're not sure," Sam's mother said. "Somehow, he was struck by a train."

Sam, gone, struck by a train. I could not believe it, but knew I had to say something. This was his mother on the phone, and she needed some comfort. I said, stupidly, to this voice that was his mother's, "Now he will never be a part of the evil!"

I would stop short of leaping into the open grave, but my grief in the days ahead would be unseemly. Tears would flow down my face in the Nice airport and on the Air France plane to London, then on the Northwest flight to Minneapolis. I accepted exploitation I'd have fought had my strength been intact. The airlines refused to honor the return tickets we already possessed for a few weeks later. We had to pay outrageously to board an underbooked flight.

No matter. My son was dead. What did money matter?

A Chinese philosopher said that one grieves "for a wife three months, for a son one year," but he may have had other sons.

It still seems like disloyalty if even a small share of the grief with its incessant self-blame is missing for an hour or so. I have many times convicted myself of my son's death, though it has been persuasively argued to me that my guilt is as irrational as that of the Hiroshima father who blamed himself for his son's death when the atomic bomb fell. The father had promised to repair the boy's sandals and had he done so, he explained, the boy could have outrun the bomb. Robert Jay Lifton tells of this in his book on survivor guilt.

"If your son had been struck by lightning, you'd have blamed yourself," a psychiatrist told me. But that was simple logic, not the other kind, the kind experienced by two-year-olds and the grieving of any age.

"Of course," I agreed, with no irony, "because if I had done something else he wouldn't have been in the path of that lightning." I was thinking of the phone booth I had passed daily in the month before his death, and how I had resisted the urge to call and invite him to take a trip to France. Had I made that call, would he not still be alive? On and on it goes. What if? If I had...! If only...!

These many years later, Sam's loss is still an affliction. At least, at our last parting I had reminded him never to forget that I loved him and had called him back for a second abrazo.

"I know, Dad," he said then. I remembered that his very first words—as he toddled around the tile floor of our apartment in Spain reaching for the knob of a cupboard—had been "Help me." But now I couldn't.

A Sestina for My Son

Adrienne Hernandez

The moist earth beckons, the roots
of trees secure my feet.
My body is cold as the stone
bench in the woods,
where you sit in silence,
ready to read to me as promised.

Azaleas burst forth with promise.
Ideas take root.
Death is so much more than silence.
Though I lie many feet
below, I feel the texture of your words,
multifaceted, smooth as stone.

You pause to touch the headstone,
you, who hold the greatest promise.
I consider the content of your words,
their resonance, their roots.
Dogwood petals at your feet,
you close your eyes to hear the silence.

You read more, no longer silent,
from a treasured text, the words fall like stones,
of heroes and forces they must defeat,
to uphold the truth, keep the promise,
overcome obstacles, take alternate routes.
Enraptured, I cling to each word.

The reading ends, no more words.
You sit near me in silence.
Time to leave, to uproot,
you touch the stone.
To return, you promise,
though finding the time is no small feat.

Stretching your legs, you flex your feet.
Bid *au revoir* without the words.
Knowing you will keep your promise,
I wait, ensconced in silence,
praying for you on a rosary of stones,
pebbles, and tangled roots.

Wordless

Lena V. Roach

That day you hurried down
Into the deepest part of the valley
To walk with me
Where storm clouds hung
In blinding shades of dark.

You opened your mouth to speak,
But, like mine,
Your lips were captive
To an unrelenting silence.

And yet, I heard
Every word you didn't say.

You looked into my eyes,
Held my hand
That I might feel
The beat of your heart
In synchrony with mine,
Decoding phrases
Of consolation
In a language
Too tender for words.

        Now comes that appointed hour
        When we must say goodbye,
        That promise-word,
        Like goodday or goodnight,
        Preparing the heart
        For tomorrow's hello.

Angela

Christy Wise

I've had people die who were close to me. I've had relatives and long-time pets die. But, somehow, when Angela Mills died, even though we'd met only a few times, I was crushed. Her death was sudden and mysterious. She was twenty-eight years old.

She'd moved back to California from Washington, D.C., where we met, and was driving up Highway 5 through the valley northeast of Los Angeles when she contracted equine encephalitis, what they call horse fever, presumably from driving through farmlands, but no one ever really explained it. She died after being in intensive care for five days.

Angela was tall and muscular with straight blonde hair. She was warm, enthusiastic, frustrated by her job as a receptionist in a congressman's office, and troubled about her future. Her relationship with her boyfriend, who lived in Boston, was on-again, off-again, and they couldn't resolve where to live. Her adventuresome spirit captivated me. She spoke about getting a job as a sailing instructor in Annapolis and how much she wanted to be outside rather than in an office. I could picture her on a sailboat, inspiring others with her vigor.

After our mutual friends left town, we met a couple of times in the Longworth House Office Building corridor to talk or to have lunch in the cafeteria. She was disillusioned by her boss's arrogance, and uncomfortable with his conservative stands on several issues. I, too, struggled with the stress of working on the Hill, usually seven days a week for long hours. My boss was a taskmaster. Whenever anything went wrong, the staff member who was in close proximity was to blame. As his press secretary, that often was me.

For my work, I traveled frequently and kept up with friends sporadically. New acquaintances were often lost altogether. So I was delighted when, a few months after we met, Angela invited me to a party at her house. I looked forward to meeting some new people and envisioned they would all be as interesting as Angela. Maybe this would be the magic catalyst I was looking for to change my life.

But I drank heavily at the party and was hungover the next morning, though the pain of the hangover was minimal compared to the anguish I felt over having made a spectacle of myself the night before, especially when I'd so wanted to show my better self to new acquaintances. I was sick of living the way I was: working hard, drinking hard, isolated from people and hating myself. I dragged myself into the shower and off to work, and by mid-morning felt just barely human again. I took a break from my work to get a cup of coffee and, as I passed a pay phone, surprised myself by stepping inside and calling AA.

That was the start of my much-needed recovery from drinking, drug-using, and living irresponsibly. I associated Angela with that change.

While I was in the midst of those first few raw months of my recovery, Angela moved back to California, and we didn't stay in touch, which didn't really surprise me. We were casual acquaintances. I never knew more than superficially what troubled her inside, though I sensed her struggle, just as she didn't know the details of my own distress, though it probably became apparent at her party. But I liked her a great deal and figured that our paths would cross again someday.

So I was stunned a year later when I heard about her death. I didn't cry, but thought about her constantly for days. I imagined her at the wheel of her car, cruising fast along the long, straight freeway, windows down as she drove through the hot valley sun, blonde hair blowing in the wind. If she'd kept the windows up, would she have escaped the fever that killed her?

I read about the disease, trying to understand it. Western equine encephalitis, found mostly in the plains regions of the western and central United States, is a virus spread to horses and humans by infected mosquitoes. People with severe reactions can have high, sudden fever, headache, nausea, and vomiting. Within two to four days, the illness may progress into disorientation, seizures, and coma. There is no treatment for western equine encephalitis. Fewer than five cases are reported each year.

I could see her in the hospital, surrounded by white sheets and nurses and doctors, with tubes and possibly an oxygen tent. For weeks, I carried with me alternating images of her in intensive care or cruising happily through the San Joaquin Valley.

I asked myself all the questions I'd ever asked about death, and several about Angela's life. Had she worked out her troubles with her boyfriend and her career? What was her return to California like? Did she feel more settled? Had she spent any time sailing or living near the water?

Even though her death wouldn't change my day-to-day existence, I mourned the loss of her presence on this earth. I was now married, sober, and had a new job. It didn't seem fair that her life had ended when mine was just starting over. In some very real way, I connected her to my beginning and wished I could share that with her.

In Memoriam

Anne Whitlock

Jim died last week. For twenty years we lived
our lives, two neighbors bordered by a fence,
his canyon civilized, a tiered expanse
of ice plant sprinkled with geraniums
and trim and proper trees, my canyon dense
with lemon berry, sumac and brush oak.

On sunny days we gardened, talked awhile
and all those years Jim fruitlessly opposed
my anti-war, my anti-military stance,
my careless kitchen door that hosted hungry
skunks, and while we talked, the summer ants
marched with immunity across my yard,
in steady lines, directly into his;
my crabgrass burrowed underneath the fence,
attacked his tender new tomato plants;
my giant eucalyptus tossed and swayed
above the rooftop like a ripe grenade.
He cleared for sun; I planted for shade.

Later, his heart failing, he hired Jose
who worked like a soldier, dragging heavy bags
like bodies across the yard, and looking back,
Jim talked about the war. As a young Marine
he cleared an island somewhere across the sea
where Japanese poured out of tunnels and holes
as thick as ink, unstoppable as ants.
In jungle heat, sweat pouring down like rain,
he led his men through burning fields of cane.
Half a century passed. Watching the evening
news, he saw his country go to seed—
its sacred soil, planted with the bones
of heros, overrun by gangs and thieves.

Jim died last week. It rained and rained for days.
The canyon lay in state, draped in sheets

of gray. I watched the eucalyptus sway.
Summer with all her wealth will come again.
The bottle brush will paint the walkway red.
Ants will ink black lines across the porch.
And high above the hill, my giant tree,
dumping branches and leaves and shedding its skin
like a desert snake, will ride the summer wind.

Aftermath of a Hero

Annette Stovall

Arthur had been home, now, since June, 2007 and was amazed how the land had suffered and still was suffering. In places, the earth looked so downright crusty that he wondered when the rain would gush enough. Still, he was happy to be home, where his hopes and purpose for living were as firm as his renown.

Everywhere in town, people recognized him. This was easy in a small town like Statonville, Utah, where everyone knew each other's business. So, anywhere he went, people would praise and applaud his army courage, knowing that he had won a purple heart. Even in the little clothing shop he and his younger brother stopped in to browse through items—some on racks, some stacked on tables—there, too, it was no surprise when store owner Mrs. Gilligan couldn't help but remark, "Such a brave young fellow you be."

"I was only doing my duty, same as any soldier would have," he replied.

"But it wot not just any soldier who subdued one hundred men, thirty of whom were brought to prison camp," she returned.

"True, but I had plenty backup supporting me. I was just the one who ran out in front of my comrades," he said.

Arthur's twelve-year-old brother, Dave, who was fed up with hearing his brother all the time being lauded, said, "Yeah, anybody could shoot like that. Hada been me there, I would've shot down more'n seventy, myself."

Arthur and Mrs. Gilligan laughed. Almost immediately, Arthur flashed back on how he lost his leg, which was badly shattered during that heroic combat.

After browsing around a while, the brothers started to leave the shop. Mrs. Gilligan called to Arthur before coming over to pin onto his tee shirt a red button that said "Our Hero." Arthur thanked her and, with Dave, limped through the door on his prosthesis.

Weeks later, a cooler Arthur, reflecting, was glad for the cool spell that eased up a scorching dry spell in the pouring down drenching received the night before. Dave abruptly burst in the house. He could hardly wait to spill all to his brave big brother, since both parents were at work, and there was no one else to tell.

"Guess what?" he said. "Walking home from school, I saw a kind old lady slip and fall into a mud puddle left over from last night. Soon as I seen her down, I rushed to her side and, after I helped her up, she remarked she had never seen anyone so eager to run in haste just to help an old lady. With that, she thanked me and gave me this good luck coin." Dave held up the shimmering coin.

Arthur said it sure was gleaming a coppery blaze, enough to blind his eyes. "Good for you. Now there are two heroes in the family!" said Arthur.

That evening, while Mamma was mending Dave's socks, and Poppa was doing nothing special, Arthur decided to spring on them his plan to look for a job. After it was so stated, Mamma was first to remark that she thought it was too soon for her first-born son to start working. She had rather he'd buy some nice clothes, have fun on the town, and relax for a spell.

Then Poppa, in his southern accent, exclaimed, "Lat a boy do like he wonts to. He ain't no dat-gum baby anymore, and he ken drive my car; I sho as corn husks won't mine."

Arthur began to ruminate momentarily on the saying, that must be true, that you can't unaccustom the south from a man, whichever location he moved to. But he knew Poppa was right. Ever since he could remember, Mamma had doted on him or underestimated things he did, and she seldom blundered a chance to make decisions for him. Now, here he was a grown man, who had served in the army for two years and received an honorable discharge. He loved his Mamma right enough, but at age twenty-three, after serving in that atrocious world of savage combat, he felt he had earned the right to make his own decisions.

Arthur had been at home, now, for four months and had had all he could stand of sitting around the house or going for the weekly walk or engaging in yard work at home. By now, he had his whole heart and mentality set in looking for a job.

The first place he drove Poppa's car for an interview was a paper factory, where, as he walked inside the wood-paneled office, he immediately saw the quick-gazing supervisor notice he had a limp. "Don't worry about the limp," Arthur said. "I can work just as hard as any man. Soon as I become more facilitated with my prosthesis, I won't even have the limp."

The super, looking dumbfounded, said he was afraid Arthur didn't understand.

Hell, what was there to understand? thought Arthur.

The super went on to carefully explain that, with this job, he'd be standing on his feet a lot and have lanes of paperwork to stack. He couldn't imagine that for Arthur. "Do you have a resume?" he asked.

Arthur started to answer him with words he envisioned Poppa would say: "No, I ain't got one. If I had one I'd damn well show it." Instead he said, "No, sir," while in his heart he shouted, "I'm a man, same as you are." He could barely hear the super say, next, he could only hire people with a resume. So a bewildered Arthur left and headed next for a truck station.

On his way there, he passed the once admirable lake and felt sorrowful to see it now carved in dehydrated mud. Quiet memories flooded back of him fishing there many times with Poppa. The lake was healthy looking, then, and brimming with tiny, greenish waves. Would science at all remedy the water shortage? He wondered when and how.

The super who ran the truck station was even harder to convince that he could handle the job. He wasn't positive how long Arthur would last, driving a truck nearly every day. He felt his prosthesis would get in the way of completing the job precisely in time allotted.

Arthur could not fathom where to turn next. He only knew he wasn't ready to call it quits, not until he received some sort of confirmation, verbal or written. He drove past some men constructing a three-story building and felt he could do some simple task there, like help unload the wood, mix concrete, tote water, just something. He stopped the car, got out, and asked for the supervisor. After someone called for the boss, Arthur began to have second thoughts after meeting so many other supervisors shallow of heart. He had already been to as many as five work facilities and was, by now, on the verge of losing his cool. Didn't anybody have empathy for the handicapped these days? he thought. He really didn't want pity, but any emotion was better than what disturbed him about how unaffected those supers were, how they looked dumbfounded at his request for work, how they showed no right emotion. After all, other handicapped people had gotten jobs. He tried to keep his patience, since this was only his first day out.

The five minutes felt like fifteen to Arthur. The super came, arm in a sling, reminding Arthur of his handicap. He gave his name as John Benton, to which Arthur replied, "Arthur Clayburn." He asked the super for a job, explaining he didn't mean climbing lofty ladders or endangering himself on framework's ledger.

The super thought a minute before saying "Oh, yeah, believe I do have something. You can help with painting the rooms. They're already done with building on one story. Leave your telephone number. I'll keep you in mind for who to call soon."

Atthur said thanks and left his number. His heart pounding in his throat, he went away thinking, yes, yes! Finally, someone cares, someone has humility enough to hire a person with a handicap.

The Ballad of a Soldier

Emily Keeler

> "*Peek-a-boo!*" *say little Olaf.*
> "*Yu can't find me. Ay ban hid.*"
> *Den ay used to look all over*
> *For my little blue-eyed kid.*

> —William F. Kirk, *The Norsk Nightingale*

Little Chuck's favorite hiding place was the cubbyhole over the pedal of the Singer sewing machine, behind the chair with mother's sweater hanging on the back. Sometimes he jumped out from behind the bedroom door or hid under the kitchen table at dinnertime.

Busy as a little squirrel, he shook his mother's powder down the hot air furnace, guaranteeing fallout for the winter; he swabbed the bathroom walls with the toilet brush and filled his pockets with angleworms. You'll never guess why he called his mother "No No".

When the doctor asked at the door, "Where is your mother, young man?" he promptly replied, "She's in the bathroom, sittin' down." For Christmas he wanted a manure spreader and for his birthday a cake made entirely of chocolate frosting.

I was his little sister. My first day at school I spotted him in the hall, and I was so happy to see someone I knew, I ran up and hugged him. He knocked me down. To prove they were not sissies, he and his buddies had contests to see who could spit the farthest across the road.

He woke me early one morning. "Here Tiny, here Tiny." Holding up his pajama bottoms with one hand, he spread out oats with the other, enticing the cow into the corral. Together we laughed at her newborn calf, all wet and wobbly on its legs; he showed me how he taught the calf to drink from the pail, and I stuck my thumb in the milk and let the calf suck. That calf won a ribbon at the fair.

He attempted once to read to me. Every time I talked or asked a question, he started all over again at the beginning, never finishing the story. In the summer we played kick the can, in the winter Monopoly, while we filled up on popcorn and apples. In Chinese Checkers, he showed me a series of moves, and I won every time.

Our family regularly sat together at the Community Church. On Children's Day, Chuck's sides shook, and he let out squeals impossible to hold in. A kid, rattling off the books in the Bible, solemnly recited, "Genesis, Exodus, Little Bitty Cuss, Numbers, Deuteronomy..." We endured the special music by a howling contralto, hoping that a fly would buzz right into her Venus flytrap's mouth. At the end of services he was out the side door before the preacher could say the benediction.

His mother paid him to go to Bible School, where they did girl stuff like coloring and pasting. He could make crates: with nails lined up between his teeth, with a tap and a bang, and a turn of the slats, the boxes took shape; with pieces of scrap wood, he made a bed for my cat and her kittens.

He earned the money for his bicycle by squeezing cull apples with an old wooden press. The teetotaling preacher said it was the best cider he had ever drunk. We never told him how long it had aged. Later, against Dad's wishes, Chuck took a job delivering papers in order to have some spending money. The morning of the first deep snow, Dad got up at five and drove him on his route.

In the summer, Chuck staked out the cow and hitched up the horse and cultivator, and I sometimes followed with my cat. He laughed when the horse quickened its pace, thinking it was headed for the barn. Then he snapped the reins, and boy and horse trudged up another row.

After he and his cousin, Gordon, built a tree house, Chuck's uncle offered them an ice cream cone if they would take it down. They shook their heads, "Ain't worth it." Chuck often climbed the locust trees high above the house, knowing which limbs would crack and which would bend.

In the summer, Dad brought tomatoes, berries, and cantaloupe to the commission house. My three brothers and I rode in the back of the truck, feeling the wind rush in our faces. When it rained we sat on the porch and counted the freight cars churning beyond the corn field, dreaming of taking a train to visit our grandmother, who had a rooming house in Chicago.

One night during dinner, Chuck was unusually quiet. He finally told us what he had seen that afternoon—how a neighbor shot a pig, but missed between the eyes. The pig ran screaming round and round the pen. Several months later, out back by the stump, where the chickens were killed, Dad handed Chuck the ax. He struggled, but could not bring himself to chop off the chicken's head.

When Chuck was fourteen, Mother was bedridden for three years with tuberculosis. It was his job to help her to the bathroom and later to empty the bed pan. I can still hear his sweet voice from the porch, before she died, "Don't cry, mother, you'll get well. Honest you will."

Adolescence was a painful time for Chuck: he plastered down his hair with water, only to find it a mass of curls when he arrived at school; had pimples on his face and Charles Atlas magazines hidden in his room; his overalls hung loosely below his waist; the cuffs were frayed, his shoes untied; he got "D's" in midterm and notes from the teachers were mailed home; then there were stern lectures and some reluctant homework turned in, and he would end up with "C's". He ranked second highest in the achievement tests. Surprised, the school rechecked his scores, finding he excelled in math, science, and history, but did poorly in English.

Chuck was often late in getting ready. One Sunday morning while we waited in the car for him, he finally came down the back steps, shirt in one hand, tie in the other. In desperation, Dad slowly backed out the car, shouting, "Maybe the army will make a man out of you." Left behind, Chuck stood with tears running down his face.

At noon one day he sauntered over with Tony, a "Wop kid" from school, to a train that had stopped. War prisoners jogged back and forth for an exercise break. When Tony spoke his mother's language, a prisoner no older than Chuck broke into tears, hearing his native tongue. Boys who knelt down during Mass, here and over there, were sent out to kill each other.

After high school graduation, Chuck was drafted into the army, sent to boot camp, and then assigned to specialized math classes in New York. Suddenly, his whole class was notified they were being shipped over. He had nine days leave, so Dad sent him money for a ticket to come home. Six days he spent traveling and three days we ate leisurely meals at the kitchen table. No longer father and son, they talked as man and man. He told about seeing Grandma, how he had knocked on her door, pretending he wanted to rent a room, then laughed and told her he was Fred's son. He talked excitedly about the math classes, saying he never worked so hard in his life. He had found himself.

Months went by: his letters stopped coming. One day in November, a small yellow piece of paper arrived at the front door—"The War Department regrets to inform you…" Neighbors and friends came and sat in the living room. His Sunday school teacher walked two and a half miles across the valley. She took my father's hand—was too choked up to speak. The minister's wife squeezed my hand and benignly smiled, "God's will be done." Inside of me, a silent scream.

When Chuck heard that shrieking artillery, those piercing shells, did he shriek like that pig, running round and round the pen? Was there anyone to comfort him, as in that newspaper photo of a soldier kneeling beside his wounded buddy? It took a long time for me to fall asleep that night.

Armies do make men out of boys: dead men.

I was awakened by shouting from Dad's room; I found him on his knees pounding the bed, cursing and sobbing. I knelt and put my arm around him.

In the morning, from the kitchen window, I saw my father in the distance, plowing the field, getting it ready for spring planting.

Voices

A. G. Deutscher

> "...*You take a created day*
> *and you slip it into the archive of life*
> *where all our lived out days*
> *are lying together...*"
> —Jacob Glastein, "The Sunset Prayer"

Who was to tell him otherwise
that he would spend his life elsewhere
yet never leave this place
etched as it was, a deep blue tattoo
stained into his heart.

Today, revisiting the old farmstead,
he questions his return. So many
things changed...the barn ravaged,
its hayloft doors split, dangling,
while the house—dressed in its cloth
of emptiness—stares mutely
across the scroll of Kansas,
across fallow acres once cushioned
with golden wheatheads.

Still...
certain things remain unchanged:
the intense dome of sky above,
summer winds scuttling the
frame house corners, tree limbs,
the same voices in the air around him
(does he imagine them?)
voices that sing, call, shout, proclaim.

It was more than six decades
ago he once lived here;
his father gone to war, his
dark-haired mother seeking refuge
with her husband's parents.

That he thought them unacceptably
old still troubles him.

Especially the Grandmother
who—well he remembers—
milked cows, butchered hogs
turned the garden by hand,
her booted foot on the spade.
The Grandmother, who scrubbed
clothes on a washboard
in cellar tubs, knew things he didn't.
Never would.

That one day
when she climbed the cellar stairs,
a basket of damp clothes
balanced on her hip,
he had opened the kitchen door,
started down.
They met half way.
She, face flushed, country apron
damp across the breasts,
he—a boy so small he could not
yet tie his shoes.
"Wait," she cried out,
"Stop Jonathan. Stop
right where you are."

He obeyed,
clung to the right stair rail.
Her hand gripped the left.
"Listen," she whispered
and lowered the heavy basket
to the step before her.
"Do you hear it?"
Fingers spread, her hand
flew across her mouth.
"Do you hear that Jonathan?"

Frightened
he stared at the stair rails,

saw the left one shudder.
"Something has happened,"
she finally gasped
and began to weep.
"Oh Jonathan something terrible and sad."

Family history records that this
Grandmother's son
did not return from the War.
Not a hint of him.
Not even dog tags.
"A crash," the communiqué read,
"Somewhere over Germany.
Wreckage never found."

Weeks later, when
a marker was placed on the grounds
of the farm, the Grandmother
declared "He was born here.
Should be remembered here."
And now, after these many decades,
he hopes to find this marker.
But why? he wonders. Why?

The afternoon ripens.
He trudges a slight rise of land
beyond the remembered garden
pushing aside dried grass
with his own booted foot.
Wind buffets him—raises his shirt collar
the back hair of his neck.
Whatever the force—there on the
cellar steps half a century ago—
now spills into his ears the
never forgotten words of yesterday
"*He was born here,
he should be remembered here.*"

At last he knows!
And with this knowing, a sweet cloak
of belonging enfolds him—leads him on.

He will find the marker, place
those old memories into the archive of life
maybe with an evening prayer.
Rest, he might say and bending
down, stroke the worn stone.
I am here now.
I remember you… I remember you.

I Don't Remember

Diana Griggs

How could I know she spent days battling shadows
that roamed the walls of our house

*my doll Clara needed to be dressed
taken out in her pram rocked and comforted.*

Maybe I didn't see her sitting on the bedroom floor
reading letters every word a sob

*Tabby the cat had kittens and I had to hide them
before the gardener drowned them in the tool shed.*

My brother and I never noticed how Evelyn the maid
chastised her at dinner for not eating her food

*We finished in haste after all I was Jane he was Tarzan
we needed to return to our tree house to battle savages.*

I don't remember her bandaged wrists raised to blow us kisses
through the window of a car driven away by our family Doctor

*I was too excited Evelyn was ironing my favorite dress
Daddy was coming home from the war.*

Dandelions for Breakfast

Joanna Wanderman

There was a magical swatch of time in my childhood, wedged between the bookends of this country's great Depression and my mother's, when I played in green fields with a leprechaun and ate dandelions for breakfast.

The happy chance of our meeting came about when my father took an extra job hauling malt to a brewery every Saturday morning to help support the plumbing business he had just opened—some said at the wrong time, and certainly wrong timing for my mother, who had to be hospitalized for the first of her many bouts with depression.

My father and I lived alone, and he had to take me with him on those Saturdays. We would leave the house while the street lights still spread their pale yellowish glow over the pavement, get into our old, ugly, borrowed truck and drive the early morning empty roads to East Los Angeles. Our first stop was a giant gray warehouse protected by growling gray dogs whose noisy barks roused idle workers who lazed on the loading dock, signaling them to get the 50-pound jute bags of hops and malt hoisted onto our truck. Thirty minutes later, we were on the highway again, the flimsy, wooden side slats of our heavily loaded truck swaying precariously back and forth to the rhythm of the potholes. I was six years old, without a mother to care for me; I wore overalls, high top shoes, a torn shirt, and a clipped, boy-child haircut; I smelled of beer and smoke from the Bull Durham cigarettes my father rolled and puffed incessantly; I was in heaven.

After crossing the bridge that spanned the Los Angeles River, we headed even farther east to the abandoned train yards, where my father picked up his helper. "Old trains are like old elephants," he said as we approached the dilapidated cluster of derelict railroad cars, "and this is where they come to die." I believed him then, but now I know it was just a place where leprechauns hung out until it was time for them to reveal themselves.

He stood on the corner waiting for my father to pull up. He was big for a leprechaun, with no pointy shoes, no cap on his wild, white hair that curled like seafoam down over his forehead and into bursts of bushy brows shading sprightly blue eyes. The rest of his face was hidden by a soft, white beard that left only his nose visible, and his glistening cheeks of rose.

"I'm Thomas Aloysius Murphy," he announced himself, as he climbed into the truck and held out one small, square hand adorned with a big ruby ring. "And you must be Ed's little girl. How do you like my house?" He pointed to one of the boxcars that stood in a weed patch of yellow flowers. "That's where I live, and every morning I get to eat dandelions for breakfast."

The truck cab was getting crowded now with the three of us, so the second best Saturday part of my day began when I got to sit in the back with the load of malt and hops. Huddled in among the coarse hemp bags that smelled better than most people and caressed me like giant warm puppies, I was the extra 50-pound gunny sack. I was family!

Afterwards, we all walked through the fields surrounding the brewery, and Mr. Murphy showed me how to find the ripest, yellowest, tastiest dandelions. Every so often, he would slip a handful into the bib pocket of his overalls and, once, even into my hair.

"You'll have blonde curls again just as soon as your mother comes home," he promised.

He didn't talk much. He whistled. "Easter Parade"! "Easter Parade" in the summer, at Christmas, on the Fourth of July, and every time I cried, telling him I was afraid my mother would not be home for Easter or ever again.

"Don't go borrowin' trouble," he'd say, and then, lapsing into the lilt of his leprechaun brogue, he would add, "You'll bid the d'vil good mornin' when you meet him."

My mother did come home soon afterwards, and my brewery days were replaced with Saturday morning catechism classes. Not long after, my father's brewery job was also replaced with a new technology, but he invited Mr. Murphy to come work and live with us in our home. This was even better than our Saturday romps, and I spent every morning going with him into the fields next to my father's store, looking for dandelions and learning how to whistle.

It wasn't long before F.D.R. kept his promise and put a chicken into our pot. Then two cars began appearing in every garage and, most important to my father's business, two bathrooms materialized in all the new homes being built, which put even more chicken into our pot.

Mr. Murphy lived with us for sixteen years. I was already working and living on my own the morning my father called to tell me Mr. Murphy had died.

"He didn't come down for breakfast this morning," my father said. "When I went up to his room, he was still in bed, a half cup of dandelion-root tea on his bedside table next to a roll of twenty dollar bills bound with a rubber band. In his hand, the one that wore the red ruby ring, he held a gold shamrock."

Will Your Destruction Merge with Another Voice and Another Light?

[Title after Neruda]

Lucille Gang Shulklapper

In the dance of her mind her body curves
toward her husband, his name now forgotten,
her memory music starts, somehow preserves
the airy tunes as though wrapped in cotton,
she's Ginger Rogers, and he's Fred Astaire,
waltzing her through waves of white caps bobbing,
past the legless man slumped in his wheelchair,
past the shrilling phones, the muffled sobbing.

Now, she can mouth gibberish, though her words
drown in violins, sink tipsy on floors
of waxed recall, like songs of mocking birds
from the murmured trees, in the gray outdoors.

one two three, one two three, Alzheimer's beat
hammers her toes on her paled shoeless feet.

Changeling

Joan T. Doran

My mother's knitting—
wooly loops, looming holes,
opening for two heads,
three arms, five feet long—
flows through a mind now knotted, too,
with webs and holes,
as this shapeless travesty unreels
onto the floor beside her chair

where not too long ago she knit
straight rows and patterns,
sleeves neat with ribbed edging,
opening for just one head,
booties for each infant on the block,
sweaters in succession for each grandchild:
mint green, shell pink, crayon red,
boldly striped and intricate
with fine designs or cabled heft,
Fair Isles for young ladies,
Icelandic beauties for their moms,
doll wardrobes for the church bazaar,
and several shy proffers that surprised her
with blue ribbons at the Dixie Fair.

I'm standing close beside her now,
bemused before my own life's
knots and tangles, remembering
how she kept us warm, remembering
how to smile, remembering how
she never let us see her cry.

Nails

Rita Ries

In the forties, Mother was in her thirties,
looked like Norma Shearer, they said.
My only formal picture shows
her lovely twenties' finger wave hairdo.
Later I remember an ultra-short chic bob,
which prompted many compliments.
She loved parties, she loved pretty clothes
and she wore artificial nails.

Mother sold women's clothing
in Denver's finest department store,
Daniels and Fisher.
Openly proud of her nails, she admitted
flashing them as she displayed
a blouse or dress or sweater.
Caring for them was a major event
when cracked or broken or snapped off.
The new nails had to be carefully cut,
shaped, filed to smoothness, then glued
over her short, ragged nails.
Nail polish and lipstick always matched,
usually bright red.

A Catholic divorcée and two daughters,
living back with her parents—
our brother with Daddy and his mother.
Then for two years or so, we three
had a studio apartment with a Murphy bed,
away from her domineering mother.
Unable to handle my fourteen-year-old sister,
Mother let her go to Daddy. Soon we two
were back at my maternal grandparents.

Life long emotional instability
led to another nervous breakdown,
a mental institution, shock treatments.

Afterwards jobs slipped away,
a bottle her way of coping in a tiny apartment.
Later when I visited my Mother
in a psychiatric nursing home,
she was in bed most of the time.
Her nails were just not strong enough.

Shadowsmith

Neal Wilgus

Shadows never scare me
    any more.
They never twist your arm
    behind your back
or slam your bleeding face
    against the wall.

Shadows were a menace
    as a kid
when you woke up late at night
    and saw them move.
You held your breath and listened
    to your heart
but in the morning they were gone
    and you could smile.

But now the shadows scurry
    'cross the wall
fleeing as the armies of the light
    come moving in.
Blinded by the glare you
    close your eyes
but somehow that just doesn't
    keep it out.

The voices and the threats
    don't ever stop—
they never never never
    let you sleep.
They know you'll always tell them
    what they want
but you never ever know
    just what that is…

No,
    shadows never scare me
any more.

Night Terrors

Kathleen Elliott Gilroy

I. What Science Verifies

Night terrors can happen even to infants, who, not fully awake nor sheltered by sleep, sob and wail as if being tortured. They are inconsolable. They cannot instantly be brought into the recognition of comforting arms, familiar scents, soft soothing sounds. What have they to fear, I wonder? Is it the subconscious journey of leaving the womb, entering this loud, light-stricken world full of noise? Is there a haunting of voices they heard through the skin of their mother, the blood velvet coating of the uterus? The murmur of the enveloping water sac?

Neuroscientists say memories are now known, having been researched and documented, as far back as to the cellular level of the prenatal stage. Then again, are night terrors the distant, far distant memory of a previous life? The cry for those who are not on this new path with them, as I and many others believe to be possible? These infants and toddlers will not remember any of these early night terrors, though, unless they are neglected, battered, or traumatized by even non-preventable medical situations. Then the memory weaves itself into the essence of being, so specifics may not be recalled full force, but the substance will leave its own mark, its perpetual linkages throughout life.

II: Lucid Dreaming

I have practiced lucid dreaming for years. Learned to insert my higher, non-sleeping consciousness into the dreams and, literally, say in the dream: *this is only a dream*, or *I am in charge*, or *get out of this dream*. Sometimes, I have heard myself ask for a different dream venue. Yet experience in lucid dreaming and even meditation prior to sleep do not always help keep ghosts of the past at bay. Like infants, I can not always explain the workings of my mind, nor the dreams that sometimes slip through my defenses. And so it was that the man who had stalked me for so long in years past gained entrance into a night terror I had four years ago, one that is still vivid in my mind.

III: The Night Terror/After Death Communication

Like an onstage play, he was at center stage, wearing the familiar deep blue jacket he had worn so often on nights that he stalked me and my closest friends. In the dream, he still wore the familiar dark sunglasses that concealed his dark, hazel-colored eyes. His dark brown hair, almost a shade of black, shone in the pool of light in which he stood.

Off to the right of the dreamscape stage, in a broken lineup, were four of the many women he had been with during the years of our marriage. All of them, wearing bright clothing that gleamed from the light he was in, shifted themselves from foot to foot, gestured, smiled toward him. I had not entered the dreamscape yet, but was aware of the women wanting to dance again, to dine, to be chosen as the one with whom he would dance magnificently, with whom he would get drunk and lusty. Whatever magnetic force had pulled us two together, it was not drinking or carousing all hours. Yet part of it had been his skill at dancing: the smooth, effortless movement in his feet, his legs, his torso, his arms and hands moving in natural unison with his partner. It was also his deep baritone voice, his façade of being ready to settle down. He had meant, of course, that only I would be settled, kept at home waiting for him. To rise from the bed and cook meals for him and his friends, no matter what hour of the night.

Now, here they were in my dream. I entered the set, stopping short of center stage. I kept my eyes moving from him to them, and my off-stage voice, the lucid mind part, said aloud, "I'm out of this dream! We are no longer together. You can stay with them."

I backed almost out of sight, not turning my back on them, but hurrying to leave the dream they wanted to be in, a dream he controlled. As I stepped backward, he said with authority, but in no haste, "Lasso her ankles and bring her back."

A long, looping rope was lifted by the women, hefted into the air, and swung towards my body. There was a whupp, whupping sound as the rope bit the air. My feet, when I finally turned to run, felt heavy, as if they were being sucked at by muck hidden under a surging river. I struggled, urgent in my lucid mind state to exit the drama laid out.

I came partially awake in that place of terror where there is no waking, nor is there deep sleep. A howling escaped my lips. My physical body responded, as well as the dream persona. In the dream, my legs scrambled to be free of the rope that would drag me back to the man who was dead. The man who had, in real life, tracked me down several times, and had now re-entered my life through a dream I could not close down.

My dream persona fought to shake off the rope tightening around legs already tied together at knees, at calves, and at ankles. Hands clawed the ground, leaving wide-fingered scratch marks, while he stood in the background, stone-faced and vengeful.

While the dream persona fought with entanglement, my body, enacting the dream sequence, slid, head and shoulders first, off the edge of my narrow bed. I felt a strong impact to my right cheekbone as I hit the nightstand. Not able to come fully awake, I cascaded down the side of the nightstand in a vertical fall.

Pain expanded like target-hit marks from a shotgun. Swelling stretched my skin outward, as if an ostrich egg had fallen from an improbable nest and was ready to rip its way free. Even through all of this, I recognized the familiar head jarring jolt of another concussion.

Through the night darkness, and in severe pain, I at last realized my legs below the knees were still trapped in twisted covers of bedding. I eased them free gradually, holding my head with fingers splayed over my face. Disoriented, I lumbered awkwardly to my knees, still holding my head immobile, my eyes closed. I braced my shoulder against the wall for support and moved at a jerking gait, letting my feet move me into the hallway, into the kitchen, without opening my eyes. With one hand, I grabbed a tall glass from the cupboard, while the other hand still covered my face. I let crushed ice chips rumble up to the brim. Grabbed a kitchen towel, dropped ice into the center, folded it twice, and put it up to my right cheekbone. The packing gradually eased a small amount of the pain in my eye, as well as the entire right side of my face.

From past experience, I knew I would definitely have a black eye. But what of the cheekbone? It felt as if it had been sliced, as well as pummeled. I sat on the sofa in the dark, glad that no one else in the house had awakened.

I felt my husband's former words pelt me: "Stupid. Dumb shit." And the sentence he had said repeatedly: "That's what you get for leaving me."

I knew it had been a dream built on resifted past events, but I did not want to return to the bedroom. I also knew not to lie down. I needed to stay awake. I had to acknowledge I felt some residue of terror lingering in the room where it was only bedding that had trapped me. Only past memories of physical abuse had propelled me to run in the dream, to move so frantically in reality. He had not struck me now to create this injury. I had hit the nightstand while running, spilled myself along till I hit the full impact of the floor.

With daylight, I went to the doctor. Along with the injuries, I carried shame and embarrassment. How many times had I lied in the past to cover the secrets of my life? Now, in telling the truth, I bore the brunt of the lies. I had a major blood clot in the eye and the eye socket. I had chipped the cheekbone, cut through the skin causing a two-and-a-half-inch wound, and deeply bruised the whole side of my swollen face. All the way to the end of the jawbone. Over to the hairline and the start of the ear.

It would take over two months to heal. I needed antibiotics to prevent infection. During that time, the right side of my face needed on-going ice packs. The injured area went through a spectrum of colors that makeup could not conceal.

When the adult daughter he and I had given life to saw it, she exclaimed, "Oh, my God, Mom! What happened?"

The son her father and I had created, one year before her birth, lives in Wyoming. When she called him to let him know what I'd done and how I looked, he remarked, "So he got her again. Even from the grave."

I prefer to think night terrors caught me off guard. Who can fully explain them? I want to be in charge of my own well being, my life without him. Yet what control do I have when he can still assert such control over me, even in a dream? Even when I practice so well, most of the time, the strategy of lucid dreaming?

I think about this sporadically, bringing up positive cognitive thoughts to allay residues of the past. And, as I do so, my fingers sometimes move over the two-inch scar below my right eye. It is then that I also acknowledge the probability that After Death Communication may very well be a viable form of 'presence.'

Messages in the Wind

Peggy Joyce Starr

A cool breeze
Blew the curtain
Across my desk
Narrowly missed my
Fragile Buddhist figurines

I took this incident
As a sign: Be aware,
Be alert. Wisely protect
The unborn voice within.

Junk Mail, the Great Beyond

Marilyn Hochheiser

Since 1995, my deceased husband, Sid, continues to receive more mail than I.

Some ask if he would like to enroll in their life insurance plans. Others promote burial through "The Neptune Society."

I have to admit that one letter did make me want to sue for emotional distress. It stated Sid had won the sweepstakes he recently entered, but they needed him to verify his address and send a small fee to receive his prize, that could very well be cash. When I calmed down, I realized the letter was either a lie, or my idea of the afterlife was totally confused.

There isn't a month that goes by without Sid being offered new credit cards or opportunities to attend business seminars. On one day, he received both a health plan and 401(k) rollover information.

Thank goodness he has not yet been sent a letter inviting him to a singles group.

In my less-than-kind moments, I have considered putting on the envelopes "moved to Oak Tree Memorial Park," and including his plot number. But then I realized all the work that goes into the buying and selling of people's names and related data, and jobs are needed!

If I wasn't really concerned about others, I could truly complain, get signatures, pass a law, or do more than I have. Since September 11, I feel more than ever for the human condition.

I can now declare it an act of mercy that I read most of Sid's mail and can laugh at the irony of it all. In some strange fashion, Sid's presence is etched into my mailbox like an actor preserved on film.

They say "old cowboys never die," and neither do the dead in the world of promotion and advertising.

Messages Everywhere

Carole Kaliher

It's amazing to me when and where we receive messages. Most of mine seem to come in a written form. A message can come from our angels, our deceased loved ones, or perhaps our deity itself.

One Sunday, sitting in church, feeling lost and lonely after my husband's death, I wondered why I was even there. Feeling such pain made me feel as if God had deserted me. This particular Sunday, I chose to sit in a different place than usual. Our church, St. Martha's, was still in the mobile unit and using the adjoining patio, as well, for seating. The altar sat in front of sliding doors, enabling the people in both places to hear Mass.

In May, we have our Holy Communion classes. It's the custom for all of the First Communicants to make banners with their name after the saying: *Jesus loves*. I looked up, and the banner in front of me read, *Jesus loves Carole*. It's very unusual to see a young girl with the name of Carole, especially with my spelling, adding the "e" at the end. I had to fight the waves of tears that threatened after seeing that banner.

At different times, when feeling Jim's loss more heavily than others, I'd come across cards from him with meaningful thoughts expressed. His cards were always found when I needed them most. The notes encouraged using my strength.

The story about the night-light is worth telling. I wanted to put a night-light in our dining room. Jim blustered, "What on earth for?"

I answered, "When our grandkids sleep over, they'll have a light to see into the kitchen if they need a drink."

"Give it up. We don't need a light in the dining room."

"It seemed like a good idea to me."

"It isn't!"

"Okay, you win."

After Jim died, I thought, *I don't have to have Jim's okay for the night-light. I can put it anywhere I like. He left me, so I'll decide where it should go.* I plugged it in, and it jumped out of the plug and landed two feet away, under the dining room table. After staring at the light until I got my composure back, I picked it up and asked, "Can I have it in the kitchen?" It seemed that my husband still had strong feelings about putting one in the dining room. Plugging it in the kitchen outlet, I waited; it stayed there. "Okay, honey," I said, "I get the message."

His books falling out of his closet on me is another example. A friend tried to encourage me to take a tour to Ireland. "Carole, this will be a once in a lifetime trip. Please think about it." The books that fell down on me were books on Ireland.

One Christmas, Jim gave me a music box with a note inside stating, "I.O.U. the island of your choice." At the time, he was waiting for his lung transplant, so the trip seemed unlikely, but I thanked him for the thought. Through another unlikely scenario, when trying to remove his name from a loan we had taken out from our credit union, the representative found an insurance policy covering the amount of the loan. We had never qualified for these policies because of his existing medical condition. The policy absolved me of $20,000 worth of debt, and gave me a refund of the money I had paid in the two years after his death. It was a total of $7,000, enough for my trip and a down payment on a newer car, which I needed and had prayed for.

After paying for my trip, I realized that Ireland *was* the island of my choice. Jim fulfilled his promise four years later and two years after his death.

When my brother, Lloyd, died, I had the responsibility of dismantling his furnishings and clearing out his personal effects so I could sell his mobile home. One day, sitting in my family room, I got the impression of Lloyd walking through my front door and smiling at me, as he had done so many times before. I mentioned it to my psychic friend, and she said, "Lloyd is around you. He'll do three things to let you know he's there, so pay attention."

The next day, the tight blossoms in a large bouquet of lilies that I had received from a friend opened completely and all at the same time. They had all been closed when I went to bed, and were all open when I got up in the morning. I've never had a floral arrangement do that. Some blooms always stay closed longer than others.

I left for La Verne, started dismantling and packing Lloyd's china and, while lifting a place setting, found three hundred dollars. I said, "Oh, Lloyd, you thought you had no money." Under the money was a picture of him waving and smiling. That was the second thing; what would be the third? Later, in his room, I found a ring of his in turquoise with an Indian decoration that signified long life.

There have been so many other times when I'd pick up a newspaper or a religious periodical that would give me the best possible message for my circumstances and frame of mind. Encouragement from friends and relatives has sustained me at just the right time.

Another and most recent example of this came as I stood at the desk in my chiropractor's office in Glendora. I hadn't been in Glendora to see her in about a year, but I had to have an adjustment, and she's particularly good. I was looking at cards in a rolodex and read: "Don't judge God's love only by the times he answers your prayers to your satisfaction." I had just complained to my sister that I was tired of not receiving answers to my prayers.

Messages are everywhere; we just need to listen and heed the advice.

When a Gopher Walks Across the Road

Sheryl Holland

Note: "Gopher" is the southern expression for land turtle

or Spanish moss sways in the wind on oak branches
like children playing on swings, when orange blossoms dress
the night in frilly frocks, or bees buzz them during the day,
I am home again, another life, another land.

If I tell you *that* land is the Land of Sunshine, do you see
bikini beauties, condo-lined beaches and Disney World?
Think the Great Escape, sun-drenched golf links and lazy palms?
Sand so white, water so blue, you'd swear it wasn't real?

Or do you see folks who live in shacks where cockroaches
slip through cracks to the ground? Trucks with shotguns,
symbols of "Leave me alone or else"?
Lake-size pits of contaminating phosphates?

Do you see churches that will save your soul
from hell, or send it there forever, if you don't
believe their Jesus? Who'll pray for you, lay hands
on your head, garble babbles in languages no one knows?

The flat sands of pristine palmetto, home to bees
and honey I worked with Dad, are secret places now.
Hotels, motels, amusement parks—homogenized
America rules the land. Beaches erode with every

hurricane, Everglades die from chemicals. But
I can still buy salty boiled peanuts, smell pink azaleas
under live oak trees, taste hush puppies, grits and okra.
You see, I know the places to worship,
where ancient gophers celebrate the earth
and honeybees gorge themselves with sweet nectar.

A Miracle of Faith at the Bird Sanctuary

Mary R. Durfee

Trevor had a face full of freckles and dark tousled hair. This cute nine-year-old boy was a student in my third grade class. Shortly before school started, I had received a letter from his mother begging me to place Trevor in my class, as she was having behavior problems with him at home.

My class had two yearly projects that were especially popular with the students. One was a musical called "The Solid Gold Dancers"; the other, a papier-mâché project in which each student made a replica of the animal of their choice. Parents were invited to participate in both projects.

Trevor had no problem with the musical. He loved hamming it up. That was when he released a lot of his pent-up energy: dancing, singing, showing off—he loved it all. But he wanted no part of that papier-mâché project.

By this time, all the children had chosen their favorite animals, and any animal Trevor could think of was already taken.

"Trevor, how about that gopher tortoise that built her nest near our condo?" his mother suggested.

"Oh, nobody would like that," he replied glumly. "And, besides, it's too hard."

"No, it won't be hard, Trevor, and I'll help all I can. I have a good picture of one I took last winter."

And so it was that Trevor accepted the tortoise assignment reluctantly.

By Christmas vacation, Trevor's behavior had greatly improved. His school grades were better, and, with the help of his mother, the papier-mâché tortoise was coming along nicely. Once again, the family left for their yearly trip to Florida, and it made quite a difference in Trevor. While he was there, he learned all he could about gopher tortoises. He watched them as they laid their eggs, and even watched some of the nests as the hatchlings emerged from their eggs. He took notes: "…a flat-headed reptile, an endangered species, environment protected by law. Unlike other turtles, lives underground in warm sandy climate. Development prohibited where they habitate." How proud Trevor was, now, to think he had picked a creature so important to our environment!

Spring came. The papier-mâché animals were finished and on display for the whole school to view. "The Solid Gold Dancers" put on their musical performance in the auditorium for parents, friends, and all to enjoy. Television crews were present, and it was later aired on the local television station. The performance was a success, and, as you might expect, Trevor turned out to be a wonderful little boy. He could do no wrong—very smart, straight A's—a complete turnaround.

The class deserved a special award. I planned a trip for the students to go to the zoo in two weeks, and the students were excited about seeing their papier-mâché animals come to life.

It was also at this time that Trevor's older brother had a birthday coming up. As with most birthdays, there was an air of excitement around the Adams's house.

"Come on, Trevor. Let's hop on the Harley and pick up your brother's birthday present," his dad suggested, "but don't tell him where we're going."

Trevor needed no urging. He just loved that Harley! So off they went, with Trevor sitting behind his dad, grasping him tightly around the waist. The road they took was little traveled and had a steep hill. On reaching the top, a huge tractor-trailer had just started to back up into a farmyard at the foot of the hill. There was no way Trevor's father could have seen that truck as he headed over the crest of the hill. He slammed on the brakes and tried to slide the cycle onto its side and avoid the huge truck—to no avail. Trevor was thrown headfirst into the side of the trailer. Even the helmet that Trevor was wearing was not enough to save his life. He died instantly.

Sadness hit our school and community. The class tried to get back to its routine of daily life, but Trevor remained uppermost in the minds of the children. Small gifts, mementos, cards, pencils, pictures, and candy were placed on his empty desk daily. Each day after dismissal, I removed the articles from his desk and packed them out of sight. Finally, when I felt closure had taken place, I had his desk removed. The children were still allowed to talk about Trevor and discuss the tragedy when it was needed.

A week had passed since Trevor's funeral, and it was time for the zoo trip. I went to the zoo a few days before the trip with a list of the children's animals in hand. I wanted to be sure I would be able to find each animal, so no one would be disappointed. I was amazed to see that the zoo had every animal the class had studied, except one—the tortoise! Oh, well, somehow it seemed appropriate, since Trevor couldn't be there, either.

And so it was that, on that beautiful spring day, Trevor's classmates boarded the bus laden down with lunch bags, sweaters, and cameras in hand. The zoo trip was a complete success. Each child found his or her animal, lunch was eaten, and squeals of laughter echoed throughout the zoo. The end of the day was fast approaching, so I gathered all the children together for the long walk back to the zoo entrance. As we walked, one little girl remarked that Trevor would have loved this trip. After all, he had always talked about it more than anyone else. And wasn't it a shame that, of all the animals, his had to be the very one that the zoo didn't have.

We reached the last section of the zoo—the bird sanctuary—and everyone entered quietly. Winding along the path, we were walking in an orderly fashion when, all of a sudden, we stopped dead in our tracks. At that exact moment, a large tortoise stepped out onto the path, making forward movement impossible. It seemed to have come from out of nowhere. It stopped and looked around, its head held high. It paused long enough for everyone to get a good look, and then it slowly ambled off underneath some shrubbery lining the path. No one said a word. No one moved. Finally, the silence was broken by the same little girl who had earlier remarked that Trevor would have loved this trip.

"Mrs. Larson, I don't think Trevor missed this trip, after all, do you?"

The bus trip home was a little more subdued than the morning trip had been. Everyone seemed to be focused on what had taken place in the bird sanctuary. Questions were being asked at a furious, but quiet pace. I was doing my best to answer the questions, but it seemed there was no plausible explanation for what we had just witnessed.

Parents were waiting to take their children home when the bus pulled up outside the school. This was one of those few times when every child had an answer to the question, "So how was the trip to the zoo?" In fact, by the next day, the entire school was busy discussing this most unusual zoo trip.

A few days later, I gathered up all of Trevor's belongings, including the papier-mâché tortoise, and took them to his mother's home. His mother took the tortoise up to Trevor's room and showed me pictures and snapshots of Trevor. She also pointed out an outstanding, beautiful bouquet of white roses that she had preserved from the funeral, in Trevor's memory.

"I just wish I knew who sent them," Trevor's mother said. "I hate the smell of funeral flowers, and these were the only ones I kept." She told me the funeral director had picked up all the cards from the hundred of pieces, tier after tier, that lined the funeral parlor. At last count, there were well over eight hundred bouquets.

I finally blurted out, "I know who sent them. It was the 'Solid Gold Dancers' group. I'm the one who ordered them. Twenty-four white roses. I collected donations from every child. They wanted to do so much for Trevor. Oh, I can't believe it! First the tortoise, and now those roses! It's a miracle!" Tears flowed freely as we clasped each other tightly.

The next year, I retired from teaching and moved to Bonita Springs, Florida. How surprised I was to learn I was living next door to a gopher tortoise sanctuary. I have learned to accept the fact that some things are not meant to be understood. And, as if to remind me of this, a rather large gopher tortoise ambles his way past my screened lanai each morning as I sit with my morning cup of tea in hand. Yes, I believe in miracles!

The Snow Globe

Margaret E. Pennetti

The Christmas that I received the snow globe was the coldest yet recorded in southeast Arkansas. Standing water rarely froze, and snow was something that happened way off in the Ozarks. World War II had ended recently enough that it was still a frequent topic of conversation, but the white stuff that stubbornly refused to disappear had finally pushed VE Day to the back burner. Cattails were frozen in their ditches, and rumor had it that ice could be seen creeping out from the banks of the nearby Mississippi river. Its tributaries looked like Fudgesicles. It was a Wonder, everyone agreed, and opinion was divided on whether it was the work of the Lord.

I was the only one who remembered later that it wasn't a Christmas present at all, but a birthday present. My birthday was close enough to Jesus's that it usually got ignored in all the fuss. "We'll make it up to you at Christmas," someone always said, but they never did. That year, things were different.

My grandfather took me with him on his daily walk around our tiny town, and the drugstore was where we lingered longest. He would hold court with his cronies, and I would get a single-scoop strawberry ice cream cone. The ice cream cone that day had sprinkles on top, making it a birthday cone. The old men sang "Happy Birthday," more or less successfully. I loved Pappy more than anyone in the world.

Mr. Cornelius, the pharmacist, told me to pick out anything I liked for a birthday present. I had never seen a snow globe before, but as soon as Pappy showed me how to make it work, I knew I had to have it. After all, this was the winter it snowed. It was clearly an Omen. My family believed very strongly in Signs and Portents.

We had Talent. For instance, Pappy was a water witch. Whenever someone needed a new well, he found the water. Mama could make me hear inside my head. No matter what time dinner was ready, or how far away I was, I always knew when she wanted me home. I had the gift of Knowing, except that I could never predict when Mammy was going to have one of her spells. Unfortunately, that sometimes resulted in me being sent outside to cut my own switch. She was, as people said in those days, "nervous." That also runs in the family.

The Talent was something we just took for granted. It never occurred to anyone that we could improve our performance, like practicing the piano. We just did what came naturally and left well enough alone. It was Ruby, our housekeeper, who became my mentor. I had been named after a famous singer, famous in some circles, anyway, although Mammy always maintained that no self-respecting white woman would name her child after a "colored girl." Mama had blithely ignored her and called me Billie. As far as Ruby was concerned, that made me "colored" by default, and she treated me like one of her own daughters, Opal and Pearl. She also had Talent, big heaps of it, and she made sure I learned how to use mine.

First, she made me practice hearing other people, not just Mama. She said that Mama had a radio dial in her head, and she could tune me in nice and clear. Other people were broadcasting, too, but they were just a little bit off the station—dim and full of static. She showed me how to tune them in, too. I never heard the words, but I could hear the tune. Sometimes, I would dance to it, and that got me some bemused looks, but what's considered strange behavior in other places is normal enough in the South, thank goodness.

Eventually, I progressed enough to become a tool-user, and that tool turned out to be my snow globe. I had developed the habit of giving the globe a shake just before I went to bed. That would remind me of the day I got it, and so I always went to sleep happy. I would watch the drifting snow, and I could feel myself slip away to where everything in the universe was happening at once. I could "zoom in" on a scene that caught my fancy and watch it for a while, then I would find myself back in my room. It was better than the Saturday serials at the movies.

I mentioned this offhandedly to Ruby one day, and I was surprised at how excited she became. Soon, she had me practicing regularly, not just at bedtime. I could never understand why Ruby couldn't see things in the snow globe, too, but I learned to think of it as being tone deaf or color blind.

The globe usually took me to strange places, but one day I was surprised to see Mammy and Pappy's bedroom. They were both there, and Mama and

Aunt Helen were with them. All the women were crying. Pappy was sitting in his rocker, and his face was very still. He was just looking out the window at the big magnolia tree. He would rock a little, stop for a while, then rock a little more.

Ruby knew what was happening as soon as I described the scene to her. "Your Pappy's going to Jesus," was the way she explained it. She was right, but the trip took a long time, and it wasn't pleasant. I wasn't allowed to attend the funeral.

I put the snow globe in Mama's hope chest, where she kept all sorts of things she never looked at anymore. After a couple of years, I forgot about it. I could still hear Mama in my head, but now she was off the station, too. Occasionally, I would frighten my playmates by saying such things as "What are you going to name your baby brother?" although they had no idea their mothers were "expecting." Generally, though, the Talent ceased to be a factor in my life.

Daddy's work as a carpenter followed the pattern of the seasons, and finally we ended up in West Texas. In summer, he would work like a demon, and he often took me to the job and taught me to swing a hammer and measure a board. The men who worked for him reminded me of the old men in the drugstore; I was their little pet. In winter, though, Daddy was often "away." Slowly, I realized that this meant he was probably in a Mexican jail; certainly, he was drunk in a Juarez cantina. He would wander back home when spring came, and the cycle would begin again.

Finally, Mama had enough. When the call came asking her to bail him out again, she refused. She simply packed up, abandoned the house, and took us back to Arkansas. The family home had long since been sold, and we moved to be near Aunt Helen and her family in Little Rock. There was no longer even any static in my head.

Now, Mama had rheumatic heart disease, which was pretty common in those days. She was not supposed to have children, but being Mama she had me anyway. She did pretty much everything she could to spite the doctors and their predictions, in fact. She played baseball with me and the neighborhood kids, she smoked (even then people suspected this was not the most healthy thing to do), and when she turned blue she would just lie down until she was pink again. She was, simply, a great mother. It never occurred to me that she was actually sick, because she didn't act like it.

On the Fourth of July, a couple of years after we returned to Arkansas, Mama couldn't get out of bed. "But you said you'd umpire today!" I wailed ineffectually. I made toast and scrambled eggs for her, but she wouldn't eat. She asked me to call her sister (using the telephone was a rare treat, but on this occasion I was unmoved by the privilege), who came over right away. Much whispering ensued behind the closed bedroom door. Mama was bundled up and taken away.

That night, both bored and frightened, I opened the hope chest for the first time in years. I suppose I was looking for something that would prove comforting. Everything in it smelled like Mama, even though it was a cedar chest. I looked at the unworn dresses, the height of '30s fashion, and the size 5 peek-toe high-heeled shoes. I looked at my baby clothes: the ruffled pink corduroy overalls and the tiny booties. I looked at the sepia photos.

I looked at the snow globe, looked at it for a long time. I don't remember what, if anything, I was thinking. Finally, I picked it up.

It was like putting my hand on the head of a much-loved dog that had been dead for a long time. We sat that way for a while, as the snow globe warmed up. When I couldn't put it off any longer, I shook it, just once. As the flakes settled, I felt the familiar sensation of going elsewhere.

I was in a room with a lot of flowers. People were there, dressed for church. Over at the side of the room was a table with a long box resting on it. Inside the box was a woman, whom I did not at first recognize, wearing a beautiful satin nightgown. Then I didn't want to look at her anymore.

Uncle Bob had come in, and he put his hand on my shoulder. We were going to take a ride, he said, to the hospital. To say goodbye to Mama.

The snow globe is still in the hope chest, but I've never looked at it again.

The Christmas Tree

Mitzie Skrbin

Friends my age, especially those who have downsized, or moved to apartments and long since abandoned putting up a tree at all, or switched to a small artificial (or, God forbid, fiber optic) tree, can't understand why I still put up an eight-foot, live tree, complete with angel on top, 800 or 900 tiny white lights, and a couple hundred hand-crafted ornaments made by me, my children, my grandchildren, or purchased at craft fairs over the years. They don't understand, because they have not experienced my quest for a Christmas tree.

When I was a child, we never had a Christmas tree. I grew up in rural western Pennsylvania during the Depression, and we were very poor. Given the era and locale, everyone was poor, but even by those standards we were poor. We did not own the farm on which we lived; we were tenant farmers.

I "discovered" Christmas trees when I started school, and I wanted one. I knew my mother shared my wish, because she had never had a tree when she was a child, but Dad couldn't justify spending money that could be put to more practical use on a tree and ornaments.

The Christmas I was in first grade, we moved from the farmhouse on the old homestead of the farm on which we lived to the caretaker's cottage on the newer, more modern part of the farm. Dad had taken on the job of caring for the owner's dairy herd.

There were two small evergreens about four feet high in the yard, and I had designs on them. Right after Thanksgiving, we started making Christmas ornaments in art class at the one-room school I attended. I had never seen paper chains before and, assuming they were my teacher's original idea, thought her remarkably clever and creative. We also made 3-D construction paper ornaments. You remember—you cut two stars, bells, ball, or trees, cut a slit halfway down one and halfway up the other, then fit them together. I thought these were magic! Even at the age of seven I was rather creative and decided to go one better. Back then, my father smoked a lot—either

Camels or Lucky Strikes. I persuaded him to smoke only Lucky Strikes until Christmas. The great thing about "Luckies" was that the packs were lined with silver foil. As Dad handed me each empty pack, I carefully removed the lining, smoothed it out, and pasted it to both sides of the construction paper with school paste before cutting out my shapes. Ta-da! Metallic 3-D ornaments. I hoarded these in a shoe box, along with a growing stack of paper chains and ornaments. A couple of days before Christmas, I took my little sisters outside, and we decorated one of the trees. It was a thing of beauty!

The only problem was that we were having a rather warm Christmas season, and on the morning of Christmas Eve, instead of snowflakes for a white Christmas, we awoke to a fine mist that turned into a drizzle and became a steady downpour. I knelt on a chair in front of the window facing the yard, tears streaming down my face, watching as the rain dissolved the paste, foil slid from the ornaments, red and green ink faded from the paper, and the paper chains fell apart, until everything lay in a sodden, pathetic heap in the grass at the base of the tree.

In the scheme of things, it didn't really qualify as a disaster. Earlier that month, the Japanese had bombed Pearl Harbor, and America had declared war on Japan, but in my seven-year-old mind, I couldn't quite relate. I didn't know where Pearl Harbor or Japan were and didn't fully understand what war was. We didn't have TV then, bringing world events into our living rooms, up close and personal. But I could and did relate to the disaster before me.

When I was in second grade, we didn't have much reason to celebrate Christmas. With the young men going off to war, jobs were plentiful, and my dad took a job at the H. J. Heinz company, where he was to work until his retirement. We moved to Etna, a small town near Pittsburgh, where we rented a drafty old house. On December 18, a week before Christmas, my baby sister, Alice, not quite three, died suddenly. She'd had a very bad cold, spiked a high fever, and went into convulsions. They continued into the night, despite the efforts of my parents and the doctor, who packed her in ice in a futile attempt to bring down her temperature. She finally lapsed into a coma, and the doctor gently told my mother that it would be better if she didn't survive. There had probably been so much brain damage that she would be in a vegetative state. Mercifully, in the wee hours of the morning, my beautiful baby sister died. She was buried four days before Christmas. On Christmas Eve day, although her heart wasn't in it, my mom went to

THE CHRISTMAS TREE

G. C. Murphy's and bought a few small toys: an easel blackboard, colored chalk, a couple of games, and a tea set. It was Christmas, and she still had children who believed in Santa. Being the eldest and going on nine, I wasn't one of them; I just played along. There was no question of a tree, holiday baking, or festivities that year.

The Christmas I was nine found us back on the farm, and I was back in the one-room school where I had started two years earlier. Our few months in the city had been disastrous, and that summer we had moved back to the country to the farmhouse we shared with my grandfather. As Christmas approached, my longing for a tree returned. Each year, Elmer Thielman, one of the big boys whose father grew evergreens, brought a tree to school on his sled. That year, our teacher, Mrs. Burford, invited any child, with their parent's permission, to bring one or more "real" ornaments for the tree.

To fit the tree in the stand, the boys had to saw off two large bottom branches. I asked if I could have one for greens and was told that I could. I happily tugged the branch to the back of the room and leaned it against the wall below my coat. After we had hung the paper chains and ornaments and tissue paper snowflakes, the teacher brought out the glass ornaments that had been brought in to hang in the empty spaces. I held my breath as the tissue was removed, revealing each fragile glass bauble; they were so beautiful. We carefully hung them, but, careful as we were, a few dropped on the oiled plank floor and broke. A couple shattered, but some only cracked or had a small hole. I thought we should still hang them, just turning the bad side in, but Mrs. Burford was afraid someone might get cut. She got a broom and dust pan and tossed them in the wastebasket. I didn't know how anyone could discard anything so beautiful. We finished off the tree by hanging tinsel icicles, one at a time, on the ends of the branches.

An idea was forming in my mind. When everyone went out for recess, I lagged behind. Carefully salvaging the least broken ornaments, I wrapped them in discarded tissue and tucked them into my empty lunch pail. I also added a handful of the icicles that had been swept up when we finished. I trudged home, happily humming carols, dragging my evergreen branch and clutching my lunch box full of treasures. I couldn't wait to show Mom; she would be so surprised!

When we got home, Mom wasn't there. A note on the kitchen table explained that she had gotten a late start and had gone into town to buy baking ingredients. She admonished us to behave, not fight, and she would be back shortly. That was even better! Now, I could really surprise her. I set my "tree" on the window sill, placing it in a heavy glass milk bottle so it wouldn't topple over, and decorated it. I turned the broken sides of the ornaments toward the branch and finished it off with the salvaged icicles, then stepped back to survey my handiwork—truly a work of art!

Just then the kitchen door opened. Mom walked in and set her shopping bag on the table. I wasn't prepared for her reaction. She looked from my eager face to the pathetic tree and back to me. Then she gathered me into her arms and burst into tears. It would be many years before I could understand.

The Christmas I was ten promised to be the best Christmas ever! Mom told Dad, in no uncertain terms, that we were going to have a Christmas tree. I arranged with Elmer to bring a tree to school on his sled on the last day before Christmas break, which was a half day. I would pay him for the tree and transfer it to our sled to take it home. Never mind that Dad had made our sled of ¾-inch plywood (he made everything to last) and that it weighed a ton, or that I had to pull it at least a mile and a half to get it home. I was determined that I could do it.

That Christmas, Mrs. Burford decided to try something new: a candlelight family Christmas party on the evening of the last full day of school. The school had no electricity, but she thought candlelight would be a nice touch. The children brought in kerosene lamps and large candles, and each windowsill was swagged in greens, with big red bows and a light in each window. We were also to put on a play for our parents. The play we were presenting was an abbreviated version of Dicken's Christmas Carol. In our version, a Christmas Fairy embodied the spirit of Christmas past, present, and future, and I was chosen to be the Christmas Fairy! My friend, Alice, loaned me a blue taffeta flower girl dress she had worn in her cousin's wedding two years earlier and had outgrown. My dad painted a pair of my old shoes silver. They were a little small and pinched my feet, but, hey, they were silver! He also made me a wand: a wooden star on a dowel, also painted silver. I could scarcely wait! I knew every word of every line of my part. Truth to tell, I knew every word of every line of everyone's part. I had committed the entire play to memory.

The morning of the party, we awoke to find a new, deep fall of snow. It was so deep that my mom put on my dad's high boots and walked ahead of

THE CHRISTMAS TREE

us so we could step in her tracks. She had told me to wear my heavy coat, but we had to wear snow pants, and they didn't match my coat. The coat was wine, and the snow pants were brown, so I wore the jacket that matched the pants. Mom asked anxiously if I was warm enough, and I assured her I was—but I wasn't. By the time we reached school, I was thoroughly chilled. Even walking in Mom's footprints, snow got in our boots, and our shoes and socks were wet. My feet felt like blocks of ice.

Mrs. Burford put a ring of chairs around the roaring fire in the potbellied stove to dry out all the wet socks and shoes. I moved to a seat near the stove and sat on my feet to thaw them out. By mid-afternoon, I was experiencing chills. By the time I got home from school, my body was racked with chills, and my teeth were chattering like castanets. Mom heated water and put me in a hot bath (her cure for everything from sniffles to pneumonia). I kept asking her to add hot water, but she could barely put her hands in it, and my little body was turning lobster red. She toweled me briskly and rubbed my throat, chest, and back with Musterole, put on warm p.j.s and tucked me into bed, piling on extra blankets. I snuggled down.

It felt so good that I began to doze off, but not before reminding her not to let me sleep through dinner, insisting I would be fine by party time. Of course, I wasn't fine. By evening, I was wretched. I watched Mom bundle up and get ready to leave. Dad wasn't home, having worked late. When he worked overtime, he missed the last train home and spent the night with friends in Etna. Before leaving, Mom went next door to get my old Polish grandfather to sit with me and keep an eye on me until they got back. Grandpap did his best to comfort me, even offering to play checkers. I remember being surprised, because I didn't know Grandpap played checkers, but I was inconsolable. I lay in a pathetic heap, shivering, sniffling, coughing, and sobbing.

When Mom got back, she said the party went rather well and, if it were any consolation, the girl who took my part didn't fit into the beautiful blue dress or the silver shoes. She had to read her part from the playbook, and she didn't read it well. Then came the final blow: Mom had told Elmer not to bring the tree to school the next day. The weather report on the radio had forecast more snow, and she wasn't sending the girls out in it for a half day. What had promised to be one of the best Christmases ever was turning out to be one of the worst.

We were not to have a tree until I was fifteen, and that one wasn't great. By that time, we were living in West Deer, near Bairdford, Pennsylvania. Dad was planning to buy a tree from Jimmy McKnight, the crotchety, stingy, old Scotch-Irish farmer who lived a mile down the road. We didn't have running water or indoor plumbing there, but we did have bottled gas and electricity, so we could have lights on the tree. When Dad had to make a trip to the hardware store a couple of weeks before Christmas, he took me along and let me pick out some lights and ornaments. That was the year they came out with bubbling candle lights. We were the first people I knew to have them. We bought three strings of lights and a dozen glass ornaments.

Dad had broken his leg badly that fall, and it wasn't healing well. The next week, when he went for a checkup, he was told he had to go into the hospital immediately for a bone graft. He wouldn't be home until the day before Christmas.

When Jimmy learned that Dad was in the hospital, he magnanimously offered to give us a tree and even deliver it. True to his word, two days before Christmas, Jimmy drove up in his rattletrap pickup and grandly presented my mother with the scrawniest, scraggliest Scotch Pine you ever saw. It was truly a "Charlie Brown" tree!

At a loss for words, my mother mumbled a thank you and, after Jimmy left, turned to me and said, "I'm sorry, Mitzie, but I don't see how we can use this."

Ever the optimist, I bubbled, "It's not really so bad. If we put it on the little table in the corner, turn the bad side to the wall, and clip the branches that are too long; it will be fine. You'll see. After we decorate it, it will be beautiful!"

And it was. It would have been hard to tell which glowed more brightly: the tiny bubbling candles, or the eyes of the teen who finally got her Christmas wish.

We were to have a tree every year after that, and they did get bigger and better—a lot bigger and better. I have carried on the tradition, and that is why, even now, the Christmas tree is a very important part of my holiday celebration.

In a Sort of Christmas Card

Manuel Torrez, Jr.

In a sort of Christmas card,
A light cord of green and red
Sags across a boulevard,
Dancing in a winter breeze
That also teases the white in a street Santa's beard,
Who, cheered by noble deeds of local gents with heartstrings,
Rings bells for eager children
Standing on a sidewalk's curb,
Observing and, with wishful eyes, imagining.

While moms, not unlike Mary
In long ago Bethlehem,
Attend to babes too young to fantasize,
And dream for them—peace and an angel for a guide—
Wide the subject matter displayed
For those with a Yule-time heart,
In a sort of Christmas card.

I Met My Million Dollar Baby in a Five and Ten Cent Store

Trudy Barton

It was Christmas Eve, and I had just finished my shift as a sandwich girl at Woolworth's Five and Ten Cafeteria in Pittsburgh. We were celebrating the holiday after the store had closed. Charlie, the Porter, had a bottle of whiskey, which we were using to spike cokes for added Christmas cheer. I was just a girl of sixteen, so this was my first real drink. I was also smoking a cigarette for the first time and enjoying it immensely.

Now, at that time, there happened to be a girl working in the store whose last name was the same as mine. Her brother, George, had recently been discharged from the Marine Corps and had just finished a holiday job as a delivery man for Kaufmann's Department Store. It seems he and some of his buddies had stopped at a few bars on Fifth Avenue before arriving at Woolworth's, and George was feeling very happy. He decided he wanted to meet the girl with the same last name as his. So his sister brought him up to the balcony cafeteria and introduced us.

All the girls said, "Isn't Marylee's brother cute?"

I said, "He's all right."

We went on with our celebration, while Marylee and her brother sat with some of her friends at a back table. Sometime during the festivities, George decided to kiss my boss, Rose Beck, to wish her a Merry Christmas. Rose was a wild and crazy lady. Then someone said, "Get Trudy."

"Oh, no, you don't!" I said and ran behind the soda fountain, the sandwich board, and the steam table with George on my heels. Well, he caught me behind the water cooler, and when he kissed me fireworks went off. He held me a long time with everyone screaming for joy. I got a special feeling and thought he did, too.

As a group, we all decided to move the celebration to the Penn restaurant. George was there ahead of us and sat at the end of a long table with his arms around two of my co-workers, who were a little on the wild side.

Sitting at the other end, I thought I had been mistaken about his feelings. I stayed a short while, trying another cigarette and having fun. When I left the restaurant, I called a friend and went to a dance, after letting my mother know I was all right.

On Monday morning, as I came through the kitchen at Woolworth's, Marylee stopped me and said, "Hey, Trudy, guess what? My brother has a crush on you."

"Me!" I said. "When I left the restaurant he had his arms around Judy and Tillie, and I heard he asked Judy out for New Year's Eve."

"Well, he really likes you and wants to take you out," she said.

Later that day, George came through the cafeteria line with everybody teasing him, his face turning bright red. When he got to me, he asked me to go out with him on New Year's Eve.

"I heard you already asked Judy out," I said.

"Well, I'm not taking her out," he replied.

"Well, you're not taking me out, either," I said. "Anyway, I don't know you well enough."

Every day, he would come in and have lunch with me. After a week of meeting, he said, "When am I going to get this date? I'll take you wherever you want—even a play."

"I've never seen a play," I said.

So we went to see "Oklahoma" with Shirley Jones. George kept apologizing for our tickets because they were on the third balcony. I remember we couldn't eat at first, we would just stare at each other.

After a year, we got engaged, and six months later we were married. The nice thing about it is that I never had to change my name. Years later, every time I would take my small children into the store for a visit, Charlie would say, "Lordy, Lordy, Trudy. It all started that Christmas Eve with me spiking your coke."

So that is why I can proudly say, "I Met My Million Dollar Baby in a Five and Ten Cent Store."

The Ring

Lois Chorle

He took his lady out to dine,
Where candles burn and memories linger,
Within his pocket, a ring so fine,
To grace this woman's lovely finger.

At order time—and it's not funny—
He got the shock of his life.
His lady had a bottomless tummy,
That he had chosen for a wife.

Antipasto, hors d'oeuvres for a beginning,
Soup, steak, and potatoes are fine,
And an order of pasta (not thinning)
Is great with expensive wine.

With pie and cake for dessert,
The meal was now complete.
And this is the part that can hurt.
She couldn't get up on her feet.

This calls for a change of plans,
Marriage could not be it,
And even if metal expands,
The ring would never fit.

She ate like there was no tomorrow,
And now the strangest thing.
Instead of money to borrow,
He had to hock the ring.

The Prince of Amour – Maltese Cat on a Mission

Lolene McFall

Old Blue, past his prime,
sooty as a chimney sweep
still strident in his lust for life and love;
he hones his prowess to ever greater
expressions of habitual seductions.

Perfection is his aim.
No obstacle looms to splinter
his passion or menace his chance
to possess the cutest of cats
while on his nightly saunters,
ever on the lookout for the female feline
who will swoon to be wooed
by sooty old Blue; in his own view
the most excellent of experienced lovers.

Surely no silken kitty can resist
the prince of amour, midnight troubadour,
old Blue.

Portrait of a Lady in Red

Adrienne Rogers

When Milton Ben Zion Cohen entered the dining room of the Hotel Excelsior in Zurich, his practiced glance almost immediately singled out a lovely blond woman who was alone. Though she was seated, her visible upper body suggested she was likely on the *zaftig* side, which did not, in his view, detract from her appeal. His taste in women tended toward painters' models, such as Renoir bathers, rather than modern Hollywood notions of slim beauty. Determined to meet the lady, Milton gestured to the maitre d' and slipped him a generous tip while surreptitiously indicating what he wanted by a glance at the woman in question.

With Milton close behind, the maitre d' approached the lady's table, and asked her in French whether she might perhaps like the company of a gentleman while dining. When she looked up, Milton got a first glimpse of big blue eyes, which added to the magnetic attraction he had already begun to feel.

In response to the question, she looked around the dining room as if to say, "There are plenty of empty tables. Let's see what you have in mind." She pursed her lips, and then nodded assent.

"Milton Cohen," he said, as he sat down opposite her. "Do you speak English?"

"Perfectly," she replied.

"That's a relief," he said.

She smiled. "Well, I also speak Russian, Polish, German, French, and a smattering of Italian, so I imagine conversation would not have been impossible, in any case." She offered her hand as she introduced herself. "I am Nadia Ivanovna."

"Russian?"

"Yes and no. My grandparents were Russian, but they left at the time of the Revolution. I was born in the States, but we spoke Russian at home."

"What are you doing in Europe?" Milton asked.

"Visiting a school friend I haven't seen in many years. We knew each other in boarding school in Switzerland. After another friend told her I had gotten divorced, she wrote to invite me to come see her. And you?"

"I'm retired. Actually, when my wife died a year and a half ago, I decided to make a drastic change and spend the rest of my life doing only what I want."

"You are from New York, are you not?"

"Yes. So how much of an ear does it take to hear that I'm from New York?" Milton deliberately exaggerated the singsong intonation, and a shoulder shrug accompanied his upturned palms.

"How about the neighborhood? I think I hear Nostrand Avenue." Nadia laughed at his amazement. One of her many linguistic achievements was the ability to pinpoint accents, and sometimes she had fun using it socially, as well. "Tell me about the things you want to do."

"I'm interested in art," Milton said, a little hesitantly. "It's something I've always wanted to learn more about. So I'm making a kind of pilgrimage to major museums to see the paintings I've so far known only from reproductions."

Nadia was taken aback. "How odd," she said. "I'm here partly because of art, too."

Milton looked at her with still greater interest, though he had not yet recovered from his amazement at her "parlor trick" of correctly pinpointing his origins.

"The people I'm here to visit," Nadia said, "—I only know the wife, and I haven't seen her since we were in school together years ago—own a very important art collection I have always wanted to see. I'm supposed to go there tomorrow."

Milton wanted to ask if he could possibly join her, but didn't have the nerve. But then Nadia said, "Why don't I call them and ask if I may bring you?"

"That would be great!" said Milton, trying, unsuccessfully, not to look like a kid to whom someone has just given free run of a candy shop.

The next day, Nadia and Milton took a tram to Kilchberg, an outlying suburb of Zurich, where the Braunsteins had a large, isolated house situated high above the lake.

At their ring, a maid answered the door and took their coats. They found themselves in a large foyer from which a long, well-lit hallway led into the living room. They could see the music ell and, beyond it, a glassed-in terrace. The whole length of the entry hallway was like a museum corridor, hung with a dizzying display of paintings that ran the gamut from Impressionism to Modernism. At intervals between the entry and the end of the corridor, red lights and camera eyes signaled the presence of a tight security system.

The Braunsteins came to greet them.

Nadia looked at Hilde, and hoped her face did not give away the shock she felt. It was more than a question of age; Hilde looked ravaged. To make it worse, Hilde said, on seeing Nadia, "My dear, how beautiful you have become!" and then, laughing with self-deprecation, she added, "Don't bother to reciprocate the compliment. Nadia, this is my husband, Heinrich."

Heinrich acknowledged the introduction with a bow and a handshake. After Nadia introduced Milton, the Braunsteins took them into the music ell they had seen from the foyer, and then the rest of the living room was visible. Again, the art display was dazzling, but the focal point was a portrait over the fireplace.

It was a portrait of a young woman, perhaps in her early twenties, wearing a formal, red satin gown, elbow-length red satin gloves, and a pearl necklace that set off her full bosom and lovely complexion. She stood by a fireplace, one arm on the mantel, body in profile, but her face turned as she looked over her shoulder towards the viewer. Her expression was self-absorbed, but rapt.

It took a moment for Nadia to recognize the model as Hilde. The figure in the painting had an ample décolletage and rounder contours than either teenage or present-day Hilde.

"What an interesting painting!" said Milton. "Who is the painter? I don't recognize his style."

"He is a Polish painter named Jacov Walski," Heinrich answered. "The portrait was done while Hilde was a student in Paris. Walski is not yet very well known," Heinrich continued, "but I expect he will be, someday."

Hilde interrupted. "Before we have tea, would you like us to show you around?" Then, turning to Heinrich, she added, "Liebling, why don't you and Mr. Cohen look around together, so that you can get acquainted? That will give Nadia and me a chance to catch up with each other. You don't want to hear our girlish reminiscences, do you?"

To Nadia's surprise, instead of showing her around as she had suggested, as soon as they were upstairs, Hilde took her arm and led her directly into her own bedroom. She slumped into a chair, allowing her face to release its social mask, and gestured to Nadia to sit opposite her.

"I am so sorry to have to curtail your visit," she sighed, "but there is so little time. I need your help."

"Of course," said Nadia, astonished at the tone of urgency in Hilde's voice. "What do you need?"

"A very important errand in Paris. It is a highly confidential and very personal matter. There is no one else I can ask. I need a friend both intimate and distant, whose discretion I can trust absolutely."

"Yes, gladly," said Nadia, flattered, mystified, and curious.

"I have a packet you must deliver to the person I will tell you about—the painter of the portrait you just saw."

After another few minutes in urgent conversation, Nadia again promised to take care of Hilde's errand.

"Good," said Hilde. "I am so relieved and grateful knowing you will do this."

They both took a moment to compose themselves before going downstairs to rejoin Heinrich and Milton.

At dinner that evening, Nadia and Milton had an opportunity to compare notes about their visit.

"Well, what did you think of Heinrich?" Nadia asked.

"Interesting fellow," said Milton. "I asked him how he got into art collecting, and he told me he wanted to add to his father-in-law's collection."

"I'll have to wait for another visit to really see the paintings," said Nadia, somewhat ruefully, "but what did you think about what you saw?"

"I was awed by it. But living with that collection must be very constraining."

"How so?" asked Nadia.

"Well, it must make you a little paranoid. Didn't you notice all the little blinking red eyes? Those are the security cameras. There was an electronic pad at the front door, which must be the code to control the alarm system. The system must be based on sound and light sensitivity, so that any kind of presence sets it off. Living there must make you feel as though you're an inmate, sharing a cell with the paintings."

By the time dinner was over, Nadia and Milton had made plans to visit museums in Zurich and a neighboring town the next day.

When they returned from spending the following morning at a museum in Baden, there was a message from Heinrich asking that Nadia call as soon as she returned. When she came back from making the call, Milton saw she was upset. Pale and shaking, she told him what Heinrich had said.

"Oh, Milton, I can't believe it! She's dead!"

"Who? Who's dead?" asked Milton stupidly. "Hilde? Hilde is dead?"

"Yes," said Nadia, choking on sobs. "She killed herself sometime last night after we left. Heinrich wants to see me because I was the last person she talked to, except for him, before she died."

"Do you want me to come with you?" asked Milton.

"Oh, yes. Please."

Once again, they were shown into the music ell, where a somber Heinrich greeted them.

"I'm so sorry for your loss," Nadia began, taking Henrich's hand in both of hers. She looked as though she might hug him, but thought better of it. Milton and Heinrich exchanged nods, but said nothing.

Heinrich motioned for them to sit down. "I don't know when she decided to do this, but she took an overdose of sleeping pills last night. She has been so very ill for so long that she must have been saving the pills to use when the pain got to be too much."

Nadia managed to look surprised, but sympathetic. In fact, Hilde had told her of her illness—ovarian cancer they had not caught in time and which had metastasized—but if she had hinted at suicide, Nadia had not picked up on it.

The maid entered, excused herself for interrupting, and said, "Herr Braunstein, there is a rabbi here to see Frau Braunstein. I told him she had passed away, but he said he wanted to come in anyway to offer condolences."

Heinrich looked puzzled, but told her to show him in.

The rabbi, a short, dark man, gave witness to his vocation only by long sideburns and a beard. His clothing was dark, but not noticeably clerical.

"Herr Braunstein," he said, going toward Heinrich with outstretched hands, "I am Rabbi Lev Minsky. I am so sorry to learn this terrible news about Frau Braunstein. Please accept my sincere condolences."

Heinrich pulled back from the effusive gestures of this unknown rabbi. He introduced him to Nadia and Milton and then invited him to sit down.

"What brings you to see Frau Braunstein?" asked Heinrich. "I don't remember her mentioning you."

"I'm not surprised. I have never met her, but I wanted to acknowledge a debt of gratitude I owe her." The rabbi was having trouble expressing himself in German. "You see, Frau Braunstein has been a generous contributor to a fund to help relocate Soviet Jews, and I am one of the fortunate beneficiaries of her generosity. I just wanted to come thank her in person. I'm so sad to learn that I can never do this."

"Yes, well, Frau Braunstein was a very generous person," said Heinrich, "although she usually did not like to publicize her offerings."

"And so she did not," said Rabbi Minsky, "but I wanted so much to know to whom I owed my freedom that I made a great effort to find out. Is there some way I can help you, Herr Braunstein, since I can do nothing for my benefactress?"

"No, thank you," said Heinrich, clearly ill at ease and at a loss to know how to handle this unwelcome presence. "I shall arrange for a last viewing of the body in a few days, and then cremation."

"I see," said the rabbi. "Then there is nothing more I can do here. Please accept my condolences again, and excuse the intrusion."

After the rabbi left, Heinrich seemed dispirited. Seeing this, Nadia said, "Please be assured, Herr Braunstein—Heinrich—that your wife's final conversation with me gave no hint of unhappiness. On the contrary, she spoke glowingly of her love for you and of the quality of your marriage."

"I'm not sorry her suffering is over, but I shall miss her very much, all the more because we have no children." At this, he looked around at the paintings, as though they had stood in for the absent children. "Thank you for coming. You were the only ones I could bear to see just now," said Heinrich, shaking hands with both of them.

Milton, for the first time, offered condolences. Nadia did hug Heinrich this time, and they left.

~

The next morning, as Nadia and Milton were having coffee in the hotel, she opened the newspaper to read the most interesting items aloud to Milton. As soon as she opened it, she exclaimed, "Oh, my God! Milton, can you imagine!"

"What? What is it?"

"There has been a robbery at Braunstein's!"

"When? How?"

"Last night! After we left—again! We seem to be terrible jinxes."

"What's missing?" asked Milton.

"Hmmm," mused Nadia. "Of all those valuable paintings, only the portrait of Hilde is missing…and the pearls she was wearing in the portrait. I'll bet the police will be looking for us mighty soon."

"If they thought we had a hand in it, they would have been here already," said Milton. "My guess," he went on, "is that they went after that rabbi who isn't a rabbi."

"Not a rabbi?" asked Nadia. "What makes you think he's not a rabbi?"

"I know he's not a rabbi. For one thing, when he came in, he offered condolences. But Jewish tradition requires that one not speak of the dead person before the bereaved does.

"Furthermore," he went on, "Jews bury their dead as quickly as possible. They do not view the body; that would not be respectful. By the same token, cremation is out of the question. No rabbi could have listened to such talk and kept quiet."

"Heinrich must have realized, too," said Nadia.

"He may or may not have. Heinrich is not Jewish."

"Of course, he is. That's why Hilde married him and not Jac—" She put her hand to her mouth.

"She wanted to marry Jacov Walski?"

Realizing it no longer mattered whether she shared Hilde's confidences with Milton, Nadia told him what she knew. "She was in love with Walski. In fact, she was pregnant with his child when he painted her portrait."

"What happened to the child?"

"She went to live in Paris with her grandmother, Jacov's mother, who raised her. She's grown up and married now."

"Why didn't Hilde marry Walski? Or, rather, why did she marry Heinrich if she was in love with Walski?"

"Walski wasn't Jewish. And he was poor. She didn't have the courage to go against her parents. Heinrich was an ambitious young businessman. His parents had been killed in the Holocaust—that made him Jewish enough for her parents."

"I see," said Milton. "So it was a marriage of convenience?"

"Maybe at the beginning. But I told Heinrich the truth when I said she loved him and was happy in their marriage."

They both fell silent, as they considered the situation.

"Another thing, Milton," Nadia continued, "if the rabbi was no rabbi, I'll tell you something else he was not."

"What's that?"

"Russian."

"He wasn't Russian?"

"No, sir, not with that accent from Cracow."

"But he was speaking German."

"Maybe, but the accent was Polish."

"So the rabbi was—"

"Jacov Walski. And I assume he got out of the country with the painting."

"Got out? Tell me first how he got in to steal it," said Milton, mystified.

"Easy. Hilde wrote him the security code when she wrote him a farewell letter telling him her condition. She wanted him to have the painting to remember her by, and for their daughter to see."

"But why didn't she just bequeath it to him?"

"Because," Nadia said, somewhat irritated at his obtuseness, "that would have hurt Heinrich. And, of course, she couldn't bequeath anything directly to her daughter because it would have killed Heinrich to know she had a child by someone else when she couldn't have any with him."

"Well, that still doesn't explain the pearls. Why did he steal the pearls?"

"He didn't take the pearls."

"He didn't? How do you know?"

"Because, silly," she said with a sigh, as though it were the most obvious thing in the world, "I have the pearls."

"You? You stole the pearls?"

"Of course not. Hilde gave them to me to take to Paris, along with a letter for her daughter. She also gave me a letter to protect me in case anyone questioned my right to have possession of the pearls. Anyway, Milton," she said, as she got up from the table, "I expect we will be having dinner with Jacov and his daughter by tomorrow night."

"We will? Where?"

"In Paris," said Nadia, "where I made reservations at the Lutece. How long will you need to get packed? Our train leaves at three."

She was gone before Milton had a chance to answer, but he packed his bag in no time flat and was waiting for her in the lobby before two.

End of Summer

Jean Doing

Time for layering
light covers
rather than kicking back
or peeling away.
Best to tuck something
at the foot of the bed
to pull up
promising an extra measure of comfort
your back to Ushas
resisting the clock
that changes the season.

The Last Letter

Michael B. Mossman

It was the fall of the year, and the leaves were in full color. I watched them sail to the ground as I sat on a bench under a huge oak tree. I held an old letter in my hand.

I had been here many times before. I was visiting my old college campus in Bluff City, the college I had attended more than forty years ago. Time hadn't destroyed the beauty of the campus.

I had driven down to visit the college earlier in the week. I wanted to check some old yearbooks in order to obtain a picture of my best friend, who was killed in Vietnam. I found the picture I was looking for. I planned to make a copy of Jim's picture and place it in my Vietnam War Memorial display. However, I also came across another picture that gave me pause. It was a picture of my long-forgotten girlfriend, Kathleen McClarnen.

I had met Kathleen at a dance in the fall of 1965. She was an attractive dark blond, and her friends called her Catty. One look at Catty and I knew she was the girl I had always dreamed about. She was popular and had lots of charisma. Besides being beautiful, she was also an outstanding student. In short, she had it all!

I asked Catty out right away. Catty and I dated the rest of that year. We took walks in the park and climbed the bluffs overlooking the river. In the evening, we frequently hung out at the local college pub, the Midway Inn, along with the rest of our gang from school. Life couldn't be any better for us.

Catty and I often double-dated with Jim Thompson and Carol Wilbanks. The four of us went to the Star Liner Drive Inn movie, rode horses, and went swimming together. We declared ourselves, "Best Friends for Life."

However, by the end of that year, the winds of change had begun to blow.

Jim and I were drafted into the military. We volunteered for the Marine Corps and were sent to San Diego, California for basic training. It wasn't long before we heard that we were going to be sent to Vietnam.

I returned home in October after completing basic training and spent most of my time with Catty. We renewed our love affair by revisiting our old familiar haunts. We sat on the bench under the beautiful oak tree. We spent many hours talking as we watched the leaves fall to the ground. Catty told me she loved me and would look forward to my safe return. We planned to be married and live in Bluff City after I got out of the service.

Jim and I were stationed near DaNang Airbase in Vietnam. Our job was to unload supply trucks that frequently drove into the area. On one particular day, I started to climb up on a truck. Jim put his hand on my shoulder. "It's my turn to be inside the truck today," he said.

Soon after, an enemy rocket slammed directly into the truck that we were unloading. Jim was killed instantly. I was standing a few feet away from the truck when it exploded. The last thing I remembered was holding Jim's lifeless body in my arms. Then I blacked out.

I was immediately airlifted out of the area and flown to a nearby naval treatment facility. My wounds were serious, but not fatal. I had suffered a punctured eardrum and various shrapnel wounds to my arms and chest.

I was soon transferred to the Naval Medical Facility in Okinawa. From there, I was on the road to recovery. While in Okinawa, I received a letter from Catty. I opened the letter with great enthusiasm. However, upon reading the letter, my heart sank. Catty had written to inform me that she was going to marry another man. He had been her friend since high school, and the relationship had blossomed into a serious love affair. His name was Rich Collins, and he was already employed as a teacher. Catty explained that she would return my engagement ring in another letter.

I had never felt so low. I felt a tremendous loss. Never in my life had I been so emotionally hurt. My feelings for Catty turned from love to anger, and I made up my mind that I would never speak to her again.

Catty's last letter arrived in a couple of weeks. I never opened it. I stuck it in my sea bag and never gave it another thought. I never wanted to look at that ring again.

I returned home the following year. I did not attend Catty's wedding and destroyed the newspaper that showed a picture of the happy bride. I went on with my life and returned to college. I reasoned that I would just have to live with the loss of Jim and Catty.

One day, I was walking alone through the woods when I spotted a young girl fishing on the bank of Miller's Pond. She seemed to be having trouble pulling her line out of the water. I came up behind her and asked if I could be of any assistance. Startled, the girl turned to look over her shoulder and lost her balance. She fell backwards into the water. I hurried to pull her out of the pond, but I also lost my balance and fell head first into the cold water.

The girl scolded me as I picked myself up and helped her back to the bank. "I wouldn't have fallen in the water if it wasn't for you," she said. Then she looked and saw water dripping off my nose.

We both started laughing.

I helped her gather in her line and walked her home. I could see that she was a lovely girl, even though she was dripping wet. She had brown hair and beautiful blue eyes. I liked her right away.

I asked her if I could see her again, and she said yes. Soon, we began serious courting.

The girl's name was Jenny. She worked as a seamstress in her mother's dress shop. I soon fell in love and asked her to be my wife. We were married in a little chapel in Colorado. After we returned home, I finally finished my college education.

The years began to drift by. I taught high school for thirty-three years. By the time I retired, Jenny and I had seven children and twelve grandchildren.

It was after my retirement that I decided to gather together a Vietnam War Memorial for my friend, Jim Thompson. That was when I went looking for the picture I found at our old college. However, I had not expected to come across a picture of my old girlfriend, Kathleen McClarnen.

Before I stumbled across her picture, I had thought of Catty only once in the past forty years. That was twenty years ago, when I heard she had died of cancer. I always knew I had a letter from her, one I had never opened. I was sure it still remained in the pocket of my old sea bag. But the pain of losing Catty had long disappeared, and I now felt prepared to deal with the old memories. I decided to return with the letter and open it under the same oak tree where Catty and I had spent so much time together in our youth.

Sure enough, I found the letter and went back to Bluff City the following week. I thought about the past as I sat on the bench. Much of what I had loved in my youth was now gone. Jim was killed in Vietnam, his girlfriend, Carol Wilbanks, had since died, and Catty had been dead for over twenty years. The house I grew up in had been torn down, and our old college pub was no longer in existence. All of my other old friends had married and moved out of town. It seemed as if everything in my youth had slipped through my fingers like loose sand.

On the other hand, I had lived a happy life and had not reminisced much about the past. This is what convinced me to retrieve Catty's letter and return to the bench at our old college.

I thought about all this while sitting under the same tree where Catty and I had spent so much time talking about our future together. The leaves were falling, and it reminded me of that October when I was home on leave from the service. Where had the years gone?

I finally opened the letter. The ring I had given Catty was still inside and fell out of the envelope into my hand. Then I began to read what she had written so long ago, in June of 1967:

My Dearest Mike,

I want you to know that I love you. I will always love you! I know that you love me, too. However, I can't marry you. I don't have time to wait for you. I have been diagnosed with cancer, and I don't know how much time I have. Rich has asked me to marry him, and I can't refuse. He is already working, and we will be able to start a family right away. He is a good man, and he really loves me. I love him, too.

But I know it will never be the same as my love for you.

Sometimes in life, things do happen for a reason. I don't know if it's divine planning, or not. I would like to think that God has a plan for all of us.

Please do not think too badly of me. Instead, think of all the magic moments that we have shared together. Remember, true love is never lost and can never be taken away.

Love always,
Catty

Tears came to my eyes as I read the letter. Catty had loved me after all! Once again, I felt great love for her and knew, in my heart, I had never stopped loving her. I now understood why she couldn't have waited for me.

I asked myself, "How can things that are lost in the past have such a tremendous influence on one's future?" If I had married Catty, I would never have met Jenny. Life without Jenny was unthinkable. And if Jim hadn't taken my place on that truck, I would have been killed in Vietnam.

A tear began to roll down my face as I realized the tremendous effect that the past had played in my life. It was as if Jim and Catty made it possible for me to complete my life's journey.

I now realized that we never lose the people we truly love. I had never really lost Jim and Catty. Their handprint would always be on my heart. They would be with me forever.

On the sofa together

Irma Sheppard

they make a familiar sight—
he upright, she reclining,
her feet bare on his lap—
how he'd sat with my mother
countless times watching
Lawrence Welk.

Here in the dayroom,
daytime TV, lost
to his macular degeneration,
murmurs in a far corner
to other nodding grey heads.

Dad is tuned in to the shape
of soft feet wrapped in his hands,
as if Mom has not been long dead,
as if his wife were not standing
amused next to me here,

as if all the spaces of his wayward
mind, emptied of racial slurs, fear
of conspiracies—are lulled now,
holding the frail feet
of this little Jewish woman.

Love Remains

Nancy Sandweiss

She sits apart in the senior center
still beautiful at eighty
with sensual red lips, wavy hair
strong Filipino features.

Nearly deaf, demented, her responses
are rarely to the point, always gracious.
She smiles, utters serial *thank yous*,
slips back to a private place.

Some days memories erupt.
Anger pinches her unlined face,
a shock of dirty words relives
racial slurs from her youth.

Then a new man arrives—
also demented, wife at home.
He focuses her drifting senses,
unleashes an inner vixen.
She bats her eyes, pats his arm.

He receives her little kisses
with an absent-minded grin,
betroths her with his ring
later reclaimed by his children.

Stirred by their innocence
I hear her whisper *I love you*,
watch her take his hand,
place it on her breast, murmur
Feel the pounding of my heart.

Prized Possession

Natalie Gottlieb

I'm in my living room looking at the cloisonné dish
given to me by his mother
who wanted to thank me properly for making dinner
one night long ago when I was in love.

How dare he ask for it back because it was his favorite?
He says he couldn't bear to be without it
now that we are no longer together.

Each time he calls, after I threw him out,
he asks about the fucking candy dish.
"You know," he says, "the one whose lid is painted blue and gold
with the woman in the meadow dressed in a beautiful gown and

the man leaning toward her with his arms outstretched…"
"Enough," I say, but he continues with "the one my mother gave us."

"Us!" I slam the phone down. *There is no us.*

I'm back in my living room lifting the lid of my prized possession.
Orange, purple and white flowers are painted inside
like a bridal bouquet plucked from the garden

where we picked our own flowers,
placed them in crystal vases,
inhaled their fragrance

until they
died.

The Room I Grew Up In

Ron L. Porter

The room I grew up in, the room I had as a child is in Des Moines, Iowa. That's over two thousand miles away from where I live now. I still go there at least once a month, sometimes every week.

My family moved to that house before I remember. A plain-looking, two-story white house that had seen better days, with a very large yard and a cement driveway that wrapped around to the back where everybody parked. My room was upstairs to the left. Not large, but not small. White ceiling with pale blue walls. Because of the slanted ceiling, you had to bend over everywhere except right down the middle and one odd little area that protruded at a right angle into a gabled window. There was a small built-in wooden desk in front of that window, and a view of the backyard, the driveway, and a one-car garage.

The reason I visit that room almost every week is Michelle Casber. Michelle and I met in high school art class and instantly became best friends. She was talented, unpretentious, a little on the plump side. Most said she was pretty, a few would say cute, but to me she was unbelievably gorgeous. And she was nice. Everyone wanted to be Michelle's friend. I was her best guy friend, and we did practically everything together. It took about a year, but when I fell, I fell hard. I didn't just love her; I was in love with her. I loved the way she looked at life. I loved her complete ignorance of anything mechanical. I loved her innocence and her sense of wonder—how she wanted to explore this life and not just let it happen. I loved the way she smelled, the way she cut her hair, the way she dressed. I loved the way she talked, the way she laughed, even the jewelry she chose. To me she was a Monet, stained glass windows, and a Mozart symphony all in one.

Michelle was also very honest, and very clear she wanted to stay friends. I learned to accept that. I'd tell her about the girls I'd dated, and she was always encouraging; she talked about guys she dated, and my heart ached. We still hung out, did a lot together, and had a lot of fun. The first time we went to the Des Moines Art Center and Museum was in the spring of 1978. I was waiting for her in my room, sitting at that desk in front of the window overlooking the driveway. The window was open, and the breeze foretold a warm summer to come. As usual, Michelle pulled her car around back. As usual, she popped out, flipped her hair back and gently closed the car's door. But something was different this time. This time, all I could see was an incredible gift from God. She was stunning, literally a vision. That day at the museum lasted forever.

But the summer went by fast. Disco fever infected the nation. Every time you turned on the radio, Frankie Valli kept insisting that "Grease was the word."

In September, Michelle left for college. We kept in touch with cards and letters. She may have moved out of Des Moines, but not out of my heart. Around New Year's, she wrote that she had met someone special. He was transferring to a college out of state, and she was going to follow. I knew her well enough to know what that meant. I had to let her go. I stopped writing after that letter. A little while later she stopped writing to me.

Please don't take this the wrong way or read into it more than is there. I love my wife, I love my kids, and am very blessed to have the life I've been given. I regret nothing and would not change a single thing.

Still, I can't go to a museum without thinking of Michelle. And I don't know that I want that to stop. So this room I go to isn't the one I played in as a kid. It doesn't have painted blue walls, or a bed, and most certainly doesn't have a door. All this room has is a small built-in wooden desk. The only view is out a window overlooking a one-car garage and a driveway. The window's always open, and there's always that same warm breeze. And Michelle's always just getting out of her car, at that exact time on that exact day, over and over again. And I'm always there, always looking out that window. And in this room, I'll always be in love with Michelle.

What A Blessing

Barbara Watson

What a blessing it was that I was at home on that evening in September 1949, rather reluctantly working around the house instead of going out with my friends. My mother needed me to stay at home to help her with some chores and had exerted some pressure on me to change my plans. I never argued with her; my sister, Joan, and I knew better. My mother would draw herself up to her full five feet and zero inches, all ninety-five pounds of her, and we would be ready to do her bidding.

It was truly a blessing when the front door bell rang that evening. First, it offered a brief escape from my work. Second, when I opened the door, there on the doorstep stood a tall, handsome, bronzed young man, and I immediately fell in love.

My mother had recently bought a house in Whitley Bay, a seaside town about eight miles from Gosforth, where I had spent the first sixteen years of my life. The plan was to turn the house into a bed and breakfast, or a boarding house operation. In the summer we would take in visitors from nearby Scotland, since Whitley Bay was only fifty miles from the Scottish Border. For three months each summer, vacationers from damp, drizzly Scotland would flock to England and coastal towns like ours, where they would soak up some of the sun that northeast England offered one or two days each summer. In the winter, we planned to provide student housing for students attending King's College in the nearby city of Newcastle.

So back to the young man waiting on the doorstep. "My name is David," he told me. He had recently returned from the Middle East, where he had served two years in the British army—hence, the tan—and now he was enrolled at Kings College and needed a place to stay for the next two terms. My heart sank, knowing that all our rooms were rented. There was no room at this inn. I did not have the heart to turn him away, so I excused myself and ran back to the kitchen to plead with my mother to find a place for him. "There is a student at the door who needs a room," I exclaimed breathlessly.

"We just have to make room for him." My mother attempted to calm me down and led me back to the front door, and invited David into the hallway. She explained to him that we had no rooms left except for an attic room we had not had time to paint and furnish before the term started. My mother was smitten, too, I could tell, because she almost immediately agreed to get the attic room ready for him by the coming weekend. He would need to find a place to stay until then, but he could move in on Saturday.

I was more than willing to help with the necessary scrubbing and painting. We found a secondhand bed, dresser, and chest of drawers to furnish the bedroom, so it was all spruced up and ready for him when he appeared at the door on Saturday morning. I happily helped him move his few belongings into the newly decorated attic bedroom.

My room was at the bottom of the stairs that led to David's room. After he moved in, I would often sit on my bed and listen for his door to open. When I heard his footsteps on the stairs, I casually ventured out of my room to force a greeting or maybe even a few words, if I was lucky, from this very shy young man. He played flute in the college orchestra and often stayed late after classes to practice. One of the house rules for the students was that they were to be back for dinner at five o'clock. If they weren't, they would miss the meal. On the nights when David stayed late to practice, my mother would set aside a plate of food and keep it warm in the oven for him. When he returned, one of us would sneak him into the kitchen so none of the other students would discover that he was getting preferential treatment.

I worked hard during that year to try to get to know our handsome boarder. I flirted outrageously, but got nowhere. I regularly went out on dates, but it was really David I was interested in. I had the odd chance meetings, occasionally bumping into him, but after many months I was still anxiously awaiting a sign that my feelings were reciprocated. The spring term would soon end, and in about two weeks he would be packing his bags to go home for summer vacation. Time was running out. I had to make a move, or I would have to start pursuing him all over again when he came back next term. I couldn't wait another three months to find out how he felt about me. So, one evening after work, I decided to pay him a visit. I plucked up my courage, raced up the stairs and boldly knocked on the door of his room. I don't know if he was surprised to see me when he opened the door, I only remember being invited in and sitting on the edge of the bed talking to him. Our conversation was interrupted by the sound of footsteps on the stairs. One of the other students was coming up for a visit and, no matter how innocent this meeting might be, being discovered in David's bedroom would not look good. To avoid discovery, I dived under the bed. Cohn, a student who also boarded with us, had decided to pay him a visit. Maybe he heard me come up the stairs and was hoping to catch me out. I'm not sure what his motives were, but he stayed in the room for what seemed like a very long time. While I lay cramped under the bed, he talked to David and paced around the room, primping in front of the mirror as he talked. I was certain that I would be discovered any minute. As Cohn looked in the mirror I could see him, so surely he could see me. Just about the time I thought I could not stay still one minute longer, I heard the door close. I heard his footsteps retreating down the stairs, and I was able to come out from my undignified hiding place, feeling very relieved that my presence under the bed had gone undiscovered and my reputation would remain intact. David and I both felt a sense of relief as we left the room to say goodbye.

On the landing outside his bedroom door, standing close together, I could feel the warmth of his body next to mine and felt sure that a kiss was imminent. We were leaning against the bannister, standing shoulder to shoulder and looking over the railing at nothing in particular, talking, but not really saying anything significant. We had never been this close before, and I, for one, did not want this moment to end. Heads close together, I was waiting breathlessly for something to happen. All I had to do was turn my head, and he would have to kiss me. I turned towards him, leaned forward, and our lips met. The months of waiting were over, and the kiss told me that he felt exactly as I did. Many kisses followed, but none so special or as meaningful as that long-awaited first kiss.

Two Roads Diverged

Susan Cummins Miller

Dodging raindrops and lightning bolts
I ducked into the back-street bar
in Montello, Nevada. Bud Country, but
Dave rustled up a warm Guinness
from the back.

My brown hair was long then, twisted
up off my neck and secured
with a piece of leather
and a wooden pick, sharpened
at both ends.

Played pool with three geologists
and a cowboy—just a way to pass the time,
a way to drive the geologic puzzles
from my mind so I could sleep. Lost,
on both counts.

Walking back to the motel
in the sultry darkness, under restless stars,
the Leach Mountains at my back
the valley stretching east forever—
or to Utah,

whichever came first—I passed
that cowboy, smoking behind the store.
He tossed out a proposition
like a half-smoked Camel.
Unfiltered.

The wind rifled the cottonwood leaves.
Black shadows played tag. A killdeer piped
from the sage-covered slope.
A horned owl answered.
Awkwardly,

laughing, I turned on my heel,
grinding the metaphorical butt
into the muddy road. Yet,
thirty years later, I'm still
wondering.

Shards

Teresa Flanagan Sheehan

we wed in love and in earnest
with youthful confidence
that we could mold ourselves
into perfect partners,
could fill the other's
every need and whim.

in the love-sick phase,
we almost made it work.

then it was all pretending
to be what we weren't,
to like what we didn't,
to swallow the lie that
the two shall become as one.

God knows we tried.

efforts be damned,
we didn't fit the molds,
so rigid and claustrophobic.
they strained and groaned,
reluctant to release us.
but when, weary of struggle,
they burst apart, a sea
of stifled dreams and differences
spilled out in front of us,
bold and undeniable.

relieved, we wept together
over the shards.

Too Late for Hello

Eleanor D. Little

A strange woman answered:
the wife of Tom, an old friend I dated
from school days.
I hoped to talk half a century of memories,
how he is, what he does these days,

where his family lives, does he have kids?
Once he brought a box of Valentine candy
then months passed. I was
too busy to look for him before,
lost in a telephone book somewhere.

We drove and talked those summer nights,
then went to school to plan our lives.
I still hear his voice,
feel my cold ears when he pulled off my hat
to play catch with the boys in the school yard.
Always I hoped I would see him again.

Today I called to say 'hello'—
his wife said he's already gone,
so instead I said goodbye.

Love, Tai Chi, and Regret

Steve Snyder

White crane spreads wings, steps
back to repulse monkey, smooth, slow motion
concentrated exercise storing more Chi,
quickening circulation as robed students,
in sync with master's pace and calm music,
move through the form. Ecstatic energy dances
along nerves, grows as you smile at me,
vanishes the sense of self replaced with
greater awareness, peace, and bliss…oh such bliss!
Beyond normal parameters of consciousness
and enamored with your warm brown eyes
I forget to ask for your number.

First Runner-Up: Best Fiction Contest

Second Chances

Richard O'Donnell

The women in my family haven't had much luck in choosing men. My great-grandmother Dorothy started the awful trend back in 1927 when she married the man of her dreams instead of one who had a steady job. He had the hair and the profile of John Gilbert, the reigning romantic star of Hollywood, but that was it. He came to the marriage with a starter set of tools, but no idea how to use them. They lived in borderline poverty as he flopped from one unskilled job to another, and those were the good years. The advent of the Great Depression, when jobs for unskilled laborers started drying up, only made things worse. As a last resort, he joined the government's new Civilian Conservation Corps, a public works program that had men chopping down trees and building roads and dams in remote parts of the country. The last she heard from him, he was working on a ranch somewhere in Montana. He didn't expect her to join him, he wrote, as the distance was so great, but he did want her to know that he was doing well. After that, great-grandmother Dorothy drilled it into my grandmother, Betty, never to look for romance in a marriage. Fine for dating, she told her, but when it came to choosing a mate, you looked for a good provider. Grandma, who well remembered the lean years growing up, took her mother's advice as holy writ.

In high school, Grandma Betty was sweet on a nice boy who loved books, but had no mechanical aptitude. When the time came, she settled for Bob Nettles, a guy who worked in the building trades. Grandpa Bob could install plumbing, run electrical wiring, build rooms, hang wallpaper, do his own landscaping, and tune up the family car on weekends. Most of the time, he came home from work, had dinner, put in a couple of hours in his workshop, then hit the sack because he had to get up early. The guy was a boarder in his own home. He never took Grandma anywhere that I was aware of, and when she spoke to him it was mostly to ask if there was anything he needed from the store.

You'd think that Grandma Betty would have learned something from the experience, but no. She was resigned to the idea of marriage as an accommodation that allowed two people to get through life. She passed that wisdom along to her daughters, Anne and Ellen. Anne, my mother, bought into it when she married my dad, Ernie Schiller. He was outgoing, assertive, and seemed always to be on top of things. He not only took care of Mom, the house, and the finances, but also relieved her of having to make decisions. That's how we ended up with colonial furniture in every room, offset with beige walls. Mom had wanted something modern, with colorful drapes and bright paint. Dad chided her for trying to be an interior decorator. "Stick to the classics, and you can't go wrong," he told her. That's what his mother had done.

Oddly enough, it wasn't his indifference that finally pulled the trigger on the marriage; it was his preference for the heavy German cooking he grew up on. Sunday dinners with the Schillers were an ordeal for Mom. Her digestive system balked at the sauerbraten, bratwurst, and other rich fare she was suddenly foisting on it. She said it took a week of vicious belching to purge herself of Grandma Schiller's boiled beef and cabbage. Dad didn't help when he gave Mom a bound copy of Mother Schiller's prized recipes one Valentine's Day. It was the only Valentine's gift he ever gave her. That was another thing about Dad—he'd squeeze a nickel till the buffalo bellowed. Mom learned that early. On his first birthday after they were married, she presented him with a card and a calfskin wallet. In return, he gave her one of his patented lectures on thrift. You didn't need to exchange birthday cards or gifts once you were married, he said. The same went for anniversaries. That was one practical thing about marriage, he explained—you no longer had to put up a front to impress each other.

Mom tolerated this behavior for years before deciding there had to be more to life than six days of indifference capped by Sunday dinner with the Schillers. When at last she told Dad she was calling it quits, he pouted, much like a teenager who's had his driving privileges suspended. But, while he accepted Mom's decision, he refused to be the one who moved out, citing some vague Teutonic custom involving a husband's natural rights. Mom's lawyer said there was no case law to substantiate his claim, but she didn't care. She said she couldn't stand living in an Ethan Allen showroom any longer. We left the house in suburbia and moved to an apartment in the north Bronx. A friend of Mom got her an office job at New York University. She didn't make a lot of money, but she knew how to manage on a tight budget. She learned that from Dad.

Despite that experience, she still maintained that it was best to marry a good provider; you just had to be more selective. As for Prince Charming, she was more convinced than ever that he didn't exist. "Forget about him," she'd tell me. "He's just not out there."

I took Mom's advice when my turn came to settle down. I was twenty-one and just home from college. As a woman who'd been forced to make it on her own, with no special skills to fall back on, Mom had insisted that I become self-sustaining. "The boy you marry isn't always the husband you end up with," she once told me. "When that happens, you have to be able to walk out the door and make a life for yourself." It was hard going, paying my tuition at New York University, even with both of us working, but I earned a degree in economics, graduated cum laude, and had a lead on a promising job. I also acquired a boyfriend in college, a bright, ambitious guy who planned to go on to law school and join his dad's firm as a specialist in corporate liability litigation. He called it a bull market for lawyers. I was eager to have Mom meet him and brought him home three weeks after graduation.

He talked a lot over dinner, mostly about himself and his ambitions, and joked about how he'd already taught me how to choose wines, order from a French menu, and dress for success. Mom seemed impressed, at least until he left. I was rocked by her real reaction.

"What a pompous egotist," she said, "not to mention a control freak."

"That's completely unfair," I shot back. "He was just nervous and trying to impress you."

"Really," she said. "Wait till he takes you to meet the family, and he preps you beforehand with a list of dos and don'ts, so you don't embarrass him."

I was hurt and angry and more determined than ever to prove her wrong. But when the time came to meet his family, and we were right on their doorstep, he said, "Try not to slouch." Mom and I had a long talk after that. I had tried her approach, I said. I looked for a breadwinner and that didn't work.

It was time to try the alternative. If I was inevitably going to marry a loser, at least I wanted someone who stopped my breath—a Prince Charming, a Mister Right, a Knight in Shining Armor, or whatever they called him these days. Mom shook her head.

"I think it's time you had a talk with your Aunt Ellen," she said. "She's the only one in the family who found anyone like that. Maybe she'll enlighten you."

I thought she was being sarcastic. Aunt Ellen was attractive, well read, held a responsible position with a major corporation, and was in every way a lady, but she was also what used to be called a spinster. If she was such an expert on Prince Charming, where was this guy?

Mom called Aunt Ellen that same day and explained the situation. She didn't ask her to talk me out of my decision or set down any conditions. But I noticed that she stressed that she be honest with me. She didn't tell me what she meant by that.

Aunt Ellen arranged for lunch at a small restaurant where people could talk without fear of being overheard and where the waiters didn't hover over you. She then proceeded to introduce me to her Prince Charming.

"I was dating the kind of guy that Mom was always pushing—upstanding, industrious, no-nonsense," she said. "He was a bore with credentials, but he treated me well. That changed after we'd been dating a few months. That's when he started to feel more comfortable about asserting himself with me. Instead of 'Are you almost ready?' it was now 'Hurry up.' He walked ahead of me when we entered a building, but no longer to hold the door, and he grew increasingly impatient and critical of anything I did, even when it was none of his business. The breaking point came on a Saturday afternoon, when we went to the Barnes & Noble bookstore on Astor Place. He wanted to pick up something on business leadership that he'd read about. The store was busy, packed with weekend shoppers and students from nearby NYU, and the checkout lines were long. While my boyfriend was waiting on line, I killed time browsing. I came across a book titled, *The World's Best-Loved Poems*—not something I'd ordinarily buy. I was turned off poetry in high school by the endless yammering about what a poem meant. Listening to the different interpretations that kids offered in class, I understood that reading poetry was a personal experience. Whatever you got from a poem depended on your perspective. When I suggested that to the teacher, you'd have thought I was preaching heresy. For whatever reason, I decided to give poetry a second chance. My boyfriend was still waiting in line, so I handed him the book and the money to pay for it. I couldn't believe how angrily he turned on me.

"'What's this?' he said. 'What do you want this for? You don't read poetry. It's a foolish waste of money. Put it back and wait outside.'

"He was so loud that people began staring at us. One of them was a handsome man standing a couple of places ahead of my boyfriend. He glared at my boyfriend, then he looked at me, and his expression changed. I could tell he felt sorry for me. I was so embarrassed, I put the book back and went outside and started to cry. I was feeling terribly sorry for myself, when I heard this soft voice saying, 'Excuse me.' It was the handsome man from the bookstore—the last person I wanted to see right then. I felt myself turning red.

"'I just wanted to let you know that I admired the way you handled yourself back there,' he said. 'It was a difficult situation. Another person might have lost it and made things worse, but you kept your composure. You carried yourself like a lady, and you're to be commended for it. I just thought you should know.'

"I was so taken aback, I couldn't speak. I just gaped at him like a fool. With that, he walked off. He never looked back. After a moment, I went back into the bookstore, got that book of poetry, handed it to my boyfriend, who was still on line, and told him to buy it. He was actually stunned. He didn't dare say a word then, but he started reasserting himself as soon as we got in the car. He said he'd drop me off at home and that he'd pick me up at seven. There was a new movie he wanted to see, and he didn't want to be late. I was to be ready when he honked the horn. I didn't say anything till he dropped me off. Then I told him I wouldn't be going to the movie or anywhere else with him ever again. He'd humiliated me in public for the last time."

"Just like that?" I asked. "You dropped him for good?"

"I knew, after the way that man spoke to me, that a woman didn't have to put up with a boor, that there were men out there who knew how to treat a woman like a lady. That man didn't know it, but he had rescued me, like a Prince Charming. I never again doubted my own worth, and I resolved that I would never accept another man except on my terms."

"Did you ever see him again?'

"No. I went back to the bookstore the following week, hoping I'd run into him so I could thank him. He wasn't there, so I came back again and again, on different days, till finally I gave up. But strangely, I didn't feel bad that I didn't see him again. It wasn't necessary. He'd already given me everything I needed. What more could you ask of a Prince Charming?"

I was barely in the door when Mom dropped the question.

"How did it go?"

"I'm not sure," I answered, then gave her a rundown on my conversation with Aunt Ellen. "Aunt Ellen seems to believe she found the man of her dreams one day, never got his name, never spoke to him, never saw him again, and yet she's happy with that. If I was supposed to learn something from her, I must have missed it."

"Now, you know your Aunt Ellen," Mom said. "She was always a dreamer. I don't think she ever read a book or saw a movie that didn't have a happy ending. And if there was no happy ending, she made one up. Do you know she once rewrote the ending for *Gone with the Wind*? In her version, Scarlett becomes a changed woman, and Rhett returns from Charleston. In the last scene, he's riding down the long drive leading to the front porch, where Scarlett stands waiting.

"She did the same thing with this stranger; she rewrote the ending. She created a whole biography for him. She gave him a name, found a great job for him as a globetrotting archaeologist or anthropologist (she couldn't decide which suited him better). In her story, she finally meets him again, signing books at the store where she first met him. Your aunt is an incurable romantic. That's why she's still single. She's living out a fantasy that keeps her from dealing with reality. Is that the life you want?"

Mom had a point. Aunt Ellen was as stable and pragmatic a woman as I'd ever met. Over the years, she'd parlayed a business degree into a job as Director of Marketing Communications for Pruitt Investments, an old-line Wall Street firm. Yet here she was, obsessed with a man she'd transformed in her imagination from a kindly gentleman into a dashing adventurer who one day reenters her life. Music up, fade to the credits. And yet…

I thought about Aunt Ellen and her fantasy over the next couple of weeks, trying to reconcile the practical woman I had always respected with the fanciful dreamer that Mom described. It finally occurred to me that there was no irreconcilable gap between the two. Aunt Ellen's approach was, for her, a practical means of dealing with reality. In her world, the ideal of a Prince Charming was valid—she had met him, however briefly, in that bookstore. All she did was dress him up and embellish him with mundane details. He could have been an engineer, an accountant, a teacher—it made no difference. Aunt Ellen was still fairly young and attractive. Who was to say that the man of her dreams wouldn't surface some day? To Aunt Ellen, that was worth waiting for. In the meantime, she was happy, which was more than Mom or Grandma Betty could claim. They shut men out of their lives because they'd made bad choices and had nothing to show for it but bitterness. Aunt Betty had escaped that. Her man was still out there. It was only a matter of time.

He turned on the bed lamp and looked at the clock. It was past midnight, and he still couldn't sleep. Tomorrow's presentation was weighing more heavily on his mind than he thought. He made his way to the kitchen, poured himself a glass of milk, and went to the living room window. He found the view more striking at night than in daylight. In the moonlight, New York Harbor shone like an expanse of slate, while in the distance Miss Liberty held her shining lamp aloft beside the golden door. The condominium in Battery Park City cost him considerably, but the view from this height was worth it. His Castle in the Sky, he called it. Besides, he could afford to indulge himself. He was single, and his position as Creative Vice President for Drake and Bennett Advertising paid him handsomely in bonuses for the millions in new billing he'd brought to the company. He'd become a master at delivering sales presentations to prospective clients. It was ironic, when he thought how shy and retiring he had been starting out. It took years before his stomach stopped churning the night before a presentation. Now the churning was back. But then, this was no ordinary presentation.

Pruitt Investments, one of the last of the private Wall Street investment firms, was planning to go public, and it needed an advertising campaign that would position it favorably with investors. A lot was riding on the campaign he'd developed. It would also be the largest single account the agency had ever landed. Heavy hitters like Ogilvie and Mather and J. Walter Thompson had already fanned out. Tomorrow, Drake and Bennett themselves would be in attendance, something they had never done in the past, to ensure that everything went well. The major partners at Pruitt were also expected to be there. They weren't the ones he had to sell, though. His challenge was Pruitt's Director of Marketing Communications, a sharp-eyed businesswoman who knew precisely what she wanted and accepted no less. She had already humbled the best from New York's major ad agencies. She would be a tough sell, but she was also vulnerable. Her own career could well be on the line if she failed to land an ad agency that satisfied her company's needs, and she was running out of options. In a way, she'd be pulling for him to deliver the goods. He had to handle her just right, though. Charming her was out of the question. Charm was never his strong suit, anyway. Polite, respectful, and professional: that was the tack to take. From what he'd heard, it was also how she preferred being treated. But first, he had to relax and get a decent night's sleep.

There was nothing on television at this hour to take his mind off work except classic movies whose dialogue he could recite even as the actors were speaking. He'd try reading. There must be something in his library that would interest him. He had well over five hundred titles, housed in a handsome bookcase of Brazilian cherrywood that occupied most of one wall of the spacious living room. He'd read all of the books at least once—some of them two or three times over. He made a mental note to buy some new ones, perhaps next week. But, for now, what did he feel like re-reading? Agatha Christie was out. He loved the old girl, but what was the point of reading a whodunit once you knew the ending? Adventure novels were okay, but the plots were all cut from the same pattern; the authors' names were practically interchangeable. His finger moved down the shelves to the classics section, then across the spines of the volumes lining the shelves: Dickens, (a touch ponderous for relaxing); tales of horror by Poe (too depressing); Henry James (forget about him). He came at last to a book at the end of the shelf that he hadn't read for some time. He slid the thumb-worn book from its place and turned it over: *The World's Best-Loved Poems.*

He'd bought it years ago, the day after he'd seen that girl with it. He turned to page 481 and read the opening lines from his favorite poem by Lord Byron: "She walks in beauty, like the night / of cloudless climes and starry skies." How like her, he thought. He could still see her face. He'd tried to console her, but ended up giving her some pretentious speech. No wonder she stared at him that way. He'd returned to the bookstore several times after that, hoping their paths would cross. They never did. He'd missed his chance.

He often wondered what became of her.

CONTRIBUTOR'S NOTES

GLORIA G. AMMERMAN, born in Ventura, California, grew up in an orphanage and three foster homes. An elementary teacher for 32 years, she was only eight when she started writing poems. She also writes dialogues and stories for her puppetry. Her specialties are haikus and lyrics. Her friends love the inspirational and humorous poems she writes for special occasions, such as weddings, anniversaries, and birthdays. Thanks to her family, foster family, and friends who encourage her, she has been inspired to write an uplifting and humorous poetry book. Gloria now resides in Sun City, California. [199]

TRUDY BARTON: I was raised in Crafton Heights, a suburb of Pittsburgh, by my widowed mother. My father passed away suddenly at the young age of 37. Mom, five months pregnant with my baby brother, was left with two little girls under three. It was the Depression and times were hard. At sixteen, I quit school to help by getting a job at Woolworth's 5 & 10 Cent store. My first Christmas on the job I met my husband. Even though it happened sixty years ago, it seems like yesterday. From that wonderful Christmas Eve long ago until he passed away, I was always his million dollar baby from the five and ten cent store. Proud mother of two sons and a daughter, with two wonderful grandchildren. [297]

HELEN BENSON: One of the fondest memories of my childhood is of my mother's garden. In the early mornings of summer before any of the family was astir, she would be out there with her hoe, waging war on the weeds and sweet-talking the plants. It all started long before in the winter evenings when she would pore over the seed catalogues and start her planning. It ended when we ate bountifully and canned and shared. Flowers were a part of it, too, and everything had its own season. Everyone had a garden in those days, but hers is the one I knew best. [177]

BOBBIE JEAN BISHOP: After the 2003 wildfire, I wrote a piece called "Cuyamaca Journal Part 1," which was published in the Miracosta College journal, *Tidepools 2005*. After our San Diego wildfire in 2007, I looked back on my journal expression from 2003 and decided to condense my feelings and experience into a poem, which became "October Wildfire 2003." It is satisfying to revisit the same material and find a similar, yet different voice. I've been writing off and on since 1969 and have had my work published over these many years in small journals and a couple of Doubleday anthologies. [128]

DOROTHY BOGGS: The Iraq war provokes questions in our hearts and minds. The Revolutionary War tumbled questions in my nine-year-old brain. That is how "Questions" was born. I'm a nurse retired, a widow busy writing short stories. Time is short, as I'm in my ninth decade. A son and his wife are active in the Bed & Breakfast business, their latest venture: Whale Cove Inn, Depoe Bay. Life is interesting. Yes! I am a proud mother, grandmother, and great-grandmother to three boys and two girls. [159]

JANE BORUSZEWSKI was born in Eastern Poland and deported to Siberia in 1940. After amnesty, her family left the place of their imprisonment. While traveling by train, she and her sister and brother were put in hospital somewhere near Bukhara. They survived typhoid, but then were alone and homeless. Jane crossed the Caspian Sea in 1942 and was brought to East Africa, where she attended school in Tengeru, near Arusha, and graduated from high school. After WWII ended she refused to go back to Poland and signed up for work in a textile factory in England, where she met and married her husband, Walt. They emigrated to America in 1950. Their three daughters were born here. Jane went back to school and graduated from Onondaga Community College with highest honors. [147]

ESTHER BRUDO: I usually write poetry, but chose a narrative style for "My Uncle Jack." I wanted to allow myself to include all of the details of this childhood experience, and to tell it in the voice of my nine year old self. "Just So Story," my other entry this year, began with choosing a body part, the umbilical cord, to fantasize about. I found myself giving life to the cord, and it is almost as though the cord then told me the story. This year I retired from my work as a psychologist. I realize that my impetus to write comes from a desire to express my own life story, and also from a lifelong interest in understanding and hearing the stories of others. [54, 190]

EVELYN BURETTA returned from California to her Midwestern roots in 1999 after completing careers in technical writing and the U.S. Army Reserve. Writing is one of her retirement projects. Her first inspirations for poetry came from childhood experiences in rural southern Illinois, where she grew up in the '40s through '60s. "Rising From Ruins," one of her first poems, was published in the anthology *Tree Magic: Nature's Antennas*, SunShine Press Publications, 2005, and "Delayed Delight," a later poem, was featured in *OASIS Journal 2007*. She wishes early teachers could have taught, allowed, and encouraged creative writing. Her poem, "Journey to Contentment," reflects sentiments about her elementary school days. Evelyn resides in St. Louis, Missouri. [35]

SALLY CARPER grew up in Eugene, Oregon and has lived in the Pacific Northwest her whole life. After she retired a few years ago, she had the good fortune to attend a creative writing class at a local senior center. She had never written before, but wanted to put on paper some of the stories her grandmother used to tell. "Our instructor, Pat Arnold, brings out the best in her students, and I have become hooked on writing and the bond created with the other students through our mutual appreciation of the written word." [175]

LOIS CHORLE was born in 1926 and raised in the town of Aspinwall. She graduated in 1943 from Aspinwall High School. She married after working eight years at Fidelity Trust Co. and attending Pitt University at night. Her interest in writing started at an OASIS Memories course, where they discussed and wrote about old memories. It's now called "The Scribes." Some of Lois's stories were published in an Allegheny County Community College book. Now she is writing a book for her four children and ten grandchildren, so they will know a little bit of what life was like from the 1930s till 2008. [299]

ANNABELLE G. DEUTSCHER is a member of the Tucson Saturday Writers. "The poem, 'Voices,' was simply plucked from the air as an overheard story—one of the many thousands of tales born of WWII that might easily have remained untold had some special person's memory not given it words." [258]

JEAN DOING is an active member of Writers' Center, Bethesda, Maryland, where she won a scholarship. Graduate of College of William and Mary. Retired human resources executive working as part-time director of nonprofit that provides job counseling for people fifty-five and older. Published in *Scribble* magazine (Maryland writers) and *LitWit*, a Washington, D.C. humor periodical. Selected four times (2004, 2005, 2006, 2007) to have poems hung in Montgomery County Executive's Poetry Project. Included in two anthologies: *Poet's Domain* and *Oasis Journal* (2006 and 2007); accepted for *New England Poetry Journal*, 2008. Published a first collection/chapbook entitled *Catch the Sun*, 2007, Live Wire Press, Charlottesville, Virginia. [310]

JOAN T. DORAN: One of the brightest spots in my "writerly" life for the past several years, has been inclusion in the *OASIS Journal,* in the good company of others who delight in putting a diversity of life experiences variously into words. There still are days I miss former attachments and occupations, but I love how the past comes back to inform the present in new ways that offer surprising gifts of understanding, insight, and, perhaps, acceptance. I wasn't able to write "Changeling" until ten years after my mother's death, and even then it took three more years to be able to finish it, with what has come to be a fuller appreciation of how much she loved us. [267]

ELISA DRACHENBERG: As a former filmmaker, I am accustomed to thinking in pictures. As a perpetual foreigner, I am used to paying close attention to detail and nuance of languages not my own. And as a writer, I mainly sit. By the time the movie in my head starts rolling and the soundtrack begins, I've long turned into all the actors who dominate the scenes with their laughs and torments, their hopes and aspirations, their insights or lack thereof. I am the daft emperor *and* the boy who points out his nakedness. Like a chameleon, I blend in, but hope to show my true colors while becoming what I create. [85]

MARY ROSE DURFEE was born in 1916, and lived her entire life in Central New York State. She began writing short stories eight years ago after one of her grandchildren asked her what life was like when she was a small child. Since then, she has written numerous articles and stories about her life and those around her. Some of her stories have been published in local newspapers. Mary was inspired to write the "Miracle" story after one of the students in her daughter's 3rd grade class was tragically killed in an accident. Her hobbies include gardening, playing cards and Bingo, cooking, and collecting antiques. Even though she just celebrated her 92nd birthday, Mary Rose continues to live a happy, independent life and just received her first computer. [281]

JOANNE ELLIS: Twenty years ago, I joined a journaling group where I met good friends, struggled with writing, helped with the publication of two books, and have continued to find the variety of mentors and assignments very rewarding. Writing memoirs in essay, poetry, and story form has challenged me to deal with the problems and joys of the past. After graduating from the University of Arizona, I taught reading to many little children, both in the public schools and in our home. Today, I live in the middle of Tucson with my husband, Bob, and Maxwell, our long-haired companion. [60]

Born in Vienna, Austria, in 1922, IRENE ETLINGER was fortunate to escape to the United States after the Nazi takeover. A kind family in Portland, Oregon helped save her life. As a half-Jewish girl, she certainly would have been in danger under the Nazi regime. So she had a life, a marriage that lasted 58 years, a wonderful, loving family, and a career. Having her story, "Goodbye, Old Vienna," published in *OASIS Journal 2004* gave her the courage to continue writing her memoirs. Since then, the Oregon Alliance of Senior and Health Services included one of her stories in their publication, *Reflections*. Also, the Terwilliger Times has printed two of her stories. Irene feels that age has given her a certain freedom and independence. [151]

HELENA FREY: "Serendipity" will be my second publication in *OASIS Journal*. I was first published in *OASIS Journal 2006*. I want to thank the editor, Leila Joiner, whose hard work has made it possible for amateurs to find their stories and poems between the covers of a book. I'm a member of Scribes, and we meet every two weeks at OASIS in Pittsburgh, Pennsylvania. Writing can be a solitary activity, but Scribes come together to share their stories, and the group keeps us focused. We all delight in putting words to paper, reading our stories and watching these same words migrate to the inside pages of a book or magazine. Over the years, many Scribes have known the thrill of publication in *OASIS Journal*. [99]

FRANK FROST spent most of his growing-up years in rural northwest Oregon on a small farm on the banks of a tidal tributary of the Columbia River. He attended a true one-room country school (nine kids total in all eight grades). There were thirteen in his high school graduating class. This was in 1944, and WWII was still raging. Four days after graduation, he was on his way to Navy boot camp. Frank has had two memoirs and one short story published in previous issues of the *OASIS Journal*. Two of those, plus this year's "Kids and Cars," had their genesis in the period of his life outlined above. [201]

DOLORES GEUDER, born in Los Angeles, California, moved to Tucson at the age of five with her family. She has lived the last sixty-four years within a ten-mile radius on Tucson's southwest side. Dolores is the mother of two daughters, Karen and Paula, and grandmother to Erin and Brent III. After retirement, she studied Spanish at OASIS and has traveled to Uruguay, Brazil, Argentina, Costa Rica, and Canada. With encouragement from her writing group, *The Misfits*, Dolores is writing of her experiences growing up in Tucson at a time when speaking Spanish was not allowed in the schools. She enjoys sharing her stories with family, friends, and others. [51]

KATHLEEN ELLIOTT GILROY: My focus is living a spiritually cognizant life, empowering my family toward their own unique qualities, sharing time with friends, being a child and animal advocate. I have had poetry, short stories, and curriculum materials published. I am a retired special needs teacher with a master's degree and multiple credentials, who has taught grade levels K-12. I have been a guest speaker at college courses. I am a life-long survivor, including stage 3 colon cancer. I volunteer for a Feral Cat Coalition, and volunteer tutor children occasionally. I value the gift of writing, revising, and sharing what I have written. I believe in contemplative prayer and definitely require more and more time for solitude. [30, 271]

NATALIE GOTTLIEB is a retired psychotherapist and a practicing fine artist. Recently, writing has been added to her pool of creative expression. Counseling people, painting them, or writing about their struggles all seem to mirror one another. Natalie strives to extract the hidden emotional kernel that stirs just beneath the surface and to translate that feeling into a painting, poem, or story. It is her constant search for the unseen that motivates her. She is deeply concerned with the human condition and how people's desires, disappointments, and triumphs affect their lives. Her own experience of the consequences of lost love prompted her to write "Prized Possession." [318]

DIANA GRIGGS thanks Mary Harker's OASIS poetry class for awakening a new passion that has become such an important part of her journey. [206, 262]

SANDRA STURTZ HAUSS is a retired teacher of gifted/talented students. Her poetic essays have been published by Blue Mountain Arts and have appeared in several journals and on the Internet. She enjoys writing inspirational and tribute pieces. "At the Gazebo in Larchmont" was written to her grandfather, who also wrote poetry and was Sandra's mentor. Her interests are mostly linguistic: reading, writing, theater, word games, crossword puzzles. As a member of the Poetry Caravan, she gives poetry readings in various rehab centers, hospitals, and assisted living facilities throughout Westchester. She is presently working on a poetry book for children. [78]

ADRIENNE HERNANDEZ, a retired teacher, has been published in "The Mid-America Poetry Review" and various small presses. Her poem, "A Sestina for My Son" is dedicated to her son, Matthew. [242]

MARILYN HOCHHEISER's work has been widely published in the United States and England. "You Touch My Life" won Marilyn membership in ASCAP in 2005. "Afraid To See" won her Tony Diamond's Brotherhood Rally of Veterans Organizations Life Membership certificate and has been read on television several times. Marilyn was one of the founding members of National League of American Pen Women, Simi Valley Branch and served as poetry editor for *Ventura County Woman Magazine* and *Verve Poetry Magazine*. Recently, "Woman Eighty Stranded in Desert Dies" was placed into *So Luminous The Wild Flowers*, an anthology of California Poets. Marilyn has also been an ordained minister through Glory House ministries since 1990 and had a poem accepted for publication by Imago Press in 2007. [53, 276]

ANDREW HOGAN received his doctorate in development studies from the University of Wisconsin-Madison. Before retirement, he was a faculty member at the State University of New York at Stony Brook, the University of Michigan, and Michigan State University, where he taught medical ethics, health policy, and the social organization of medicine in the College of Human Medicine. Dr. Hogan published more than five dozen professional articles on health services research and health policy. The story included in this volume is his fourth published work of fiction and was prepared for the Advanced Fiction Workshop at Pima Community College, where he is a student of creative writing. [117]

RUTH WEISS HOHBERG is a survivor of the Holocaust. She arrived in the U.S. in 1947. A graduate of the Cooper Union School of Art and Architecture in New York City, her art has been exhibited in the New York, New Jersey, and Connecticut area, winning prizes in local organizations, and places in National juried shows. In California she often exhibits her work in Poway and Rancho Bernardo. As an author, she has published a memoir titled *Getting Here*, several interview pieces in a local paper, a story in *The Firing Line*, and has been accepted by *OASIS Journal 2007* and *2008*. She has completed three other sections of her autobiography and written various pieces on travel and observations. [73]

SHERYL HOLLAND is a relative newcomer to poetry writing. She has taken workshops at Pima Community College in Tucson, Arizona with Sheila Bender, at Ghost Ranch in Santa Fe, New Mexico, with Joan Logghe, and with Janice Moore Fuller at Wild Acres Poetry Workshop in Asheville, North Carolina. She is an avid poetry reader; favorites include Dorianne Laux, Billy Collins, Marie Howe, and Rainer Maria Rilke. Deborah Butterfield's sculpture at the entrance to the Cantor Arts Center, Stanford University, inspired "Aging Horse." "When a Gopher Walks Across the Road" was inspired by watching a land turtle cross a busy road in Tucson, reminding her of the many she saw as a child living in Florida, where land turtles are colloquially referred to as "gophers." [174, 280]

In July of 2006 JANET IRVIN served as a work fellow at Antioch Writers Workshop in Yellow Springs, Ohio, where she had the great fortune to study with Cathy Smith Bowers. A poem Cathy shared with the workshop created such an immediate connection that Jan requested permission to write a prose piece based on "Groceries." The result is "The Price of Plums." Cathy also suggested Jan write a collection of stories based on poems, an idea she is in the process of developing. She hopes to find just the right works to serve as catalyst for the stories, and that poets will be equally excited to have their work highlighted in a cross-genre work. Jan would love to hear your ideas. Contact her at: irvinjgdm@yahoo.com [23]

HELEN JONES-SHEPHERD was born in Brooklyn, New York, April 19, 1931. Elementary education at Immaculate Heart of Mary School in New York. Moved to California with family in the 1940's. Received B.A. and M.A. in English Composition and Literature from California State University, San Bernardino. Worked as Adjunct Faculty at Riverside Community College on Riverside and Moreno Valley campuses and Cal State University for over 23 years. Since retiring 2½ years ago, she continues to write poetry, memoirs/perceptions of her world travels, essays, and short fiction/non-fiction. Attends Writers' Workshops, volunteers at church as Advocate on Canon law. Enjoys reading, especially classics and Shakespeare, nature hiking, square dancing, tennis, and listening to opera and classical music. "Color Coordinated?" was inspired by a true incident in her life. [52]

CAROLE KALIHER was born in New Orleans, Louisiana in 1938. Her family migrated to Rosemeade, California in 1946. She graduated from Mark Keppel High School and worked for Pacific Bell Telephone in Alhambra, California. She married Jim Kaliher in 1959 and from that marriahe they produced six sons and fourteen grandchildren. Together, they were active in their childrens' baseball for fifteen years. Carole began writing seriously in 1997 in tribute to her husband after he died. He'd encouraged her to write and submit her work, but she dedicated her time to family and Jim, when he was incapacitated with emphysema. She facilitates a creative writing group where she resides in Murrieta, California and has been published locally. [68, 277]

EMILY KEELER is a sojourner: her childhood was spent on a farm in the Spokane Valley of Washington State; she has lived in five states and across the Pacific in Japan; she jokes that she moved from Siberia (Lansing) to Calcutta (Houston) to paradise (San Diego), where she lives near her son and his wife, their three children, and a dog named Rambo. She enjoys her retirement from teaching; attends two reading groups (peacemaking and Great Books), and a UU church community strong in social justice; she walks daily in Balboa

Park and exercises at the Y, volunteers, and participates in classes at OASIS. She feels grateful to Mary Harker and Ann Whitlock for editing her writing, and to Leila Joiner for the *OASIS Journal*. [254]

RUTH MOON KEMPHER has owned and operated Kings Estate Press in St. Augustine, Florida since 1994. Now retired from teaching at St. Johns River Community College, she continues with her own writing and editing that of others, taking time to travel whenever possible. She lives in the woods with two dogs, Sadie and Mr. Frost, and is blessed to have a large extended family, including her 99-year-old father, living next door. [146]

JANET KREITZ: In the folly of youth, I shrugged off my college English teacher's recommendation to change my major to writing. During a recent conversation about life regrets, my brother encouraged me to write. I stumbled onto the OASIS website and, once I calmed my fear of failure, signed up for a six-week creative writing class. "Day" is the result of a class assignment to use twenty unrelated words to create a poem. I wrote "My Dad" because the too early death of my father left a void in my life, and I wanted to share his spirit with others. These first two submissions are hopefully not my last. I don't know where my writing will take me, but I look forward to the ride. [79, 192]

LOUISE LARSEN has been published in *OASIS Journal 2005* and *2007*. In 2008 she was selected to write an "Opinion Shaper" column for a local suburban newpaper, *West Journal*. For the past nine years, she has participated in the OASIS Writing Class in St. Louis, Missouri. Her work has been published in the following magazines: *Story Teller, Byline, Beginnings, New England Writers Network*, and *Good Old Days*. Louise is 90 years old and loves to write. She graduated from Washington University, St. Louis, Missouri in 1939, where she was assistant editor of the university magazine. She is honored to be included in *OASIS Journal 2008*. [65]

ELEANOR LITTLE was born in Detroit, Michigan during the depression. She began piano lessons when she was four and studied classical piano until she was 14. She attended Albion College in Michigan and is a graduate of Wayne State University, Detroit. She taught high school, then moved to San Diego in 1958. Eleanor taught piano there for 10 years, worked at the UCSD Department of Music and began to write poetry in 1998, after she retired. She leads and plays piano with a traditional jazz quintet called *Senior Moments Quintet*, as well as with other music groups, takes classes, writes, gardens, and spends time with her family and "Scooter," a beloved mini-poodle. [327]

CLAIRE WARNER LIVESEY: Born in Los Angeles, grew up in Carmel, California. Two comedies she wrote in high school were staged in her senior year and were well received. Attended Mills College and U.C. Library School at Berkeley. She was a children's librarian at Alameda City Library for fifteen years. Married to Herbert Livesey in 1958, widowed in 1962, when she began to write poetry and children's books. Moved to Tucson, Arizona in 1970 for reasons of health. Claire studied poetry with a number of teachers: Ann Demier, Richard Siken, Nancy Wall, Barbara Cully. Children's stories published: "At the Butt End of a Rainbow," 1970; "Our Polliwogs," 1999; to be followed by "Bees, Bears, and Black Cherry Jam" sometime in the next year or two. [112]

In the last year, ELLARAINE LOCKIE has received a poetry residency at Centrum in Port Townsend, Washington, her eleventh Pushcart Prize nomination, the 2008 Writecorner Press Poetry Prize, the 2008 Skysaje Poetry Prize, the 2008 Deane Wagner Poetry Prize, the 2007 Elizabeth R. Curry Prize and finalist status for the 2008 Mudfish Poetry Prize, the 2007 Joy Harjo Poetry Award, and the Creekwalker Poetry Prize. Recently released publications are *Mod Gods and Luggage Straps*, a poetry/art broadside from *BrickBat Revue*, and her fifth chapbook, *Blue Ribbons at the County Fair*, a collection of first-place contest winning poems from PWJ Publishing. [29]

JOLLY ANN MADDOX has been teaching English since 1970 and is an adjunct instructor for San Antonio College. She received her Bachelor's degree in English/History from Texas A&I Kingsville, and her Master of Arts in English from Southwest Texas State University. The poem about her father is her attempt to paint a snapshot of a man whose experiences not only defined his life, but that of his family. It is one of several poems she has written about her four brothers, her sister, and her parents. [82]

RONNA MAGY began writing after she entered mid-life. Having grown up in Michigan, she now calls Los Angeles her home. In Ronna's memory endure the intimate moments of childhood shared between mother and daughter. "In Her Mirror" frames the reflection of a daughter crossing into the world of mother, and a mother crossing into the world of her child. Ronna's short stories and memoir pieces have appeared in several anthologies; her textbooks are used by adults studying English as a Second Language in many parts of the world. [57]

VERA MARTIGNETTI was born in New York City and lived on the East Coast until she moved to Tucson, Arizona, where she has lived for 34 years. She has four children and six grandchildren. Although she has journaled all her life and written about her family for her family, this is her first effort at publication. She is currently working on a piece about the first twelve months of being a widow. [223]

This is LOLENE MCFALL's first experience in submitting written work. Her interest in poetry began in 2002 with a writing group in San Diego, California. Her interests then were essay and memoir. There was only one poet in the group, and he wrote free verse, which caught her attention. Pursuit of poetry became her passion. "Authentic Self" resulted from musing over change and areas of personal growth as she neared the eighth decade of her life. "Prince of Amour" evolved from an experiment in creating a poem from random words quickly jotted down. This has become one method Lolene uses to surprise herself with a new poem. [77, 300]

Tucson writer/geologist SUSAN CUMMINS MILLER, a research affiliate of the UA's Southwest Institute for Research on Women (SIROW), edited *A Sweet, Separate Intimacy: Women Writers of the American Frontier, 1800-1922*, and authored the Frankie MacFarlane mystery novels, *Death Assemblage, Detachment Fault, Quarry*, and *Hoodoo*. Her poems have been published in regional journals and anthologies, including previous *OASIS Journals* and *What Wildness Is This: Women Write about the Southwest*. An encounter during one summer field season in northeastern Nevada inspired her poem, "Two Roads Diverged." She is currently working on her fifth novel, *Fracture*. [324]

CAROLE ANN MOLETI is a nurse practitioner and midwife in New York City. In addition to professional publications, she writes speculative fiction, memoir, and opinion pieces that focus on health care politics and women's issues. Carole's work has also appeared in *Tangent Online Short Fiction Review, Vision Magazine, The Internet Review of Science Fiction, The Fix*, and *Noneuclidean Café*. "On the High Seas" is an excerpt from Carole's memoir, *Someday I'm Going to Write a Book*, which chronicles her career working with medically underserved families in The Bronx, Harlem, and Washington Heights. [107]

MICHAEL B. MOSSMAN was born in Alton, Illinois. After serving honorably with the U.S. Marine Corps in Vietnam, he graduated from Southern Illinois University at Edwardsville with a degree in Educational Psychology. He received his Master's from the University of Oklahoma at Norman. Michael spent thirty-three years in the fields of elementary and special education. Since retiring, he has spent his time writing stories and doing art. He wrote

"The Last Letter" because of personal experiences at college and serving with the Marine Corps in Vietnam. The story centers on a girl he once knew and a friend who was killed in Vietnam. "I have been spiritually touched by both of these wonderful people, and felt the need to share my feelings with others." [311]

MARILYN J. MORGAN: I am recreating old stories into new myths for the 21st Century. This story emerged after I was initiated as Elder in my spiritual community and is one of many multicultural stories I write for the Soul seeker in everyone. I am keeper of the Medicine Way Spiritual Path and an ordained minister. Inspiration for creative endeavors comes from nature in Mt. Laguna in San Diego, California, and sharing women's wisdom in many circles. I am writing a memoir for my children and grandchildren. My poems and essays have been published by the *American Pen Women*, the *Del Mar Spectator*, and the *Light Connection* of Encinitas. I'm a member of San Diego Writers/Editors Guild and San Diego Writers, Ink. [113]

MIMI MORIARTY is the producer and host of "Write Stuff," a cable access TV program in the Albany, New York area. Her short fiction, poems, essays, and articles have been published in many journals, magazines, and newspapers, including *Margie, Alehouse, SLAB, Thema, Rockhurst Review, Connecticut Review, Peregrine*, and *Irish America*. Her chapbook of 23 poems about the aftermath of war, *War Psalm*, was recently published by Finishing Line Press. This chapbook is dedicated to her father, as is the poem, "Capsized," written shortly after her father died. [98]

J. R. NAKKEN: I sat down to write a story about my experience at the Celilo encampment on the first gathering after Elder Brother Art Shilo went to his grandfathers. "Twice a year they gather here," I began. The computer screamed at me, "I'm a poem, you fool!" And indeed it was. "Bendemeer's Stream" was begun in a motel room in 1980 and finished twenty years later. It is the "stream" in the title of my recent book, *Stream and Light: A Woman's Journey*, Imago Press, 2008. My eccentric felines are now Cataline, Periclaws, and Pandora, for the reservation is hard on cats who venture outdoors. Still, life goes on swimmingly here on the Tulalip Indian Reservation, north of Seattle in God's Country. [61, 116]

ELEANOR WHITNEY NELSON has enjoyed a career as an exploration geologist traveling worldwide with her geologist husband. A longtime Tucson resident, she holds degrees in English (BA) and Geology (MS). Always interested in writing, she has kept detailed journals of her wide-ranging experiences, often drawing on them for inspiration or background material for short stories, memoirs, and poetry. Her published work can be read in *Chicken Soup for the Dog Lover's Soul, A Way With Murder: An Anthology by Arizona Mystery Writers, The Story Teller 2005*, and *OASIS Journal 2004, 2006*, and *2007*. Eleanor has been a horse lover since childhood, riding for pleasure and in competition at home and abroad. Today, she credits her four trail horses with helping her keep fit. [165]

JAN RIDER NEWMAN has been published in *Louisiana Literature, Denver Quarterly*, and *New Orleans Review*. This year, the State of Louisiana, Division of the Arts, has accepted her application for an Artist Services - Career Advancement grant, which she will use to research Acadian history and culture in Louisiana for developing a series of novels. "Goose Chase" grew out of childhood experiences. Her father was a sharecropper, and they lived on a little side road surrounded by rice fields, along with a few other families who worked for the same landowner. One year, a couple of the other men got into trouble after an illegal nighttime goose hunt. The serious part of the story grew out of the unfulfilled longings of someone close to her. [37]

MARLENE NEWMAN, mother of four, grandmother of two, shared her knowledge of reading, writing, and library skills with her students and fellow teachers. She has always found words and language fascinating. She served as editor of *Fuse News and Views*, the newsletter of the New Rochelle local of New York State United Teachers. In September 2005, *Barefoot Books* published her story, "Myron's Magic Cow," about a boy who was sent to the store for milk. Her story about her husband's family is posted on the Ellis Island immigration stories site. She is a computer tutor at the Bethlehem Public Library in Delmar, New York. She enjoys reading, doing crossword puzzles, and watching the many visitors at her back yard birdfeeders. [31]

KATHLEEN A. O'BRIEN: I began writing poetry in 2002, two years after the death of my husband. I was walking around a small lake and my first poem, "Permission" (to be happy) came to me. I've written over 500 poems now and can't stop. I'm in a foul mood if I don't take time to write. In "Another Spring," I just wrote what I saw from a window. I wrote "It Will Not Last Long" as I rested in bed and a gentle summer rain began to fall on the roof. I was a teacher. I'm now an LPN, currently working two days a week. I love reading, writing poetry, dancing, gardening, and volunteering for hospice. I'm the mother of four grown children and "Nanny" to three grandsons. [72, 222]

RICHARD O'DONNELL, a native New Yorker, has been writing since he won a citywide essay contest while in high school. "After that, I never wanted to do anything else," he says. Following a hitch in the Marine Corps, he followed a career in public relations, writing news and feature articles, annual reports, technology articles, and executive speeches. He now works freelance, writing business profiles for a marketing firm, as well as articles and commentaries on developing electronics technologies for a scientific journal. He recently turned to writing short fiction and has since produced several stories, one of which was named second runner-up in *OASIS Journal 2007*. [329]

SHIRLEY OPPENHEIMER: "At the Y" is based on snippets of actual conversations that I participated in at the Lohse YMCA downtown. A couple of years ago, four or five other retired people and I began having coffee together after we worked out in the morning. We would sit at a round table in the lobby, donating for the coffee and cups which are provided by the Y. There are no subjects out of bounds, so we often laugh uproariously. Recently, the Y moved us into a room where we don't disrupt the working environment. Our table is larger but, even so, we have outgrown it as more and more people are drawn to the lively discussions at the Y. [200]

MARGARET E. PENNETTI: I've had one other article published, in the American Mensa *Bulletin*, so now I guess it's officially not a fluke. My 11th grade English teacher would be so proud! Biographically speaking, well, you've just read a piece of it. Subsequently, I've been, and in some cases still am, a Sagittarius, an underemployed Humanities major, a wife, a mother, a Wiccan, and a gun-totin' liberal. I recently received my Medicare card, much to my horror. Currently, I live in the Seattle area, along with the rest of the unregenerate old hippies. My writing heroes include Oscar Wilde, Mark Twain, Lewis Carroll, Ernest Hemingway, and Hunter S. Thompson. The rest "is subject to change without notice." [285]

LEILA PETERS taught English and reading in middle school for 39 years. Her best friend, Sue Ritter, was part of many adventures: buying a farm, raising cows, then horses. When Sue became terminally ill with cancer, Leila made a promise to herself that Sue would never go to a nursing home. That promise was rewarded with the "perfect gift." Her dog, Honey, is her companion now. In the summer, they go to her cabin in Montana and hike to the high mountain lakes. [219]

RON PORTER lives with his wife, Erika, in the rural community of Valley Center in San Diego County, California. His writing includes short stories, spiritual essays, and poetry. In his words: "I try to write daily, just putting down on paper what comes to me. I really don't control what comes out. Also, credit must be given to the wonderful inspiration and support of others during our weekly writing class at OASIS." He is currently writing a spiritually based monthly editorial column for the Philosophical Library of Escondido, California. [319]

DIANA M. RAAB is a poet, essayist, and memoirist. Her award-winning poetry has appeared in national magazines. She has two poetry collections, *My Muse Undresses Me* (2007) and *Dear Anaïs: My Life in Poems for You* (Plain View Press, Fall 2008) and a memoir, *Regina's Closet: Finding My Grandmother's Secret Journal*, which won the 2008 National Indie Award for Memoir. She's editor of the anthology, *Writers and Their Notebooks*, forthcoming by The University of South Carolina Press in Spring/Summer 2009. She teaches in the UCLA Extension Writer's Program and at the Santa Barbara Writer's Conference. She also teaches writing and journaling in the community. [64]

Since moving to Tucson as a teenager in 1959, DIANE RAU has cherished its cloud-shadowed, lavender-blue mountains and desert terrain. Indulging her passion for language—which began with writing short stories in fifth grade—she thrived in journalism and English classes at the University of Arizona, learning to craft lean, yet lyrical, prose. Subsequently, while raising her son, she taught English and reading, became a substitute teacher, and later a home health aide. Although unpublished, Diane sculpts ideas with words by reflecting in her journal on life's experiences, nature's beauty, and individuals' courage, and writing impassioned letters on social issues. Miraculously blessed with recovery from recent end-stage cancer, she is practicing gratitude and self-forgiveness. Sharing her story through publication in *OASIS Journal* is a privilege. [207]

DAVID RAY's recent books include *When* (Howling Dog Press), *After Tagore: Poems Inspired by Rabindranath Tagore* (Nirala Editions, India), and *Music of Time: Selected & New Poems* (Backwaters Press). Other titles include *The Death of Sardanapalus and Other Poems of the Iraq Wars* and a memoir, *The Endless Search*. The essay included here, "Return to Provence," is from another volume of his memoir-in-progress. David lives in Tucson, Arizona, with his wife, poet and essayist Judy Ray. [236]

JUDY RAY's most recent publication is a chapbook in the *Greatest Hits* series from Pudding House Publications. Other chapbooks are *Fishing in Green Waters* and *Sleeping in the Larder: Poems of a Sussex Childhood*, and earlier books are *Pebble Rings* and *Pigeons in the Chandeliers*. Judy's essay, "Jury Duty," won the *OASIS Journal 2007* non-fiction contest. Since she and her poet husband, David, moved to Tucson, Judy spends some of her time as a volunteer teacher of English as a Second Language to adults in the community. [43, 184]

CONSTANCE RICHARDSON worked in film and video for 25 years before retiring to Tucson in 2001. She has written and directed many educational films, worked as an editor on features, and was a Director Fellow at The American Film Institute. She is just completing her first book, *Swimming Upstream*. "Across" is a eulogy for her daughter, Nina L. Boden. Constance wrote the poem in 2001 while driving from the east coast to Arizona after her daughter's tragic death. Publishing credits include "A Work in Progress" in *Art.Rage.Us & Writing by Women with Breast Cancer*, Chronicle Publishing, 1998; "Circles" in *OASIS Journal 2005*; "The Path" in *The Storyteller*, the Society of Southwestern Authors, October 2006. [234]

RITA RIES: This is her third publication in OASIS Journal. She has been in an ongoing poetry class at OASIS in Los Angeles for seven years and a church poetry group for six. "I get so much more out of a poem in a class where it is discussed." At eight she wrote about the death of her grandfather from pneumonia but did not write again for almost fifty years—a gift of the golden years and retirement. She recently participated in an annual poetry fest at a local library. Her Presbyterian church group, Poetry & Spirit, is about to publish a third book, *Grace Revealed*, geared for the Advent season. [268]

LENA V. ROACH: When asked to give the eulogy for my older sister, Hermence Vidrine, I remembered the comfort she offered me after the death of my husband, Ed. I wanted to honor that special bond between us that began as we grew up in Evangeline Parish, Louisiana. Now *OASIS Journal* has added to that honor by publishing my poem, "Wordless," for which I am truly grateful. My love for poetry began in fifth grade when my teacher praised my six-line effort, "Little Red Rose." A first sale, "Success," appeared in *Young People's Paper*, Philadelphia. During my career as an English and history teacher, I wrote poetry and articles for regional and professional periodicals, besides a syndicated "Dear Teacher" column for several newspapers. Today, fiction has my undivided attention as I revise that first novel. [244]

ADRIENNE ROGERS: "Portrait of a Lady in Red" was written for a proposed monthly publication of mystery stories. To kick it off, there was a contest for short mysteries. A series of thirteen clues were offered, and the story was to use any three to create a mystery plot. The three clues chosen here were a painting, a string of pearls, and a red dress. This story was not selected, and the magazine never got past the initial two issues. However, with publication in

OASIS Journal, there is renewed incentive to find more adventures for Nadia and Milton. The portrait in the story is a product of my own imagination. However, the art collection is real and has been exhibited worldwide. [301]

ALBERT RUSSO, who has published worldwide over 55 books of poetry, fiction, and photography in English and in French, his two mother-tongues, is the recipient of many awards, such as The American Society of Writers Fiction Award, The British Diversity Short Story Award, several New York Poetry Forum Awards, Amelia Prose and Poetry awards and the Prix Colette, among others. His work has been translated into a dozen languages, including Greek, Turkish, and Polish, and broadcast by the World Service of the BBC. He was also a member of the 1996 jury for the prestigious Neustadt International Prize for Literature, which often leads to the Nobel Prize. His websites: www.albertrusso.com and www.authorsden.com/albertrusso [135]

NANCY STEIN SANDWEISS was born in Detroit and developed an early love of reading and writing. Her father transmitted his reverence for language and the conviction that words have meaning and should be used with precision. As a medical social worker, she learned a great deal about human nature in times of crisis and confusion. "Love Remains" was inspired by a woman whose longing for love and connection survived the erosion of her cognitive faculties. Nancy credits teacher Mary Harker and her fellow classmates at OASIS-San Diego for demonstrating how to write with economy and make every word count. [317]

TERESA FLANAGAN SHEEHAN, born and raised in Somerville, Massachusetts, is mother to seven adult children, as well as a retired junior high school counselor. After relocating to Arizona in 1990, she began studying Spanish and later enrolled in a Creative Writing class taught by Dan Gilmore at OASIS. Her short stories, published in the 2002, 2003, and 2004 editions of *OASIS Journal*, reflect her Irish heritage. Some of her poems were also published in *OASIS Journal 2002*, and another recently appeared in *Spirit and Life*. With the encouragement of her writing group, The Misfits, she is working on a childhood memoir about her distorted perceptions following the death of a sibling. Teresa enjoys traveling, reading, gardening, yoga, and visiting her far-flung children and grandchildren. [326]

In private practice as a psychotherapist, IRMA SHEPPARD has lived in Tucson for the past twenty-four years with her husband and a succession of cats. A recent move to the foothills north of Tucson allows her to include coyote concerts, snakes, scorpions, and tarantulas in the pool, and strolling bobcats in her list of so-called cheap thrills. Her short stories and poems have been published in numerous journals across the country. [316]

A workshop Leader for The Florida Center for the Book, the first affiliate of the Library of Congress, LUCILLE GANG SHULKLAPPER writes fiction and poetry. She has won awards and competitions from the National League of Pen Women: Nob Hill Branch, Icarus International Poetry Competition, The Florida Chapter of The Mystery Writers of America, Palm Beach Repertory Theater, the R. Rofihe Trophy, and others. Her work has been anthologized and appears in many publications, as well as in her four poetry chapbooks, *What You Cannot Have, The Substance of Sunlight, Godd, It's Not Hollywood*, and *In the Tunnel*. [266]

MITZIE SKRBIN is 74, retired, widowed, mother of six, and grandmother of eleven. She is active in her church, a volunteer usher for Pittsburgh Cultural Trust, belongs to an AARP chapter, takes classes at her senior center, and is enrolled in "Creative Cards" and "Scribes" at OASIS. Her poem, "In My Dreams," was published in *OASIS Journal 2006*; her short story, "My First, Last, and Only Fishing Trip," in *OASIS Journal 2007*. She was inspired to write "The Christmas Tree" because every year she is inundated with holiday ads for expensive electronics, jewelry, and toys and the "wish lists" of her grandchildren and their peers. She remembers her own childhood when Christmas was simpler, but more meaningful, and wish lists were more down to earth. [289]

JEAN RITTER SMITH: I am almost 81, with warm memories of living for a number of years in Central Oregon while raising our young family. Exaggeration based on basic truths is lots of fun for me—I hope also for everyone reading "Those Letters from Sally." [185]

STEVE SNYDER, a native Tucsonan, has had one short story and several poems published in *The Laughing Dog, Erete's Bloom, The Tucson Poet, The Black Hammock Review*, and *Poetry At The River Annual Review*. He won second place in a local poetry contest in 1995 and honorable mentions in a national contest in 1990. "About a year after I began learning Tai Chi some new students joined. During a 'push hands' exercise with an attractive brunette I sensed some fear and smiled to relieve her tension. She smiled back, and I planned to ask for her phone number, but forgot due to distractions at the end of class. She never returned, and my efforts to find her failed. Needless to say, I felt some regret." [328]

BILL SPEIGHT SR. is retired from the U.S. military, a self-employed consultant currently facilitating computer and life skills classes for residents who live in public housing in Tucson, Arizona. He was encouraging class attendees to write for *OASIS Journal 2008*. Driving home from work, it came to him to follow the advice he was giving others: "You write a story." "My Little Red Wagon" is the result of that internal dialogue. It will become part of the "Our Little Red Wagon" Learning Environment (a series of workbooks) he is working on that includes: "The Other Side Of Anger," "Defensive Behavior," "Creating Accidental Adversaries," "The Other Side Of Accountability," and "Team Communications." E-mail: billsp8@msn.com [69]

PEGGY JOYCE STARR: "Messages in the Wind" is one example of many ways I experience intuition and insight into living mindfully. In 1974, after a series of major life challenges, I wholeheartedly set foot on a sacred journey to find Inner Peace. At age forty, I left administration at a university to live for fifteen years in ashrams and monastic communities, after which I completed an M.A. in Transpersonal Psychology. Through studies in Western Sufism, Buddhism, spiritual practices, journal writing, dream guidance, and art I slowly found in me the person I sought to be and reentered the workforce. Opportunities arose to integrate my spiritual training into a 'Life Counselor' position. Today, I live in a retirement center where I offer meditation practice to my neighbors. [275]

ANNETTE STOVALL: "Aftermath of a Hero" began at a clinic writing group as one hand-written page that I enlarged upon and completed later at home. I elaborated on his difficulty finding a decent job because handicapped people, soldiers and veterans included, do have trouble finding a good job. It is especially a shame when it happens to a military person who has sacrificed so much for his country. "At an Age When" was written after I read Frederick Douglass's autobiography. I wanted to reveal some things that occurred in a time of slavery that we never imagined as occurring. I also wanted to express the happy ending—showing them freed from slavery—since I am an African-American. [162, 250]

JOANN SUNDERLAND: "Just Another Day at Golden Acres" is more truth than fiction. The names have been changed but the location, characters, and most of the incidents are real. I just recorded their story and made up the dialog. I would like to dedicate this piece to Ivan and Audrey, who worked so hard to provide a haven of compassion and dignity for the residents of "Golden Acres," and who made a difficult period in my life not only bearable, but actually fun. [193]

The 2003 death of a beautifully eccentric friend, "Pearly," and the desire to archive her memories motivated JANET K. THOMPSON to write about Pearl. Later, as more friends died, she found writing about them and other living friends and relatives revealed the facts of her own life in a fun way.

A boarding school survivor who can document over 40 address changes, Janet went through many life experiences and two marriages along the way. She was a 1951 Polio epidemic victim, college dropout, office manager, and self-employed bookkeeper. In more incarnations, she was a historic property renovator, urban pioneer, slumlord, construction company and water well drilling partner, financial winner and loser. Now retired, she volunteers, writes a newsletter, reads, and relishes politics. [179]

TONI TIMMONS, a graduate of Marylhurst University, is a retired teacher from N. Clackamas School District in Milwaukie, Oregon (near Portland). Mt. Hood, Mt. Adams, and Mt. St. Helens are short distances away. The area is covered with earthquake fault lines that sometimes give a shake or two. Scientists continually check the mountains for any sign of activity. Toni felt feelings aroused by living here were important to write about, but she wouldn't live anywhere else. She also writes science fiction/fantasy, romance, and currently has a little mischievous boy living on Mars. She enjoys life with her husband, Archie, three grown children, and their families. [129]

MANUEL TORREZ, JR. belongs to the McCreeles Branch Library Writers' Support Group in San Antonio, Texas. His most recent poems accepted for publication are: "River city Christmas eve," "Little girl mortified," and "Experiencing progress." They will appear in the anthology, *Voices along the river*, in October, 2008. Manuel writes from past experiences and knowledge that he may have on a particular subject. Research is very important to him, as is revision. [295]

JOANNA WANDERMAN began writing after she entered mid-life when she discovered "Emeritus," a college for seniors located in Southern California. "Emeritus" refers to people retired with honor, and Joanna enjoys the feeling of self-worth that comes from sharing her life experiences with fellow students. [263]

BARBARA WATSON: "What A Blessing" is one of the chapters from my book, *A Funny Thing Happened on the Way: a Memoir*, which I self-published earlier this year. I was born in England and emigrated to the United States in 1955 with my husband, David, and our eleven-month-old daughter, Judith. Feeling the need to tell my story of growing up in England during World War II, I enrolled in a memoir writing class in 1998 to learn how to go about writing my story. I discovered that I loved to write and started compiling chapters, which I planned to organize into folders for each of our four children. A funny thing happened, I decided to publish, and a book was born, a legacy for my children. It has taken ten years to write, organize, and publish, but it has been a wonderfully rewarding experience. [321]

TILLIE WEBB has been attending OASIS-sponsored writing classes for three semesters. She has a doctorate in Secondary Education and visited Machu Picchu while teaching in Latin America. As for most others who have had the opportunity to visit this extraordinary place, her experience was unforgettable, so when her writing teacher assigned the topic of "Remote" to the class, some of the details of her journey into the past of the Inca Indians of Peru sprang to mind. She is happy to share them. Tillie is now retired and resides in Rancho Bernardo near San Diego, California. [133]

MEGAN WEBSTER is a Welsh-born author, teacher and freelance editor. Her third chapbook, *Bipolar Express*, won the San Diego Book Award for Best Unpublished Poetry Chapbook and was a finalist for the New Women's Voices Award. Her poems have appeared in numerous publications, including *Connecticut Review, Sunshine /Noir, Wordgathering, ONTHEBUS, California Quarterly*, and five previous issues of *OASIS Journal*. Reach her at: Web5089@aol.com [218]

ANNE WHITLOCK shares a home in San Diego with her two cats, "Baby" and "Fuzzy". In 1979, when she bought a house on a canyon, it seemed like a romantic idea. The property came with "tenants"—squawking blue jays, marauding skunks and possums, and plenty of lizards for the cats to chase. Eucalyptus, jacaranda, and bottle brush vied with each other to litter the canyon floor, already densely populated with native scrub. For someone who had never gardened in her life, the maintenance was overwhelming, but through gardening she grew to know and appreciate her neighbor, Jim, a former Marine, whom she honors in her poem, "In Memoriam." [248]

NEAL WILGUS has no computer. He does have three clipboards next to his bed and writes almost everything by hand, then finalizes it on a typewriter as old as he is. He still uses carbon paper. Originally from Arizona (B.S. in English, NAU), he's lived in Corales, New Mexico for several decades. Thirty years ago, he wrote *The Illuminoids: Secret Societies and Political Paranoia*. He is also author of several chapbooks of poetry and a collection of LEAK News Service satires. His short story, "Blink," appeared in *OASIS Journal 2007* and "Galápagoed" won the 2006 short fiction contest. "Shadowsmith" is fantasy, not autobiographical. [270]

JO WILKINSON, originally from Los Angeles, has now been living happily in Tucson, Arizona for the past seven years. She is the mother of two adult children, Eligh and Sara. Although she made her living as a legal secretary for over twenty years, her passion has always been her singing and songwriting. She describes her music as "contemporary folk." She has an album coming out this fall with her band, *Grains of Sand*. She also has recorded a soon-to-be-released CD entitled *On Sacred Ground: Mother and Son,* with her son, Eligh, a renowned hip hop artist. Both albums are original material (see jowilkinson.com). Jo helped form a local writing support group to stretch her writing into other areas. "A Child of the Fifties" is her first published memoir vignette. [45]

MARIAN WILSON is the dancing queen of South Marvin Avenue. Now that she is retired from Tucson Unified School District, she has time for her neighborhood activities as detailed in her prize-winning, 2002 book of humorous poetry, *Why Pencils Are Yellow.* Marian also reads, walks, and plays bridge. [178]

CHRISTY WISE, author, essayist, paper artist, and freelance writer, lives in Washington, D.C. with her husband, two teenagers, a dog, and two cats. Her essays have been published in *The Sigurd Journal, O!TemporaMagazine,* and the *Wall Street Journal,* and her news and feature articles have been published in numerous magazines and newspapers. She is coauthor, with her mother, of *A Mouthful of Rivets: Women at Work in World War II,* a book about women who held nontraditional jobs during the Second World War. [245]

JOAN ELIZABETH ZEKAS: I continue to moderate our memories writing group (the Scribes) at OASIS in Pittsburgh, Pennsylvania. Wonderful people! Wonderful stories! Writing "An Immigrant Life: Snapshots" helped me bring back to life my cherished ones—the early family pioneers. My story comes from my own first-hand experiences and from those of my dear departed Uncle Frank (Grammie Rose's son). He shared the scary story of the Ellis Island refusal, and he was present at the house raising. (Grandpa's 1923 contract shows the house raising cost him $800.) While researching how houses were raised, I learned of a millionaire who had his house moved *up* and *over* a grove of trees, rather than cut down the trees. Wow! The things you learn along the way. [155]

ORDER INFORMATION

Copies of *OASIS Journal 2008* are available at:

www.amazon.com
www.barnesandnoble.com

Copies of *OASIS Journal* from previous years (2002-2007) may be ordered at a discount from the publisher at the address below as availability allows. Please enclose $10.00 for each book ordered, plus $3.00 shipping & handling for each order to be sent to one address.

Please make checks payable to Imago Press. Arizona residents add $0.81 sales tax for each book ordered.

Proceeds from the sale of this book go toward the production of next year's *OASIS Journal*. Ten per cent of the net proceeds are donated every year to The OASIS Institute. Your purchase will help us further the creative efforts of older adults. Thank you for your support.

Imago Press
3710 East Edison
Tucson AZ 85716

www.imagobooks.com

Printed in the United States
208424BV00001B/103/P